The Christian
in
Politics

WALTER JAMES

London
OXFORD UNIVERSITY PRESS
NEW YORK   TORONTO
1962

Oxford University Press, Amen House, London E.C.4

GLASGOW NEW YORK TORONTO MELBOURNE WELLINGTON
BOMBAY CALCUTTA MADRAS KARACHI LAHORE DACCA
CAPE TOWN SALISBURY NAIROBI IBADAN ACCRA
KUALA LUMPUR HONG KONG

PRINTED IN GREAT BRITAIN

24848

Preface

WHILE I had no intention of writing this book until little more than three years ago, I must, looking back, acknowledge a large debt to those of my friends who at various stages of my life stimulated my interest in its subject. Many years ago, when we were still at the university, Mr. Gordon Phillips, now chaplain to Anglican students in the University of London, introduced me to the literature of Christian Socialism. His forceful enthusiasm was usefully tempered by Mr. D. E. L. Haynes, at present Keeper of the Greek and Roman Department of the British Museum, whom I met first at the British School at Rome. Later, when I was working in Manchester, I came across Dr. Alec Vidler, then Warden of St. Deiniol's Library at Hawarden, now dean and chaplain of King's College, Cambridge. Off and on over the years we have discussed the relations of Christianity and politics, and he made some valuable suggestions for the present work. Through him I met Dr. J. H. Oldham, and I, like many others, came under the spell of this self-effacing man with his instinctive sense for new ideas that mattered and great human powers of drawing contrasting minds into common enterprises. If I must admit how much the writing of this book owes to the varying influences at different times of these four friends, no one of them, of course, may be saddled with any responsibility for its main arguments.

I am indebted to the following for permission to quote from the works mentioned: Lutterworth Press: *The Divine Imperative* by Emil Brunner; Cassell and Co. Ltd.: *The Second World War* by Winston Churchill; Raymond Postgate: his *Life of George Lansbury* (Longmans Green and Co. Ltd.); Victor Gollancz Ltd.: *Throw Away Thy Rod* by David Wills. For permission to quote from Archbishop Temple's letters I am indebted to his widow. My wife has given me invaluable help and support in preparing the book for the press. I have a debt also to Mr. R. L. W. Collison, the librarian of the B.B.C., who unearthed books in London which I should not have been able to lay hands on myself.

W. J.

Contents

secular interests of members — Support limited by Christian title —
Some Christians wish to make lay appeal to whole electorate — Others
believe Christians strengthen their cause by associating closely with
co-religionists — But Christian parties become saddled with sin and
mistakes of political action — While Continental experiment in Christian
parties not disastrous, nothing in it advises English to imitate them — In
politics Christians should work beside their fellow men.

10. INSTRUMENTS OF GOD

Tensions of Christian's dual allegiance, to this sinful world and to
Kingdom — Christian love not to be generalized and applied to public
affairs — But Christians must serve this world, God's creation —
Politician an instrument of God's purpose — Politics a vocation — Even
under Communist régimes — The dire choices politicians have sometimes to make — Assassination discussed — But Christians may not
escape these terrible responsibilities.

The special temptations of a party politician — Pride and self-
advertisement — Conflict between requirements of politics and commands of God's Kingdom — The need to advocate causes in which
politician does not believe — The 'urge to be first' — Politics unfavour-
able to Christian living — The Christian politician must watch himself
narrowly: and in his personal dealings he must show love.

Politicians one day to face God's judgment — What his contemporaries say of him means little — how may we judge Bismarck? — We
cannot foretell the nature of God's judgment of the politician — But Our
Lord understood his predicament — Words to Pilate.

I

Introduction

CHRISTIANS believe that the world was redeemed and men offered the opportunity of salvation by Jesus Christ who in his teaching of a new relationship of love between God and man, and between man and man, revealed the whole purpose of human life. The power of Christianity in personal lives, and its relevance to them, is illustrated by the saints, and a multitude of ordinary people will also bear witness. But if we move out of the sphere where man meets God in prayer or his neighbour face to face and consider instead the more impersonal world of great societies, the relevance of Christianity becomes immediately less clear. If love be admitted the foremost principle of Christian faith, how may this love which is a certain means of overcoming any personal difficulty be applied by States to their subjects, or by one side of industry to another? If attempts at such application have often been made, it must be confessed that they rarely if ever have succeeded. When a Christian in a formally Christian country takes stock of the world around him, its politics and business, he is unlikely to differ greatly from the verdict given by Henry Scott Holland, a leading figure in the Christian social movement in England, during the course of the war of 1914–18:

If only the world had been Christian, it would not be at war. . . . It must be its [sc. Christianity's] representation by its accredited organs and institutions that has so piteously failed to make it effectual. It has been allowed to lose its grip on the real facts, so that the big affairs of the world go on their way as if it were not there. In the World of Diplomacy, of International Relationships, it does not count. In Trade and Industry it has hardly any place. Over the dominating motives and aims by which our enormous wealth is created, it has little or no control. In many departments of Business it is openly denied. It exercises no authority over the wealth, after it has been made. It establishes no over-ruling conscience, no paramount sense of responsibility. . . . So men are bitterly aware . . . and they trace the curse of Materialism on us within, as on those without. They do not see that we, churchmen, contribute an ideal element to solid affairs . . . politics are not changed by our taking part in them. We take our colour from them, not they from us. In our Business and in our Political interests we are too often just as other men are. The world is not aware of any difference in its temper or habits because we take part in its doings. So men assert.

The assumption throughout this passage, that Christianity is relevant to politics and business, was never made in the Early Church and occurred to few in the Christianized Roman Empire after Constantine. By the thirteenth century, however, it was the accepted orthodoxy of medieval Christendom and years after that civilization's break-down in the Reformation, the right of Churches to lay down rules for politics and economics was claimed, if not effectively exercised, by Protestants. But by the eighteenth century in England the idea that Churches were concerned only with the religious life and possessed no authority to pronounce on secular affairs was thoroughly established. Puritan laymen had insisted on it in their dislike of priestly meddling, and in the course of time the Church of England made their views its own. Her bishops were virtually silent on social and political questions for a century.

It will be seen therefore that the prevailing Christian attitude to politics has varied from first to last. When Scott Holland wrote, however, the pendulum had begun to swing the other way. F. D. Maurice, Ludlow and Charles Kingsley preached the social gospel in the mid-nineteenth century, the successors of the Tractarians carried it on, and by 1918 the movement began to gather power. The Conference on Christian Politics, Economics and Citizenship (C.O.P.E.C.) at Birmingham in 1924 was a milestone in this development. In 1925 Söderblom, Archbishop of Uppsala, called a Universal Christian Conference on Life and Work, and an offshoot of this was the Oxford Conference of 1937 on Church, Community and State at which almost all the non-Roman Catholic Churches were represented. The leading British figure after 1918 in this movement to re-state Christian responsibility for politics and economics was William Temple. The movement reached a peak during his short tenure of the see of Canterbury, and one would have to go back to the Middle Ages to find an Archbishop as convinced as Temple was of the relevance of Christianity to everyday political affairs.

The meeting at the Albert Hall in London on 26 September 1942, in the midst of war, usefully illustrated the claims some Christians make for their religion's bearing on politics and the ensuing correspondence in *The Times* not only brought out different views held by other Christians but raised several of the many difficulties with which this great matter is infested. With Temple on the platform were Cyril Garbett, Archbishop of York, and Sir Stafford Cripps, then Lord Privy Seal.

The Church, Temple said, had a right and a duty to declare the principles which should govern the ordering of society. Everyone accepted that the Church should lay down principles for the conduct of individuals, but what was disputed was the right of the Church to lay down principles for the action of trade unions, employers' federations or national States. In his view this distinction between the individual life and the various groups in which it was lived was untenable. The understanding which the Church had concerning the nature and destiny of man gave it a qualification for deciding what kind of structure of society was wholesome for man and what unwholesome. After this statement of general principle, Temple came down to detail — though here he was careful to explain he spoke as a citizen, not as the head of a Church — and proceeded to criticize the profit motive, the unrestricted private ownership of land, and the creation of credit by the banks which as a monopoly function ought to be taken over by the State.

For these political utterances, the more obnoxious because they were Socialistic in origin, Temple was taken to task by a string of critics in *The Times*. Conservative M.P.s counselled the Church to stay within its own limits, and W. R. Inge, the former Dean of St. Paul's, who had a reputation as a popular journalist in the *Evening Standard*, made reference to the 'court chaplains of King Demos' and quoted Burke:

'Politics and the pulpit are terms that have little agreement. Those who quit their proper characters to assume what does not belong to them are ignorant both of the character they leave and of the character they assume. Wholly unacquainted with the world in which they are so fond of meddling, and inexperienced in all its affairs, on which they pronounce with so much confidence, they have nothing of politics but the passions they excite.'

Burke's taunt of amateurishness and ignorance was echoed by other correspondents but effectively silenced, in so far as it touched Temple, by the Cambridge economist, Professor A. C. Pigou:

Expertness is a matter of degree. It is really not the fact that, because a man is active in one sphere of life, he is, therefore, necessarily a complete nincompoop about everything else. . . . Everyone knows that the Archbishop is a highly intelligent man and has been deeply interested in these matters for many years. It is difficult to believe that he is not far more expert at them than the vast majority of letter-writers and leader-writers in newspapers. Why then should he not say what he thinks? Of course, if he were to claim for his views on these matters special authority on account of his ecclesiastical position, that would be very improper, and, indeed, very ridiculous. But in the most express terms he has disclaimed anything of the kind. So what is all the bother about?

While Temple claimed no special authority for his views on account of his headship of a Church, it must be allowed that the most striking thing about them was that they were proclaimed by an Archbishop. Temple might say he was speaking as an individual citizen, but he was too good a man to waste an Archbishop's time on matters which he did not consider to be of grave importance for the Church. In fact, it is extremely difficult, when an Archbishop mounts a political platform, not to feel the Church is in some way committed however much he may protest that he speaks for himself alone. It was the obviousness of this deduction which led a Lancashire country clergyman to declare the case against ecclesiastical interference in politics: 'The gospel contains no social programme, and the Church as an institution has no right to put forward such a programme; its business is not to reconstruct society but to convert individuals.' Another correspondent noted one consequence of the Church's having such a programme: 'The objection to the Church "taking part in politics" is that it must take sides; and those who are on the side opposed to that which it takes feel a sense of injustice in being attacked, not by the ordinary arguments of political controversy, but by a body which claims divine authority.'

It will be seen even from these quotations that a Christian form of politics, at least one generally acceptable to Christians, is not easy to lay down. The distinction frequently drawn by Temple was that it was possible and right for the Church to declare political principles, but wrong to go into details of application which must be left to individual citizens. For example, the Church might declare the necessity of proper care for old people, but on the question of whether their pensions should be contributory or non-contributory it was not the Church but an expert or a politician who should speak. Most would agree that it was ordinarily a Christian duty to care for the aged, but one can imagine political situations in which they might have to be sacrificed to the young, for the sake of ensuring a particular society's survival. Even if it were possible to arrive at Christian political principles of absolute validity, the difficulty of politics lies surely more in applying principles than in drawing them up. Is there value in agreeing on principles, but parting company on detail? If the Church's contribution to politics stops short of telling the politician what he should do, is it of much use? In the realm of personal morality the Church has no such diffidence. Adultery, for example, may be more or less heinous, but Christians would agree that it was always wrong. But when it comes to aggression between States, it has first to be decided whether it has happened and then whether it is justified, and to these questions, as invariably in politics, there are no clear answers — or rather, there are many answers that appear blindingly clear to those who make them, but they are not agreed answers and so resolve nothing.

There is something disturbing to easy assumptions when we come across, as we still may, two Members of Parliament, both Christians, both sincerely believing that they are applying Christian principles in politics, but the one belonging to the Conservative and the other to the Labour Party. If principles issue so differently when put into practice, the suspicion is that they were too widely drawn or obscure in the first place. When Mr. Aubrey Jones, later Minister of Supply, wrote in his book *The Pendulum of Politics*, 1946, that 'True religion and socialism are incompatible with one another, and he who would cling to his religion must abandon his socialism', he appears in sharp contrast with William Temple who remarked, at the time of his joining the Labour Party in 1918 (he remained a member for seven years), 'Churchmen ought to consider very carefully the formulated programme of the Labour Party, and whether they should individually subscribe to it.' Yet if we take the Christian social principles set out by Temple in his *Christianity and Social Order* — Freedom, Social Fellowship, and Service — we can well see how one man may choose Socialism and the other Conservatism, seeing that such principles are so broad that they may be held to include the whole range of decent politics. British parties are anyhow so close together that for Christians to stray into one rather than the other could be a mere consequence of upbringing or environment. There is everything to be said, in a professedly Christian country, for Christians being spread throughout the politicial spectrum, for nothing is more certain to stir up anti-clericalism or hostility to religion than for all its followers to club together in one party. However, where Christians belong to several competing parties, they must necessarily disagree much about detailed policy, and indeed possibly in their general attitudes to society, and this again suggests to us that what Christianity has to say of politics is by no means precise.

There is a further difficulty. In the West it is now taken that politics to be respectable must operate within some form or other of Anglo-Saxon democracy. Is it not in such a setting only that Christian politics may develop? While this book will concern itself mainly with the West, and with England particularly, there are grave objections to supposing that political forms evolved by English Protestants are the most typically Christian that can be discovered. It could indeed be argued, and often has been, that Western democracy is the most perfect expression of the Christian spirit and its emphasis on personality, and is, as it were, the peak of its development in the political field. Aquinas himself would seem to have regarded a mixture of monarchy, aristocracy and democracy as the ideal government, and this view of his has sometimes been worked into panegyrics of the British system (where, however, the balance between the three constituent parts has been in constant process of change, the democratic element being now far more prominent than the other two). But it would seem reasonable to suppose that wherever in a State Christians hold the main positions of power, some form of Christian politics is in operation. It may not be ideal; it may be declared by many to be actively un-Christian; but any government administered by professed Christians must be allowed to offer evidence useful to our discussion. Spain under General Franco offers a spectacle of Christian politics and if his rule is widely judged offensive it is mild beside similarly authoritarian régimes conducted by Christians in the past. Franco Spain is a fossil that cannot be disowned; it is a Christian fossil. There are few parts of the world today where Christians of the Eastern Orthodox Church can be said to be in power. But their helplessness in Soviet Russia represents little change in the effective political influence of the Church in that country. From the days of the Byzantine Empire the Eastern Orthodox Church has disclaimed all concern with politics, and has been content with a position which at its best might be described as that of a religious department of State. What must be remembered is that the authoritarianism of Franco Spain and the political indifferentism of the Orthodox Church spring naturally out of the history of Christianity. Nor are they mere survivals. They emphasize certain permanent attitudes in Christian thought about the world which still exist, quite strongly, within the Churches of the western democracies as well. How often in local meetings in England have sympathetic murmurs greeted some worthy's heartfelt exclamation: 'What we want in politics is more Christianity!' Little can he or his hearers realize the complexity of that aspiration, the difficulty of deciding what Christianity has to say about politics (for almost every conceivable political opinion has at some time received respectable Christian backing), and what part of that is relevant to our own day-to-day

B

affairs. The great divergences between the various Christian approaches to politics have their roots in the history of the Early Church and these origins will be considered more closely in the next chapter.

Some readers will have by now grown restive at an approach to the problem which they regard as cynical in its scepticism. Members of Christian political movements, like Christian Action in England, are firmly convinced that the command to change the world politically was given to them by Christ. As He would not command the impossible or the too difficult, the appropriate application of Christianity to politics must necessarily be discernible to men of goodwill. If 'Thy kingdom come, Thy will be done, in earth, as it is in heaven' is interpreted as a prayer, taught us by Christ himself, that the Kingdom of God be realized on earth, then the command to develop a Christian politics is indeed clear. This is how many modern Christians concerned with politics do interpret it. Diana Collins in her book *Christian Action* says (p. 11) that 'we have, indeed, an imperative and absolute duty to labour for the establishment of God's kingdom here on earth, and that means that we must try to bring His love into the whole of life, public as well as private, in the international field, and in our own country'. Victor Gollancz, the publisher, who was the chief speaker at a 'Call to Christian Action' meeting in Oxford in 1947, a meeting chiefly concerned with Anglo-German reconciliation, declared that he 'would go so far as to say that there is the gravest element of spiritual falsity in any religion for which the establishment of God's kingdom on earth is not the very centre of its hope and striving'. Sir Stafford Cripps in his *Towards Christian Democracy* constantly reiterates a conviction that 'we must concentrate upon the task, both individually and as members of the Church, of creating the Kingdom of God here on earth'. If this reading of the passage in the Lord's Prayer were correct, then the Christian's political duty would in principle be clearer. It is however wholly incorrect. The Church has at no time given this secular interpretation to the idea of the Kingdom of God and its roots lie, not in Christianity, but in humanitarian utopianism.

For the Christian, the Kingdom of God is already come. It

came with Jesus Christ. But it is still in process of being made, is not complete, and cannot be completed in this world. Sin which is built into this world prevents the perfecting of any human endeavour and sin infects the lives and action of all men, Christians included. In this world, the special sphere of the Kingdom is the Church, for in the Church the divine community is forming. The perfection of the Kingdom is never to be expected in this world, where sin rules out perfection, but in the beyond. The Kingdom of God on earth which some Christian politicians pursue is a secular conception concealing a profound injustice. For what is its promise? That future generations may enjoy conditions of happy plenty in a world where equality and virtue are lastingly established. Apart from the promise's incredibility to the student of human nature, its fulfilment would amount to the sacrifice of past generations to their successors. Christians believe that God is lord of history, but they cannot accept that He is concerned to prepare, with or without human co-operation, an earthly paradise for men and women of the twenty-first century, say, whose satisfactions men and women of all previous centuries can never enjoy. The Kingdom of God is open to all, and because of that it must lie outside the world. We may imagine this divine community forming in the beyond, increased by every human generation, but never realizing its perfection until the world and history end. This is the orthodox Christian view of the Kingdom. Those Christians who talk of bringing the Kingdom on earth or of building Jerusalem in England's green and pleasant land have mixed into their religion ingredients entirely foreign to it. The perfectionist hopes of the nineteenth-century reformers, with their grand idea of human progress (which supplied Communism with its own hope of the earthly paradise of the classless society and the withering away of the State), have worked themselves into the heads of some Christians but have no foundations in Christianity.

If the notion of creating God's Kingdom on earth is presumptuous, a product of spiritual pride and ignorance of man's proven incapacities, this does not mean necessarily that Christians are not called upon to improve the world, or at least to try. There is

nothing in Christianity, of course, which guarantees that the world
will become more just, more civilized, more prosperous, as the
faith spreads. Although marked by many evils, the Roman
Empire in A.D. 1 was a far finer example of man's handiwork, on
any score, than its former territories could be considered 600
years later, after all those years of Christian belief. No informed
Christian would ask that his religion be judged by its results
in history. On purely pragmatical grounds, from the study of
societies non-Christian and pre-Christian, and a comparison of
them with Christian societies, it should be clear to the detached
observer that Christianity has less of its own to contribute to the
lives of States and nations than has been supposed in principle.
Such a study of history would seem to show that Christianity's
main bearing was not on public life and politics at all. But if its
real concern, as this book maintains, is with relationships between
God and men, and men and men, this still enjoins a secondary
concern with the setting in which men live their lives and work.
How man stands with God, how man lives beside his neighbour
— these are all-important. Everything else on earth is no more than
the setting, the background, against which these vital relationships,
themselves the purpose of life, are brought into play. This framework must exist. As man must till his fields, so he must attend to
politics, for both are needed to sustain the important side of his
life which is to do with relationships. This digression is introduced
only for the sake of those who consider that politics and social
welfare are supreme activities and would test the worth of a
religion by its relevance to them. But it is difficult to see how a
Christian can regard politics as a human activity of the first order.
It ranks secondary, and we may find in its comparative unimportance in the Christian scheme a possible reason for the dubious
and mixed results of Christian activity in the political field. We
cannot change the seasons and there seems something almost as
immutable in the political behaviour of human societies. There is
an evil, a perpetual frustration, a regular falling short which cannot be eradicated from political action.

I may at this point attempt to meet a possible criticism which
rejects as dangerous and misleading my analogy between the work

of politics, which is wholly by, through and for people, and that of tilling the land, which is an activity directed to the non-human resources of the earth. If Christianity is about personal relationships, how can it fail to affect politics, which is one great mass of interwoven personal relationships? It is certainly true that personal relationships exist in politics, in the sense that Asquith, Grey and Haldane were close friends and Lloyd George in 1916 a bitter opponent of Asquith. Such face-to-face dealings are matched by those between men working together on a farm. These close relationships are within the personal sphere to which Christianity is chiefly relevant. But they are rare in politics. Politics is mainly impersonal. Men appeal to men whom they do not know and accept the leadership of men they have never met. Political parties are made up of persons, and seem to have a life of their own, but they are not themselves persons and it is a mistake to personalize them. Groups like trade unions are not persons except in a technical legal sense. The conflicts of politics are fought out between organized interests which are directed by persons but behave in many ways impersonally. A crowd listening to a political speaker is not unlike an audience watching an actor, or, at one further remove, a man looking at a painting by a famous artist. Something of personality comes through; there is communication, but it is indirectly rather than immediately personal. A Parliament passing a law concerning the treatment of prisoners is acting abstractly, generally and impersonally, compared with the father who is deliberating on the punishment of the disobedient son standing before him. A Government deciding whether or not to declare war is far removed from two people on the edge of turning from words to blows. Such thoughts are enough, perhaps, at this stage, to permit the argument that if Christianity is mainly about personal relationships it is less applicable, or applicable only with much greater difficulty, to the more impersonal realm of public affairs.

But if there is little in their religion to tell Christians that they will succeed in making politics work better than other men, any more than Christians may expect to get more out of the soil, there is much in their religion to suggest that they ought to take part in politics and do their best. A Christian is taught never to set his heart on the things of this world. 'Here we have no abiding city', he is told, and 'Labour not for the meat which perisheth, but for the meat that endureth unto everlasting life.' This is a deeply held attitude, but there is the other side. 'I have compassion on the multitude because they have nothing to eat.' The Church and its members must have a concern for men's ordinary affairs, because they must show the love for men that God has, and cannot love people without taking an interest in what they do. The love of one's neighbour comes out as a sense of responsibility for him and this responsibility must be exercised, not only in personal, but in political and social affairs. Christians have little assurance from either faith or experience that they will do better in these fields than anyone else, but to show less willingness to try would be flagrant disobedience to the Commandment of love; they must try more.

They will meet with oddly disappointing results. It is not perhaps in these days realized how much Christians had to do with creating the atmosphere in which the first Labour Government with a solid majority of its own came into power in Britain, to establish our version of the Welfare State. Many of the votes that went to Labour for the first time in 1945 were cast by middle-class people whose consciences had been disturbed by the teaching of Church leaders. 'Every child', wrote William Temple in 1942, 'should find itself a member of a family housed with decency and dignity so that it may grow up as a member of that basic community in a happy fellowship unspoilt by underfeeding or over-crowding, by dirty and drab surroundings, or by mechanical monotony of environment.' That, of course, is an aspiration proper to an industrially developed country with a favourable balance of trade. There are many countries today, in the East particularly, where the statement of such a principle would be ludicrously inapposite. It would be happy for them if they could say, 'No child should starve.' But in the England of 1942, in spite of the hunger marchers of the thirties and the monstrous unemployment of those years, Temple's principle was fair enough. A year before he declared it Temple had presided over the conference on 'The

Life of the Church and the Order of Society' at Malvern. Among the findings of that conference was one that began by declaring the sovereignty of God over all human life and the call to His children to be brothers one of the other. The Church, it went on, should point to features in existing society which are contrary to divine justice and 'act as stumbling blocks, making it harder for men to live Christian lives'. The report continues:

In our present situation we believe that the maintenance of that part of the structure of our society, by which the ultimate ownership of the principal industrial resources of the community can be vested in the hands of private owners, may be such a stumbling-block. On the one hand it may deprive the poorest members of the community of the essentials of life. On the other, while these resources can be so owned, men will strive for their ownership for themselves. As a consequence, a way of life founded on the supremacy of the economic motive will remain, which is contrary to God's plan for mankind.

Twenty years later, after some years of experience of nationalized industries, that finding of the Malvern Conference rings strangely. It is not that the nationalization of coal and the railways, for example, has turned out badly. There were many sound economic reasons for removing these basic but intractable industries, unprofitable in many of their parts, from private ownership. On technical grounds, more industries than these may seem suited to nationalization. It is when we search for the effects of the changes already made in the ownership of industry which might have significance for a Christian that disappointment sets in. Are industrial relations in coal and railway transport better for nationalization? Can it be claimed genuinely that there is a new spirit inside these industries? It is possible to point to all manner of technical improvements and modernization schemes, most of real economic value, which might never have come about except through State control. But the question for the Christian is not whether carriages are cleaner and trains run more to time, or mechanization produces coal more cheaply, but whether the old bitterness between masters and men has disappeared in more harmonious relations between managers and men. It is early, of course, to speak, but experience suggests that suspicion and resentment still exist, and that if they are to be removed it is not by changing systems but by new attitudes. Twenty years later, can it really be argued that nationalization of their industry has made it easier for railwaymen 'to live Christian lives'? Is it not reasonable now to suspect that the question of private or social ownership has little to do with Christian living, and that Christians who once thought it had were misled by the political fashions of their times? Those Christians who advocated nationalization on purely natural, that is to say technical, grounds, were surely right to busy themselves for the common good, working towards humdrum decisions beside other men, and not standing apart in pietistic aloofness. Those, however, who based their arguments for nationalization on the sovereignty of God and the brotherhood of man must necessarily be dismayed by the pedestrian results of hopes set altogether too high.

If those Christians who supported the policy of nationalization on religious grounds cannot regard the product of their labour with unalloyed satisfaction, it might be held that their part in creating the Welfare State, with its greater equality of income and its recognition that proper provision must be made for the weak or unfortunate, has borne happier fruits. The Gospels are filled with warnings addressed to the rich and blessings conferred upon the poor and when we come later to discuss those few political tendencies and attitudes which have a specifically Christian mark upon them — for in our view they will be found to be few — room must be made for that enduring concern for the poor which the Church has always shown. Yet if one surveys the Welfare State in the early 1960s, with its fairer shares, reformed educational system, full employment, and payments to people sick or in other ways in need, one does not have to be a Christian to detect much that is disappointingly wrong. In the middle of the want and waste of the 1930s, an argument commonly urged by Christians upon their less socially conscious fellows was that the mind of a man with an empty stomach was too concentrated on the business of filling it to have time for thinking of God. The argument brings out the point that for a Christian the end of all his activities, social, political and personal, should tend to the greater glory of

God. Ultimately the Christian in politics — and the Malvern Conference was right in emphasizing this — must aim at removing stumbling blocks which prevent men and women from coming closer to God and so discovering what, for a Christian, life is all about. Certainly political action has a part to play in this, but it is an uncertain instrument and too much faith cannot be placed in it. Many social evils have been removed under the Welfare State, but some have been created, and the tremendous surge of social progress between the 1930s and the 1960s illustrates the same inescapable mixing in of evil with good which attends humanity's best efforts. English society is in every way more prosperous in the 1960s and the prosperity more evenly spread, but crime, particularly among the young, is increasing and the widespread opinion that 'getting on' in life is its main purpose — the theme of C. P. Snow's very representative novels — does not suggest that the Welfare State, whatever injustices it has removed, has made it easier 'for men to live Christian lives'. There remains some point in William Wilberforce's complaint, unpopular though it may be with the humanist: 'I declare my greatest cause of difference with the democrats is their laying, and causing the people to lay, so great a stress on the concerns of this world as to occupy their whole minds and hearts and to leave a few scanty and lukewarm thoughts for the heavenly treasure.' As Lord Hugh Cecil pointed out in *Conservatism*, although the Gospels underline the Christian's responsibility for the poor, their approach is radically different from that of the secular reformer. 'In the Gospels', he writes, 'riches and poverty are invariably considered only in their bearing on the spiritual well-being of the rich or poor person. Accordingly poverty is invariably treated as a blessed state; riches as one full of spiritual peril.' The Christian planner of the Welfare State has to think of the next world as well as this, whereas his humanitarian fellow-worker has no such concern. The worldly judgment is that it is better to be rich than poor, but the view of the Gospels is that it is safer to be poor than rich, and the disagreement erects a permanent difference between the Christian and the ordinary man of the world.

In spite, however, of the inevitable disappointment of Christian hopes in political activity, we have argued that Christians ought to take part in it, to accept responsibility for society beside their fellow men and to work in their company. Enough has been said of the difficulties of this field from the Christian point of view to indicate that Christians in politics should work humbly and easily in partnership with men of goodwill who do not share their faith. Elsewhere in this study we shall draw attention to political attitudes and contributions which may possibly be described as specifically Christian — elements which we should not expect to see as strongly represented if Christianity had not come into the world. But it is essential to remember that politics existed and were practised well and badly, virtuously and wickedly, before Christianity came into the world. Not only does this fact demonstrate the ease with which Christians should be able to co-operate with others, but it urges them to refrain from the habit, irritating to non-Christians, of assuming that all good action is inspired by religion. Clearly in a country which has been Christianized for as long as Britain, our ideas of right and wrong must be profoundly affected by Christian influence. But this does not allow us to claim natural virtues like honesty, compassion or justice as belonging exclusively or even predominantly to the convinced Christian. However much we may argue that they are fortified by religion, or that they are found at their highest only in the religious man, we certainly cannot say that in the politics of non-Christian countries the natural virtues are not to be found. It is possible for a non-Christian to be a good and honest politician and for a non-Christian country to have good and honest politics. Indeed, such a view finds its justification in an important branch of Christian thought which could do with more attention than it receives today. The medieval Church inherited from Rome the theory of Natural Law. Outlined by Aristotle, it was developed by the Stoic philosophers whose general belief may be summed up in the formula: Nature is Reason, and Reason is God. All men for them, whatever their State or country, were members of the city of God, and they were all subject to the law of that city, the law of Reason, the law of Nature. In their separate States men lived under many varieties of man-made positive law which all reflected in some degree the majesty of the true and universal Law of Nature and of God. The early Christian fathers took over the Stoic idea of the Law of Nature and incorporated it in the Church. They had to fit it into the teaching of the Fall and Original Sin, and to make this possible a division was drawn between an absolute Law of Nature, proper to man's state of grace before the Fall, and a relative Law of Nature applicable to his present fallen condition.

The Law of Nature was vague enough before medieval schoolmen began to argue about the content of the two halves into which it had been divided. It was nowhere codified or written down — in fact, it was not discoverable except by the reason of individual men. But as an idea, it still has much usefulness. The Declaration of Human Rights adopted in the General Assembly of the United Nations in 1948 may be derided as ratiocination in a void but it testifies to the value of the Natural Law idea even today. How, it was asked by one side in 1948, can human rights be recognized or granted except by States? How may men talk at one moment of their 'inalienable' rights and in the next turn to their State with a request that they be allowed to possess them?

Yet, however difficult the theory of Natural Law may be to apply to the real world, it, or something very like it, is needed by that world. If men feel strongly that they are entitled to 'Life, Liberty and the pursuit of Happiness', and their State denies these goods to them, to whom can they appeal but to their Creator, or, if they do not acknowledge one, to Nature, or to the experience of man, or to some such ultimate source of rightful law? In all societies, there are certain rules of neighbourliness, prohibitions against acts which disturb communal life, and though social customs and accepted morality may vary greatly there is still a recognizable residue of what would pass for morality anywhere. Any man, whether he be a Christian or not, might reasonably conclude, merely from looking at human societies up and down the world, that there are certain broad human necessities for men to observe if they wish to live quietly together, that there are general laws only under which human beings can live together and these might as well be described as the Law of Nature as by any other name. It is not entirely fanciful to imagine this law of human conduct as something really existing, though not apparent, nowhere written down, but to whose behests the customs and positive law of all good societies approximate more or less closely.

Certainly the Christian is driven to hold some conception of Natural Law, a law of virtue for all men, for Christian and non-Christian alike, because his God is creator and judge of the world. It is wholly His and His purpose extends to all men, those born before the revelation of God in Christ, those who have not yet received that revelation and those who having received it cannot accept it. No Christian can suppose — and it was the merit of the Natural Law theory to drive this home — that some goodness is impossible to man without the grace of Christianity. The conception of a Creator God, ever thoughtful for His creation, demands that He should have made it possible for men to apprehend a pattern of natural good living. If this were not part of His purpose from the first, before ever He revealed Himself, then human life would have been faced with the impossible. It must be allowed that morality was proper to man from the first, that its tenets were discoverable by reason, that some men and some societies have reached higher than others but that all possessed enough sense of its necessity to admit a moral law.

This view must be kept in mind throughout any study of Christians in politics. It is dangerously easy, when seeking to discover the essentially Christian contribution, to slip into claiming all good actions as Christianly inspired. This would be absurd. There is a goodness — common honesty, a concern for people, a sense of justice, a hatred of corruption — which may be looked for in all politicians whatever their faith.

The Natural Law theory encourages us to think in terms of a common political morality for Christian and non-Christian, and of the possibility of co-operation between them. Realistic Christians in most Western countries will admit that such co-operation is all that is open to them. In England certainly professing Christians are a minority. It is only too easy to forget the fact of this and to discuss matters as though the control of society were still in Christian hands. This is because the classical period of thought about the Church's task in politics was the Middle Ages, when non-Christians, one might almost say, did not exist in Europe, even mildly deviant Christians being quickly removed as heretics. The main forms of a Christian approach to politics were laid down during this age of Christian ascendancy, and it is in terms of those forms that we still incline to think, although the ascendancy has altogether disappeared. Most English churchmen who in modern times have been interested in the relation of religion and politics have belonged to the Catholic section of the Church of England and it came easily to them to draw inspiration and ideas from the medieval Church. Roman Catholic writers naturally tend especially to think in terms of the medieval situation, where politics no less than religion had for ultimate end the salvation of souls, without remembering entirely how remote it is from the world confronting us today. One feels that even Jacques Maritain, who in his *True Humanism* never fails to stress the difference between the 'consecrational concept of Christendom' and the modern lay State, nevertheless has in mind a society in which Christianity is a predominant or at least an extremely powerful force. Mr. T. S. Eliot views the Western democracies, the lives of their people depersonalized by industrialism, as sinking into a kind of paganism. Our culture, however, so far as it is positive at all, is still Christian, and he believes in a still open choice of our deliberately forming a new Christian culture or accepting a pagan one. Yet it must be said that Mr. Eliot's *The Idea of a Christian Society* is a visionary speculation. He looks forward to a community whose rulers will 'accept Christianity not simply as their own faith to guide their actions, but as the system under which they are to govern'. It may well be that the movement of history will once again bring the idea of such a Christian government within the bounds of credibility. But it is not credible now, and this book is directed to discussing what Christians may expect to do through politics in the present largely non-Christian world. Clearly the setting in which they work is limiting. Recognizing those limitations is a necessary first step, for no service to Christianity is done by exaggerating the possibilities open to Christian politicians. There is a vast difference between the Christian writer in his study,

working out in one more of the many books which have already
appeared the revolutionary changes which Christianity could
bring about in the State and society, and the practical Christian
participating in some loneliness in the mainly neutral sphere of
politics as it is. There is indeed no useful connexion between the
activities of these two men. The writer in his study is presupposing
a re-conversion of society, which must come about before his
ideas can be realized; the active politician cannot pre-suppose any
such re-conversion, let alone aim at it in any way more direct than
setting an example of Christian living. He has felt a call to work in
politics, and he labours there usually, not as a revolutionary, but
as a sustainer of the present order, almost pagan though it may be,
because the lives of his neighbours need that settled order for the
conduct of their everyday affairs, their eating and drinking, their
getting married and having children. The majority of those with
whom he works will not in these days be Christians at all. He will
not gain their support for the idealistic schemes outlined in the
books of Christian writers on sociology and politics. But through
the common concerns, in the area covered by Natural Law, he
can appeal to them, and he will not find it impossible from time to
time, because he works with these men as a colleague, to achieve
some measure of settlement which is the better for the Christian
insight he brings to the shared task. There are indeed great questions, hovering between the areas of Natural Law, which all men
can accept, and of the divine law revealed by Christianity, which
Christians should discern more easily — questions of race relations, of reconciliation, and of resistance to overweening authority,
to whose solution the Christian is specially fitted to contribute.
So it need not be felt that he brings nothing more than the next
man, and that his religion is no help to him at all in political
affairs. But that Christianity is the great panacea for our earthly
difficulties, as so many seem to conceive it, is an illusion which
the study of history and politics ought to dispel. The fact of sin
contradicts the idea of the earthly paradise. Our best efforts are
not unlike those of a man who bales a perpetually leaking boat.

So far we have reviewed generally and discursively the applicability of Christianity to politics. Later we shall examine the

thoughts and actions of some consciously Christian politicians, and some of the theories of modern writers on the subject. In the light of this evidence, an attempt will be made to set out what the Christian has in fact contributed in the past and for what we may look to him in the present. First, however, it is necessary to look back to the Early Church to discover the roots of Christian attitudes to politics and then follow this development in later centuries.

2

The Legacy of the Early Church

WHAT had the New Testament to say about politics? In asking this question, we are not adopting a fundamentalist attitude and seeking to pierce through a mist of later misconceptions to the original truth of the Gospel. In trying to discover the basis of Christian politics we must range far outside the Gospels and take account of Church teaching. Too sharp a line must not be drawn between the days when our Lord was on earth and those when His message had passed to a Church guided, as He promised, by the Holy Spirit. As in other matters, in this study of politics we cannot ignore the development of the once-for-all Revelation by latter generations of Christians. But we must start with the Gospels and the rightness of this will be seen when, as we recall some of their main emphases, we realize suddenly how deeply they have entered into Western thought, so that the origins of firmly fixed political attitudes today, often maintained without any consciousness of their connexions with Christianity, are found to lie 2,000 years ago.

In the Gospels Jesus preached the Last Judgment and the coming of the Kingdom of God, in which God's complete mastery of the world will be shown and sin and suffering have no part. The timing of this programme is not specified, though the Kingdom will come 'soon' — which the early Church construed as 'any time now', a mistaken interpretation which clearly much affected her attitude to this world. The Kingdom of God is not thought of as an earthly paradise, but as the vindication of God's greatness, and it is always associated with the Last Judgment and the passing away of the earth. Meanwhile, a community of men and women, living in love for God and for each other, are preparing for the coming Kingdom. Love is the order of this community. Love God: love your neighbour. This is the whole of the matter:

everything else follows and is included. It is not possible to love God without loving your neighbour and if you love God nothing else matters. Love God and do what you wish. This saying is not in the Gospel, but it is the implication of the Gospel. It does not sanction any form of behaviour in those who love God. The assumption is that those who love God can only show the effect of that love in all they do. It constrains them to act in ways which are described in the Sermon on the Mount, but the teaching of the Sermon is not a rule. It is a description of how people who love God cannot help behaving.

Jesus showed a special concern for the poor and this concern of His has reverberated down history. The condemnation of riches in the Gospel has been appealed to by medieval peasant rebels and modern social reformers. Yet the use politics has made of the Gospel's attitudes to poverty is, in a sense, an immense misunderstanding. Jesus instances the poor man and holds him up as an example solely because the poor man, less distracted by the things of this world, finds it easier to love God. The ancient Jews tended to regard success as a sign of divine favour or reward and this self-satisfaction, a form of self-dependence, was attacked by Jesus. He attacked it because self-dependence was a barrier to loving God, in that those who feel sufficient have no sense of need. But the poor man, suffering from the pinch of failure and usually from the physical ills which went with it in those days, felt himself without hope or help. To any rope thrown to him he would cling with all his might, like any sinking man. He was thus, the poor man, more readily open to the love of God, and it was this which was Jesus's concern and not the poverty that he praised for helping and the riches he condemned for standing in its way. When St. Francis talked about 'My Lady Poverty' with a kind of whimsical affection, he was much nearer the Gospel spirit than the modern social reformer typified by Lord Beveridge who diagnosed four 'giant evils' in pre-war Britain of which Want was foremost. There is, as Troeltsch rightly argues, not a trace of social reform in Jesus's teaching. Relieving the poor, rich men selling their goods to give to the poor — these are illustrations of what happens through that neigh-

c

bourly love which runs in harness with the love of God.
Love and its relationships are the Gospel's sole theme; all else is
incidental.

During some periods this point was fairly well taken. Shaftesbury was unlike a modern social reformer and the initial motive
behind his famous and effective agitation on behalf of the factory
children was his earnest wish that they should have enough time
off work to be properly educated as Christians. Wilberforce,
although not indifferent to the suffering of the poor in England,
was also keenly aware that too great an improvement in their
earthly state might take their minds off the heavenly treasure.
Our own day, of course, happens to be one in which such
attitudes appear remarkably wicked, but the last century was
nearer the Gospel truth than our own. Jesus saw that poverty was
a painful disability in this world, but for the coming world of the
Kingdom, immeasurably more important, and for loving God
and man, poverty was an ideal starting point, a blessed state. The
assumption of our affluent society, that poverty is a curse to be
removed at all costs, lies almost at the opposite pole.

There is, however, as so often in Christianity, a genuine tension
in the interpretation of the Gospel view of poverty. If Jesus and
indeed His followers in the Early Church never thought in terms
of the need to level society and abolish poverty as such, it is also
clear that He and they regarded indifference to poverty, however
blessed a state it was, as a sinful failure in love. Charity and alms-
giving, the sharing of possessions with those who have less,
although regarded as outmoded and odious in the Welfare State,
were recommended to His followers by Jesus. 'He had compassion
on them.' Our Lord's concern for every form of suffering has left
a deep imprint. His words on poverty, though constantly misunderstood, have had a powerful influence upon Christian politicians, and indeed no less upon their post-Christian successors.
The poor, oppressed and ignored in society, were raised high in
the Gospel, whereas the rich, who lorded it in the world, were
severely criticized. This simple picture, shorn of all qualification,
has justified many revolts and agitations, from the Middle Ages
to this day. Here, broadly speaking, lie the foundations of Chris-

tian Socialism and indeed much of the *élan* of secular radicalism comes from this source.

In the Early Church, Jesus's teaching on love, combined with His special concern for the poor, produced those social attitudes and arrangements which Troeltsch has called the Communism of Love. It amounted to no more than the pooling of possessions as a proof of love and a willingness to sacrifice. There was no theory then that society as a whole should be run on these lines. These early Christians took the world as they found it and had no urge to change it. What they wished to do was to change relationships between themselves, to live in their small communities, of people of no importance to the world, according to the spirit of the Sermon on the Mount. The thought that all men should be equal, that none should possess more than another, never entered their heads. They were trying only to put love as Jesus had taught it into practice and to prepare their souls for salvation when, shortly, the Kingdom of God came. When the Church came to terms with the world, under Constantine, such efforts largely ceased. There is too much evil in a mass society for its affairs ever to be regulated by love. Law and coercion, property and legal rights are principles necessary to the maintenance of any large human society. Without them, it flies apart; the lofty aspirations of the Beatitudes cannot be a norm for large-scale society.

The early Christians were not political levellers or egalitarians — they did not think in political terms — but they had a keen sense that in God's eyes all men were equally unworthy, sinners equally needing redemption. To men and women whose lives were no more than a waiting for the Kingdom of God, differences between them in earthly place or possessions were of no account beside the hope they shared. The value of salvation was infinitely greater than that of anything else, and salvation was mediated through the Church and sacraments which were open equally and freely to all men. In the early Christian communities there appears no evidence to suggest that in secular matters any particular stress was laid upon equality. But secular affairs were not for these people important, and in what they did consider supremely important, their worship and especially the eucharistic feast, there was complete equality and fellowship. Even when Christianity later came to power there was little enthusiasm for the freeing of slaves. One can understand this possibly by noting that in what really mattered for the Christian the slave was under no disabilities. Before the altar slave and free man were on a level; the slave might as well lead the community's worship as the other man. To these fervently believing people, in the springtide of Christianity, this was the only sphere that counted.

It must be obvious how far such ideas as the Communism of Love, and the early Christian attitudes to poverty and the equal unworthiness of all men before God are from any principle of modern politics. Yet we shall also admit, as we follow the course of history down, that these dynamic religious ideas, held by people who regarded this world as evil and lived in expectation of its imminent end, have been mixed time and time again into purely secular hopes and aspirations. Ideal Christianity has exerted a profound fascination. Regularly over the centuries the notion that it can be applied to ordinary affairs and made to work has seized some men's minds, and naturally those men have tended to be the oppressed and unprivileged, those to whom the world has been least kind. Throughout the Middle Ages, heretical groups kept springing up to criticize the leaders of church and society for their riches, injustices, and un-Christian living. In the twelfth century the Humiliati in Lombardy, recruited from the poorest classes, formed little societies of their own sharing a common religious life. The Poor Men of Lyons or Waldensians were moved by much the same impulses and the Albigensian Catharists, although their heresy was more complicated and extreme, also started from the contrast between the pure relationships of the Gospel and the world they saw around them. The precursors of the English rising of Wat Tyler's peasants in 1381, preachers like John Ball and the Dominican John Bromyard, declared their reading of the social implications of early Christianity and inveighed against the rich. 'The poor for their good works', said Bromyard in a sermon, 'are not rewarded, but are so oppressed by the rich and powerful that however true a cause a poor man may have against a rich man in this world, it will nonetheless happen to him as it did to the lamb at the hands of the wolf. . . .' The same attitudes can be traced through the Lollards into the revolutionary conditions of the seventeenth century when in Cromwell's army levellers and others, in sects of every sort, harked back to the primitive simplicities of Gospel love and poverty. 'He hath put down the mighty from their seats; and hath exalted the humble and meek.' Although Jesus could say, 'I come to make all things new,' it is impossible to read into the Gospels or discover in the history of the first Christian communities any justification for changing the social order by revolutionary means. Yet in later centuries the spokesmen of the oppressed have constantly interpreted the Gospels in terms of this world and spoken as though the Kingdom of God were something we should seek to build here and now.

Of all Christian concepts, this of the coming Kingdom has supplied most hope and energy to the politics of the Left in later history. As we have seen, the secular version of this idea was false to the original, and had indeed far more in common with the Messianic kingdom looked forward to by the ancient Jews. The kingdom of Jewish expectation in the Old Testament was clearly one of this world, a kingdom to be ruled in righteousness, in time and under the eyes of the nations. It has never been easy for Christians, brought up on two Testaments, to distinguish between one and the other — indeed the Old is always stealing an advantage, because many of its attitudes are more akin to those man adopts naturally. But the Kingdom preached by Jesus is not of this world; its consummation comes as this earth passes away. That is the faith of the New Testament. Its secular effect has been to leave a powerful strain of hope, an eager looking forward, a sense that great things are round the corner if only men will exert themselves. It is the promise of reformers and revolutionaries down the ages and this unfailing optimism rises, one may believe, from the great hopefulness implanted in men's hearts by Christianity. Men retain the feeling that good news is in the air long after they have forgotten what it was about. But it is not only the secularized version of the Kingdom in the hands of non-Christian politicians that concerns us. Christians themselves, without

justification in the Gospels, are constantly caught by the fancy of
building the heavenly kingdom here and now. The attraction of
this false incentive is powerful. Charles Kingsley, one of the first
Christian Socialists, wrote in 1850 his novel *Alton Locke* with
working class politics for its theme. At the end, its crippled hero,
by now converted to Christianity from secular Socialism, expresses
well the translation of the Gospel hope of the Kingdom into lay
terms: 'Hark to the grand lilt of the "Good Time Coming!" —
Song which has cheered ten thousand hearts; which has already
taken root, that it may live and grow for ever — fitting melody
to soothe my dying years! Ah! how should there not be *A* Good
Time Coming? — Hope, and trust, and infinite deliverance! — a
time such as eye hath not seen, nor ear heard, nor hath it entered
into the heart of man to conceive! — coming surely, soon or
late, to those for whom a God did not disdain to die.' A few
lines earlier he apostrophizes 'Oh, England! Stern mother-land,
when wilt thou renew thy youth? — Thou wilderness of man's
making, not God's! — ... Is it not written, that the days shall
come when the forest shall break forth into singing, and the
wilderness shall blossom like the rose?' Here, unmistakably, in
the exaltation and the biblical language, we detect a Christian
engaged in imagining a Kingdom of God on earth.

One further implication of Gospel Christianity has had powerful
and lasting influence over political belief. Jesus teaches throughout
the infinite value of each human soul to God. A man who gains
the whole world has nothing if he lose his soul: the hairs of each
head are numbered: the one sinner who repents causes heaven to
rejoice. In Western thought before Christianity it is hard to detect
this particular note so firmly struck. The Greeks, who had a real
sense of personal and political freedom, tended to restrict its en-
joyment to certain classes and types of men; Aristotle, for example,
would reserve effective citizenship to rulers, priests and warriors.
Stoicism perhaps comes nearest to the all-inclusiveness of Christianity, but it was an intellectual doctrine that failed to move far
into the great world. Christianity made it entirely plain that each
man and woman, down to the poorest and most insignificant,
was equally the object of God's love. Everyone counted, because

God counted them. This teaching, once given a political dress, carried slowly and inevitably as far as mass democracy.

The notions so far discussed have played an immense part in the shaping of radical and popular movements in the history of Western politics; they are the foundations of the Left. But at the same time, in those early years of Christianity, the foundations of the Right were being laid also, for this is a religion which speaks politically with two voices, the one optimistic of the world and radical, the other pessimistic and strongly conservative. St. Paul's declaration of the proper Christian attitude to the State at the beginning of Romans 13 is Christian Conservatism's basic text: 'Let every soul be subject unto the higher powers; for there is no power but of God: the powers that be are ordained of God.' When St. Paul wrote, he and his fellow Christians lived in daily expectation of Christ's second coming and the establishment of the Kingdom. They saw themselves as strangers and pilgrims in a world with which they felt no sympathy, but at the same time, under St. Paul's guidance, they accepted Roman power as maintaining an ordered framework of existence. The business that absorbed them was making themselves ready for the Kingdom, by developing among themselves the relations of Christian love, and they were grateful that the Roman State kept things steady outside. They were, of course, forbidden to have any connexion with heathenism and idolatry, and for this reason certain forms of state service could not be entered by Christians, but the State as such they accepted. It is true that the writer of the Revelation, living under a persecution which had shed much Christian blood, saw Rome as the beast. Even this view has had its following down the centuries, men who regarded the State and any form of secular authority with deep suspicion. Anarchism like Communism can find its beginnings in the early Christian age. But by and large the majority opinion of the Early Church took the lead given by St. Paul: the State, which preserved order, drew its authority from God. Once again, at the very start, we are confronted with a division. There was the acceptance of the State, on St. Paul's grounds, and there was also a rejection of the State, as part of the world which Christians had been called upon to flee.

These early, almost instinctive reactions were rationalized when after Constantine the State itself became Christian. Under the influence of Judaism and Stoicism, there grew up a peculiarly ambivalent attitude to the State. As St. Paul had said, its powers were ordained of God, who had created the world and had sanctioned all that grew up in it, but those powers were a result of the Fall and were permeated by the evil released in that human catastrophe. Even under persecution by the State, the Christian saw his sufferings as trials and penalties imposed by a God who used the State as His instrument. These Christian men and women were gripped in the perpetual confusion caused by the problem of evil. On the one hand, they believed, with the Jews, that the world was a divine creation, and on the other, they faced a real world eaten out with wickedness. The paradox was lived out practically. However evil the world was, living in it was part of the religious life. There was no other stage on which the commandments of love could be heeded and practised.

The Stoics, from whom St. Paul and the Fathers learnt much, looked back to a golden age later destroyed by man's selfishness and unreason. In that idyllic beginning, man had been ruled by the Natural Law, and when intellectual Christians examined this idea it fitted in well with their own, for they identified the Natural Law of the Stoics with the law of His creation imposed by God. Anything in man-made, positive law which ran counter to the original Natural Law of creation was invalid. Yet, as they looked around them, Christians saw much tolerated by the State of which they disapproved — slavery, social customs and trading practices. How might the State, itself a product of God's creation, the maintainer of that order on which human life depended, have lost contact with its pure beginnings? Just as the Stoics explained the disappearance of their golden age under man's unreason, the Christians, turning to the Jewish Scriptures, found it in the Fall. The Christian Fathers ascribed all those institutions which they found intolerable, as well as the imperfections of the State, to the effects of original sin as it had spread outward from Eden. But Adam's sin had not destroyed the original and Natural Law entirely. Evil, it is true, had been released and it had infested the whole life of man. But there remained a second Natural Law, a shadow of its original, a Natural Law adapted to man's fallen condition, one which his reason could discover and which could guide him in the making of those positive laws and coercive system which were necessary to control and curb the vices released by the Fall. Thus this relative Natural Law, this reasonable system precisely suited to man's fallen nature, which included the powers of the State itself, was at once the result of sin and a remedy for it. Christians were in two minds about the State. Its coercive powers had come into existence only through sin, but they existed only to check it.

The notion of Natural Law, which had great part in medieval thought, may be confusing to modern minds, but the idea of it is simpler than its application. To put the discussion of the last few paragraphs more shortly, when God created the world and Adam, He established in Adam's mind a code of right living. This is the primitive Law of Nature, the law of paradise, the law of a world unspoilt by sin. This Law, suited to a perfect creation, could not fit a world into which evil had entered. Yet that fallen world still needed a Law discernible by the light of reason, and God, who had by no means deserted what He had made, guided men's minds to the perception of what might be called a second, revised edition of the Natural Law more suited to man's present state. For all practical purposes, this second version is the Natural Law which Christians from the first centuries down to the Middle Ages have seen as standing behind man-made law. It was an idea of value, not a figment of the philosophers. Medieval men would have been horrified at modern doctrines of sovereignty and the assumption that as the State is the source of law it can do no wrong. For the medieval Christian, no earthly law or decree possessed validity or need be obeyed if it ran counter to the Natural Law. As the Natural Law was nowhere written down, its practical usefulness was limited, but the idea of its existence was a powerful check to absolutism. It is good when both rulers and subjects believe that the ultimate authority in law does not lie in this earth at all. Subjects are made more critical and rulers take greater care.

St. Paul's teaching of respect for an ordered society as the desirable background to the life of Christian communities endowed Christianity throughout its history with a strong element of conservatism. It has appealed particularly to State churches like the Church of England where on one Sunday of every year, the fourth after the Epiphany, the celebrated text from Romans 13 forms the Epistle read at Holy Communion.[1] The Lutheran Church in Germany was late in developing opposition to Hitler largely because of its profound acceptance of the Pauline teaching of the God-given authority of the State.

There has never been a period in Christian history when in some part or other of the Church the rejection of the world, with its social organization and the State, has not been actively upheld. Monasticism itself was one of the formal expressions of this attitude. But in the formative centuries, the main body of Christians accepted the State and the order it dispensed with little disposition to change it and little thought of social reform. Examples can be found in the law of marriage, in which under the Christian Emperor Justinian many concessions were made to pre-Christian custom, and in the practices of trade and other daily business, but the most obvious is the early Christian toleration of slavery. While there was a definite attempt to sanctify the inward relationships of slavery — the slave being exhorted to love and obey his master, who should be concerned for the physical and spiritual well-being of his slaves — the institution was accepted as part of the general law of property and the order of the State. As Christian thinkers saw it, the right to possess slaves was upheld by that second and relative Natural Law rising from the Fall, and the institution of slavery was one that God had permitted to exist. In the eyes of religion no distinction existed between slave and free, as indeed there could be none in the coming Kingdom. But in human laws, under a system approved of by God, such a distinction did exist, and as long as slaves were not required to do anything sinful, their status might be left unchanged. In the beginning, as we have said, slaves were able to hold office in the

---

[1] The Roman Church, always jealous of superior claims by lay authority, allows no place to the passage in the Missal. It is read on 9 January at Matins, a Service in the Roman Church familiar to clergy and religious but not to the laity.

Church, but as the early expectation of the second coming drained away, and the Church settled down to live in a world where the secular authorities had become Christianized, further steps towards compromise were taken and Gregory the Great renounced the rights of office-holding by slaves. Slavery was allowed to endure right on into the Middle Ages and its disappearance was owed almost entirely to economic developments which deprived it of social usefulness. It was not in any way that Christians, in considering slavery, missed the contrast between what was and what ought to be. The admission of slavery, they saw quite clearly, was at odds with that inner spiritual freedom and equality which was the ideal of their faith. Although they believed in the principle that the world had to be renounced, and indeed did renounce it in many particulars, they nevertheless took the pragmatic view that it had to be lived in, and to live in it compromise was necessary. For those who wished to keep compromise down to a minimum, there was the safety-valve of the monastic life. In the monasteries, as later in the sects, men sought to live more purely Christian lives, where the pattern of the Sermon on the Mount might be closely followed. It seems then the lesson of these early centuries, when the fervour of this new religion was at its height, that for its precepts to be honoured some withdrawal from the world was necessary. The discovery was then first made that Christianity could not in detail be made to apply to and govern the affairs of a world shot through with evil, a world that jogged along according to slowly evolving laws of its own. Yet not its own laws entirely, for they existed under the providence of the Creator. The early Christians were not without hope of this world, to which they found it hard to make their religion apply, with which they were forced, for the sake of mere living, to make so many shameful compromises. Bad though this world had become through the inescapable results of the Fall, it was nonetheless, Christians believed, being directed by God towards his own purposes. Thinking of past and future, of all history and not only of the Christian era, St. Augustine wrote, 'God is the unchangeable Governor as He is the unchangeable Creator of mutable things, ordering all events in His providence until the beauty of the completed course of time, the component parts of which are the dispensations adapted to each successive age, shall be finished like the grand melody of some ineffably rare master of song.' Average Christians even in these early times were often driven into thinking it best to leave this imperfect world as they had found it, but they did not have a sense that this world was hopeless and nothing was being done about it at all. Quite apart from always looking forward to the Kingdom, however long its coming were delayed, they believed that in God's mysterious ways the wicked world, one day to perish, was nevertheless being guided by God sufficiently for his purposes to be achieved. They were inclined to leave much to God which in modern times men feel they should try to accomplish for themselves.

The Church was conscious of the harm and suffering caused by the social system, which she did not feel called upon to change, as such action was beyond her power, and her concern was made clear. To our previous brief discussion of the Church's attitude to slavery, we may add this last notice of her work of charity. The social evils were not viewed with philosophical detachment. If nothing could be done to alter the society that showed these wounds, they at least should be attended to for love's sake. Orphans, widows, the unemployed, the sick — all those who are in our day provided for by the State — were in the early centuries and for much later regarded as the responsibility of the Church, but this obligation was quite different from that borne by the modern Welfare State. We today regard it as a public duty, still more a Christian duty, to abolish poverty. But in the days when Christianity was establishing its image in the world, no such duty was thought of. The relief of the sick and the poor was solely to illustrate and to quicken that spirit of love which Christ imparts, because through it He can make known to men God's nature. After Constantine the apparatus of charity became large and organized. There were hospitals, hostels and free canteens, as we should call them. In them and through them the one aim of the Church was to show love and to awaken the response of love. She sought to illustrate the nature of God. The idea of what we should call a social programme was entirely missing. The saying of Jesus 'Ye have the poor always with you' was taken quite literally. No call was felt to improve the world, though love should always be shown. In the world was sin — it was the realm of Satan, though his will for the world could not prevail against that of its Creator — and consequently it was a testing ground, a place of pilgrimage, a preparation for heaven. Christians did not feel called to change the rules of the game, to remove the obstacles to good worldly living which were in themselves proving points in the life of the soul.

What may we learn from our short glimpse at this vital early period that can help to clarify the proper Christian attitude towards politics today? It is clear that the germs of most possible views of the State were already in existence. By choosing out a particular series of texts illustrating one line of thought, it is as easy for a modern Christian to convince himself that the true mind of the early Church regarded State power as satanic as that it was divinely ordained. St. Paul has been thrown overboard before now by later Christians. Further, the adherents of the whole range of modern political parties might all discover some sanction for their activities in one early Christian attitude or another. But the point is, surely, if we restrict our field to the first four centuries, and try not to be selective but to catch the Christian position then as a whole, we shall find that it consorts as uneasily with modern pure radicalism as it does with unmitigated conservatism. A facile solution would be to say that the Christian politician should be half a radical and half a Conservative. (One can usually detect conservative strains in the Christian Socialist: George Lansbury liked taking children round the Houses of Parliament, because it helped to illustrate to them the continuity of English history and their place in it: the language of the Prayer Book had for him the same historical appeal.) But it is easier to imagine such a half-and-half politician than to be one. Where a politician is concerned enough about religion to wish to justify his standpoint by it, his usual course is to select those parts of the New Testament which support him and to ignore the others. This is naïve rather than harmful and that politicians of such widely differing aims make this appeal to the New Testament successfully should not surprise us. It merely illustrates how many may stand underneath that capacious umbrella. On the other hand, this fact supports the view that however far back in the development of Christianity one ventures, any clearly accepted set of Christian principles that may be applied to politics is hard to discover.

Richard Niebuhr, in his book *Christ and Culture*, attempts in some passages to defend the Christian from the question: If attitudes to the connexion between Christianity and the world differ widely at any one time, and still more over the centuries, where is any core of precision to be found? Dr. Niebuhr unrolls rather more attitudes, five in fact, than have been discussed here, and suggests that it would be easy to define more. 'Yet it must be evident', he says, 'that neither extension nor refinement of study could bring us to the conclusive result that would enable us to say, "This is the Christian answer." ' If we were to say this on politics in general, he seems to suggest, we should be usurping the 'Lordship of Christ'. On the other hand, if no settled opinions of what precisely to do may be gathered from the differing attitudes of Thomists and Lutherans, Tolstoyans and Augustinians, the Christian is still faced with the decision to act in politics here and now. 'The problems of Christ and culture can and must come to an end only in a realm beyond all study in the free decisions of individual believers and responsible communities.' In making our decisions, it is on the whole good for us to study how other men at other times made theirs, but our choices, like theirs, will be 'free, relative, and individual'.

Dr. Niebuhr's argument will repay study at length, but it remains unsatisfactory, because while refusing to concede that Christianity is irrelevant to politics, he is unable to produce evidence of any consistent Christian opinion about where it does relate. Nor does he hold out any hope that one will be reached in the course of time. His difficulties may rise from the general human attempt to insist that anything men judge important must necessarily have a similar importance in the scheme of things as apprehended by God. Politics are important to us and therefore Christianity must relate to them. But metallurgy is important to some of us, and Christianity has nothing to say about it. The objection will immediately be made that the analogy is ridiculous, for how can a field of applied science, ethically neutral, be compared with politics, an activity serving man's highest aspirations and efforts. If the analogy is ridiculous, then it is human beings who see it so. For all we know, *sub specie aeternitatis* it may appear more to the point. What everyone who considers the matter must be prepared to agree is that Christian guidance on politics is obscure and hard to deduce from the Scriptures or tradition. If one believes that through the original revelation, and in the guidance of the Church by the Holy Spirit since then, God has given to man all that he needs for salvation, then these difficulties about politics may be taken perhaps to indicate the relative unimportance of this sphere beside personal living.

Nevertheless, so powerful are the early texts of a great religion that they take their effects down the years. There are men in our own day whose political outlook is still deeply conditioned by St. Paul's teaching. His acceptance of constituted authority is engrained in many Christian minds, who rarely stop to consider that his views of man's future on this earth are different from their own. Everything St. Paul said about the powers that be must have been affected by the belief, which he shared with all his Christian contemporaries, that the present order was shortly to be swept away. He had no thought that there would be any further development, that one day Christian Emperors would go before Christian bishops to be crowned, that Christians would have in their hands full power to mould society as they judged right. All this he failed to foresee; what he aimed to give was interim counsel for a time of waiting. Now it is entirely possible, if we speculate only in Christian terms, that we may fall into an error the reverse of St. Paul's. He and his followers made the mistake of expecting the Second Coming within their own days. Modern Christians have got into the habit of supposing it to be extremely remote, whereas it might be almost upon them. It is, however, what men think that matters and while many good Christians in these days will carefully prepare themselves for their own deaths, it cannot be plausibly maintained that more than a handful at a time of people generally regarded as religious maniacs now expect the Second Coming to be imminent. In other words, the context in which the Pauline teaching was delivered was markedly different from that in which in these days it is received. While the discrepancy does not destroy its relevance, it must be held to lessen it, and to make efforts to apply it today all the more difficult.

We may proceed to a smaller point in the same field of argument. The poor, the weak and the suffering lay all about the Roman world. They figure largely in the Gospels and were ever among the chief concerns of early Christian communities. And, in truth, they have been long with us. In the side alleys of medieval towns and the back-to-back hovels of the Industrial Revolution, the poor have lain, a challenge to the conscience of Christian men. Right up to our own times in Britain, in the writings of Christians who concerned themselves much with politics like Gore and Temple, the condition of the poor has been in the forefront and in fact has supplied the driving force of much Christian political activity. But (although this is a development so recent that it must be viewed with caution), the poor have disappeared from Britain and from a large part of western Europe. They exist in Asia, Africa and in broad tracts of South America, but if the economic processes which have procured their disappearance in Europe may be extended, and there is no reason why they should not, this particular object of Christian concern may no longer exist. Professor Alan Peacock began his lecture to the Liberal Summer School at Cambridge in 1960 on 'The Economic Role of the State in an Affluent Society' with these striking words: 'It could well be that during the next twenty years or so, unless an important war finishes us all off, the standard of life, of western countries at least, will improve so markedly that the fundamental economic problem of poverty will be solved.'[1] The social problem will have changed radically from the shape in which it has agitated Christians for centuries. As Keynes, who foresaw these changes, put it, the new task will be to teach man 'how to occupy the leisure, which saving and compound interest will have won for him, to live wisely, agreeably and well'. Christians will no doubt say that

[1] Published as *The Welfare Society*, Unservile State Papers, No. 2, p. 3.

their religion is not beyond supplying guidance for the proper settlement of this new problem. But they ought first to recognize the smallness of their part in solving the last. If poverty has been removed from wide regions of Europe, and is eventually removed from the rest of the world, they have had little to do with it. This is in no way to underrate the great and persistent Christian works of charity, or all the sacrifice that has been devoted to this end. It is not to ignore the more recent efforts of Christians in exposing social injustice and demanding a redistribution of wealth. The plain fact is that the eradication of poverty — and as we all know, we should not speak too soon, for war could ruin the achievement — has been brought about by a vast and sudden increase in human productivity, the result of the application of science to industry and agriculture. Nor was this itself caused by any conscious human intention to abolish poverty, for the surface impetus behind technological change, apart from the practical curiosity of scientists and engineers, has been the desire of manufacturers to make money. As often in history, this remarkable change of scene cannot easily be ascribed to deliberate human intention. Manufacturers have always wanted to make money; since the end of the War it just happens that they have been able to make it at a vastly increased rate. To return to the start of it all, why the Industrial Revolution began in England and why precisely it launched itself in the second half of the eighteenth century are questions to which the historian can supply no tidy answer. There then took place a gigantic shifting of the scenery before which human life is played, but the nature of the stage management is obscure. No body of men planned the Industrial Revolution; this revolutionary movement sprang up haphazard, unexpected and unheralded, while most of the schemes which men were consciously pursuing at that time have been forgotten and those that bore fruit have been infinitely less significant for human life than the huge economic change which came about, as it were, willy-nilly.

This digression has served usefully to remind us that the control of his environment which man seeks to maintain through politics is less certain than he sometimes supposes, but it was introduced

D

other purpose. Just as St. Paul expected this world soon to
, while we do not, so poverty was for him and for most
tians since him one of the larger facts of life, while for us,
at least, temporarily, it has ceased to exist. Distinctions and
differences between the setting of the New Testament and our
own time could be multiplied, but this is hardly necessary. We
need go no further to accept at once that political principles drawn
up and political attitudes fixed in conditions so dissimilar are
understandably difficult to relate to the choices before us nowadays.

If this is thought to be a harsh and cynical opinion, let us take a
hypothetical instance not too far removed from present realities.
Let us assume an African Christian, a subject of one of those
colonial territories which are aspiring towards independence but
whose government is still mainly in European hands. He is an
active politician and he is trying to decide between a course of
co-operation with the ruling power and a policy of agitation and
rebellion against it. (As he is a Christian, he will pray for guidance,
and he may be given it, but the effects of prayer are evidence too
individual to be brought into discussion.) For our purposes, he
has before him the history which has been outlined and the effects
of its influence on modern political ideas. There is one strain of
thought before him which would counsel him to ignore the choice
altogether. What happens in this world, it would argue, is of no
consequence; his business is with God and the hereafter He has
prepared. This pietism we can dismiss. He is next confronted with
the radical offshoot of the early centuries, with all those arguments
which declare Christianity to be the fount of democracy and
equality. The infinite importance of each human person in the
eyes of God will be pressed into the claim, now popular in Africa,
of one man, one vote. But the governing power in its wisdom will
not grant this claim. To insist upon it, for our Christian African,
is to move into paths of rebellion. Before he does this, he reminds
himself of quite another Christian attitude, almost the contrary of
the last: 'Whosoever therefore resisteth the power, resisteth the
ordinance of God: and they that resist shall receive to themselves
damnation . . . wherefore ye must needs be subject, not only for

wrath, but also for conscience sake.' How wise, in fact, is this particular Pauline direction in the situation in which our Christian African stands. The power administering the territory in which he lives is in no way hostile to the independence on which he and his followers have set their hearts. Its policy is to bring the territory and its people gradually to that standard of education and preparedness which is essential if independence is to be enjoyed successfully. But then our African is driven on by a mob of supporters animated by a force which St. Paul knew not at all and no Christian knew until almost our own time, the force of Nationalism. How then can he gain clear guidance on the problem which faces him, either from the New Testament and the Early Church or from what later Christians have deduced from these original teachings? Not only are the principles of the primitive deposit conflicting in themselves, but the circumstances in which they were declared no longer exist — for primitive Christianity knew nothing of either democracy or nationalism, which are very much the creations of the present age. If Christians consider the predicament of this African politician frankly, they will have to admit that the guidance which their religion and his offers him is by no means plain.

The moment has come to contrast this reflection, which some may find almost despairing, with views rising from the field of human relationships, to which the teaching of the Gospels is as relevant now as when it was first delivered. For an example, we may take work with maladjusted children. This is a contemporary problem, although maladjusted children have always existed, because they are at present the object of wide concern, their difficulties are studied scientifically, and special measures for their treatment are taken by the State. As it happens, we have had recently in England two books published upon how two Quaker Christians run their schools for maladjusted children, *Mr. Lyward's Answer* by Michael Burn and *Throw Away Thy Rod* by David Wills. No one who reads these books can doubt for a moment that what has been given to these children, whose troubles were largely caused by a breakdown of natural affection in their homes, is the love commanded in the Gospels. It is also obvious that this approach is exactly relevant to their condition. It applies, it works, it is what these children desperately want and it does more to cure their troubles than anything else.

As Christian love is easier to talk about than to practise, it is worth quoting Mr. Wills on the subject and how he sets about overcoming the difficulties. He is suggesting that it is possibly easier to love God than one's brother, especially if that brother be a maladjusted child:

> We may not be able to see God, but neither can we smell Him, and we can smell our brother. He stinks, because he soils his pants. What is more, his nose runs, he stuffs food into his mouth with filthy fingers with which he has just wiped it, he kicks us in the shins and repays any kindness with abuse. How can one love such a creature?
>
> It is quite simple if the will is there; not easy — simple. One merely decides that one will do so and acts towards one's beastly brother as if one did love him. It is as simple, and as difficult as that, though of course it must be accompanied by sympathetic understanding. If one perseveres one finds in time that one is acquiring a genuine feeling of affection for the child. I have said all this before and I hope I may live to say it many times again. I only wish I were better at practising it. Unfortunately for the worker, the kind of affection that is thus engendered is a real, deep-seated one, which makes him really care what happens to the child, which causes him distress if the child is unhappy or failing to make progress. . . . It is an exhausting preoccupying business that uses the whole man.

To someone dealing with disturbed children, what the Gospels teach about his problems may be difficult for him to apply, but it is not obscure. Compared with the guidance supplied by the New Testament on politics, what it says about personal relations stands out in absolute clarity. Nor, of course, are such relations important in a school for the maladjusted — and nowhere else. They can be powerfully applied in every field of life — between husband and wife, manager and man, Prime Minister and Leader of the Opposition. The outgoing Christian approach guarantees no agreements between parties in dispute, any more than in Mr. Wills' school it succeeded in eradicating all source of disturbance from every child. Nevertheless, its existence helps greatly — it profoundly affects any personal situation on which it is brought to bear — and for that reason it is alive and active. If, as some people believe, human life is not a series of battles won, bargains struck, speeches made, and ultimatums delivered, but instead is a series of personal encounters, of glances and words exchanged, of laughter and fears shared, of devotion felt — if, in fact, 'all human life is meeting' as Martin Buber said, then on this side, Christianity possesses the keys. One is bound to confess that the teaching of Christianity seems far more clearly directed to the sphere of personal relationships than it does to the business of politics. We have, however, still a long way to go before we can attempt to determine what relevance, if any, Christianity has in the political field. In the early centuries, the Church was first persecuted, then in the ascendant, but never fully in command. In the Middle Ages, which we must next consider, Europe was Christendom. It was a period when Christians were indisputedly in charge of all social activity.

3

The Middle Ages: Christians in Control

In western Europe in the thirteenth century, the high point of the Middle Ages, Christianity was undisputed master of the scene. Kings as well as priests and ordinary men believed unquestioningly that the sole object of life in this world was to gain salvation in the next. Theology dominated the universities, the greatest buildings were cathedrals and abbeys, commerce itself was strictly regulated according to Christian principle, and international relations conformed to the theory of a united Christendom.

Though what was left of ancient Rome had accepted Christianity, this victory was never then complete. The custom, traditions and ways of thought of pagan antiquity still existed beneath a Christian covering, just as many a Christian church had for its shell and foundations a Roman temple. But medieval society was a house Christianity built for itself — as far as men are able to determine consciously the conditions under which they live. The collapse of Roman rule and civilization was utter and was succeeded by centuries of anarchic barbarism. There were flashes of light, as under Charlemagne about 800, and the monasteries were scattered citadels of order, but Europe remained in turmoil until well into the tenth century. The popular memory ceased to hold the ways and ideas of Rome and when, with painful slowness, a Christian order came to be imposed, it was as much upon a *tabula rasa* as human history has ever allowed. It is true that when the Church, and princes schooled by the Church, came to the rebuilding of society much use was made of Roman examples. But now this legacy, found only in manuscripts and nowhere in existence, was filtered through purely Christian minds. Antiquity, whose influence was so powerful on early Christianity, has now been overcome and transformed. The civilization of the Middle Ages is properly termed Christian.

No claim is being made, of course, that the basic forms of society like the feudal relationship or the open field system of cultivation were invented by Christians according to principles discovered in their texts. As always, the material foundations of society were determined by processes in which human persons were involved, but processes so complicated, extending over such great periods of time, that it is impossible to entertain the idea of their being within human control. But the groundwork of medieval society fitted Christianity well. The innumerable personal ties of feudalism, those bonds holding the agrarian communities of the Middle Ages together, with the powerful granting protection in return for fealty and service from their weaker vassals and villeins, produced a network of human trust and mutual dependence in which the Church saw little to criticize. Feudalism, in north-western Europe, grew up to satisfy the needs for security and order of a society which had been forced to abandon town life for the fields, but Christianity found it easy to accept and bless. Like much else in the Middle Ages, feudalism was not created by the Church, but as with everything in that period it became infused with the spirit of religion.

In this period the supremacy of the spiritual ends of life was conceded by everyone. This acceptance made it possible for the Papacy by the beginning of the thirteenth century, after long struggles both verbal and military, to establish itself in Europe as the fount of all legitimate earthly authority and universal arbiter. The seeds were sown far back. At the end of the fifth century Pope Gelasius I advanced a doctrine which was to gather force in later years. Only Christ, he declared, was both priest and king, but priests, in virtue of their spiritual power, were superior to kings. Kings depended for their legitimacy on consecration by priests, and priests were also responsible to God for the actions of temporal sovereigns. This early statement, a classic text in the dispute between the medieval Roman Emperors and the Popes, could be turned to use as the Papacy purged itself of corruption in the tenth and eleventh centuries. The great reforming Pope, Gregory VII, wrote to William the Conqueror in these words:

For as for the beauty of this world, that it may be at different seasons perceived by fleshly eyes, God hath disposed the Sun and the Moon, lights that outshine all others; so lest His creatures whom His goodness hath formed after His own image in this world should be drawn astray into fatal dangers, He hath provided in the apostolic and royal dignities the means of ruling it through divers offices. . . . If I, therefore, am to answer for thee on the dreadful day of judgment before the just Judge who cannot lie, the creator of every creature, bethink thee whether I must not very diligently provide for thy salvation, and whether, for thine own safety, thou oughtest not without delay to obey me, that so thou mayest possess the land of the living.

Such theories appeared so logical and conclusive to medieval men that the Church could have done without celebrated forgeries like the Donation of Constantine, by which the Emperor, on leaving Rome for Byzantium, is made to bequeath to the Pope and his successors sovereignty over Italy and all the other countries of the west. As successors of St. Peter, to whom Christ had given the two swords representing spiritual and secular power, the Popes from Gregory VII (1073–85) regarded themselves as subject only to God who had set them in full authority over all other Christians, including their rulers.

These lofty principles were translated into plain fact. Naturally they were contested by lay rulers. The Holy Roman Emperors, whose landed possessions were based on Germany and Italy, opposed with their whole strength the papal claim, made by Gregory VII, that the appointment of bishops to their sees (and the lands which went with them) was a right of ecclesiastical, not lay, authorities. Half the land of Germany at the time was ecclesiastical and so for the Emperor to admit arrangements which directed the loyalty of his bishops to the Pope rather than to himself was to surrender much of his own power. But in this great controversy, producing a mass of written polemic as well as a series of wars, the military might of the Emperors was worsted by the spiritual weapon of excommunication and the forces which papal diplomacy could coax into the field. The victory was not outright; some compromise with the secular authorities over the appointment of men so important in medieval communities as bishops was unavoidable; and not even at the summit of the papal order from 1200 on were many kings given to supine obedience. But the Church's moral triumph and her victory in the argument were not to be denied. It could not have been otherwise, granted the assumptions of medieval Catholicism. These assumptions stand clearly out of Gregory VII's sentence of excommunication against the Emperor Henry IV:

> Come now, I beseech you, O most holy and blessed Fathers and Princes, Peter and Paul, that all the world may understand and know that if ye are able to bind and to loose in heaven, ye are likewise able on earth, according to the merits of each man, to give and to take away empires, kingdoms, princedoms, marquisates, duchies, countships, and the possessions of all men. For if ye judge spiritual things, what must ye believe your power over worldly things? and if ye judge the angels who rule over all proud princes, what can ye not do to their slaves?

The Papacy controlled the gateway to heaven which all the faithful, including their rulers, hoped earnestly to enter. Few in those days doubted the truth of this and it gave the Popes a moral authority which has never been wielded since. A Pope like Innocent III held all Europe in his net. The administration of his court was by far the most developed in Europe and through the Church, its bishops, priests, monks and friars, all now closely bound to Rome, the Papacy was able to create in Europe a unity of action and opinion which has not been repeated. Nor can it be said that this wordly power was amassed to satisfy the pride or provide the pleasures of an ecclesiastical caste. Whatever may have been the motives of some Popes in later centuries, the politics of men like Gregory VII and Innocent III were waged solely to secure proper conditions on earth for the salvation of souls which was the Church's God-given task.

Nor were the concerns of the Church at this time confined to high politics. The ordinary affairs of ordinary men were as closely regulated, to the same ends, as those of States. Marriage naturally came within the ecclesiastical law — but it was also to the Church and its institutions that men turned in sickness, for poor relief, and for education. The idea that economic life possessed an independence of its own was, of course, unthinkable. The condemnation of usury and the detailed arguments of the schoolmen about how to determine the 'just price' of commodities for sale were not matters of abstract debate but were applied, if not by the Church, by men who accepted her teaching, in the innumerable markets of medieval Europe. Buying cheap and selling dear, securing a corner in some commodity and profiting from it, holding produce back until the market improved — all these and many other mercantile expedients were narrowly examined and either approved or forbidden. To suppose all this worked out in practice with the day-to-day precision expected from a modern administrative machine would be wrong. Both Church and State gradually learnt how to tax with a thorough efficiency, but the markets, and other spheres of life, were constantly falling far short of the ideal drawn up for them by theorists. The point to hold to is that Christianity in this period admitted no bounds to its authority and through the confessional had a potent means of exerting it. (In the Lateran Council of 1215, summoned by Innocent III, confession at least once a year was established as a rule.) There were no islands of autonomy; every human activity was subject to the divine law whose interpreter was the Church. Although Emperors might quarrel with Popes, and kings with bishops, no sense existed on either side of any essential division between Church and State. Life was a preparation for death when, shriven by the priest, fortified by the Host, guarded by angels, the Christian soul would move to a Kingdom more glorious than any in the insignificant resting place of the world he was leaving. Church and State were agreed upon this; they shared the view that ultimately their chief business was to get men through this world without endangering their salvation. Further they accepted the fact that in this aim they were there to help each other. They were two aspects of one authority, twin servants of one God. If St. Augustine is the authority on politics with whom medieval thinkers always began, they left far behind his sharp contrast between temporal and spiritual power, the *civitas terrena* and *civitas Dei*.

This then was a Christian society. At no time before or since have Christians, not yet divided among themselves, had the total government of the world so completely in their hands. When all power was theirs, what did they make of it? If we run over again some of those elements in the Christian attitude to politics discussed in their primitive form in the last chapter, we shall notice that the conservative side is in the ascendant throughout this period. It could hardly be otherwise. The high Middle Ages, centring in the start of the thirteenth century, saw public order recovered after centuries of collapse and appalling lawlessness. The medieval Christian, with anarchy in his memory, set immense store by order. Courts of justice maintained it with implacable severity and imposed for even trivial crimes penalties which later generations would judge ferocious. But this profound conservatism did not overlook its duties to the poor. While there were odd men out in medieval times, people who suffered from failing to conform in some way or other, it was for most, including the poorest, an extremely protective society. It was mainly agricultural and in the country, under the feudal system, the ties of personal responsibility bound rich to poor. In the towns associations like the craft guilds looked after their poorer members. There could be famines and disasters and then men would starve, not because there was no one to feed them but because there was nothing to feed them with. In normal days, however, the poor were looked after and had no excuse for losing their sense of belonging. Much of this good state of affairs was owed to the personal character of feudal relationships and, although feudalism was no Christian invention, its personal basis was far more in line with Christianity than the impersonal bonds established under the money economy that came after. In the period of which we are writing, there was little money about — exchanges and payment in kind were the rule. The money economy developed in the later Middle Ages, under much hostility from the Church, whose many attempts to control it failed.

Any idea that the poor should be raised and society reformed was alien to the Middle Ages. The Second Coming may have seemed less imminent than it did to the successors of the Apostles — though just before A.D. 1000 the expectation that it would happen in that year was intense enough in Europe to disturb the pattern of ordinary life — but the picture of the Last Judgment was always in the medieval mind, as can be seen in much stone carving and stained glass. History had only one more important event to produce and that was its own ending. The idea of progress was totally absent from the Middle Ages, as might be supposed in a period when the Last Judgment was in the foreground of the imagination. The highest path of preparation for it was by renouncing the world, for in the cloister, free from the compromises necessary outside, men and women could live out the Sermon on the Mount. Where renunciation of the world is regarded as the wisest and noblest course, the thought of social reform is unlikely to occur. The Christian was assured that in the world there already existed all that was needed for his salvation. Institutions, laws and the general arrangements of society as seen around them were as God had ordained. If they were not as they should be, it was because of man's sin, and they might be restored, though the thought of improvement, in the modern sense, just did not exist. The medieval man took the Bible quite literally. 'For we have not here an abiding city, but we seek after the city that is to come.' To him this was not a pious fancy but the plain fact of his condition. Men would be wise to improve themselves, but improving a world soon to pass away was a waste of time.

It goes without saying that the modern idea that Christians are called to build the Kingdom of God on earth is not to be discovered in the Middle Ages. Their hopes were not in this world but in the next. If to William Blake, inspired by the secular hopes of the Enlightenment, it came naturally to write of building a Jerusalem here and now, for St. Bernard in the twelfth century his *urbs Sion aurea* — 'Jerusalem the golden' as we know it better — stood across the bridge of death. At no time in England were his hymns more popular than in the last century in their translations by J. M. Neale. It is strange to think of those Victorian congregations, their workaday minds tuned to the doctrine of mankind's steady but inevitable progress in this world, singing lustily on Sundays St. Bernard's hymns about the heavenly Jerusalem, the only one he believed in. The prosperous middle-class church-goer probably did not realize the difference between his own attitude and that of the words he was singing:

> The world is very evil;
> The times are waxing late;
> Be sober and keep vigil,
> The Judge is at the gate;

That one verse exactly catches the spirit of the Middle Ages. Men thought little of repairing this evil world and looked beyond it to the heavenly city. When Christians had the power to set about building the Kingdom of God on earth, they never thought to try.

Naturally this conservative and, as far as this world went, pessimistic society was extremely static. Movement over long periods of time there obviously was — there is a vast difference between the social arrangements and leading families of the chaotic seventh and ordered thirteenth centuries — but the development took place so gradually that it failed to be noticed. What men did see about them in the thirteenth century was a society hierarchically arranged, a rational pattern of classes, divinely approved and each with their appropriate functions, but between which there was no movement. The idea that people are born into classes from which they have no business to climb had a long life. In our time the passages in the Church of England catechism when the child undertakes 'to order myself lowly and reverently to all my betters' and 'to do my duty in that state of life into which it shall please God to call me' have incurred much ridicule. But however odious these views may now seem, no one questioned them in the Middle Ages. People were expected to stay in their grades and places. A letter by St. Hildegard in the twelfth century sets out this deeply held notion:

God orders every man, so that the lower estate shall not raise itself above the higher, as once did Satan and the first man, who sought to rise above their estates. And what man puts all his beasts into *one* stable: oxen, asses, sheep, goats? For them much evil would ensue from this mingling. Thus care must always be taken that not all people shall be thrown together into one herd. Else an evil confusion of morals would set in; men would rend one another in mutual hatred if the higher estate should be degraded to the lower and the lower raised to the higher. God divides His people on earth into different estates just as His angels in heaven are divided into different groups, angels and archangels — cherubim and seraphim. And God loves them all.

The only medieval channel for what we call social mobility was the Church itself, and there are many instances of poor children being educated and then rising to be bishops, which might well bring in those days high secular responsibilities at the royal court.

Nevertheless, although this picture of a united, settled, hierarchical and conservative society fairly represents Europe during the period we are mainly considering, there was also what might be called an incipient Left, reproducing, just as the Middle Ages reached their apogee, the radical or 'Communistic' elements noticed in the Early Church. In considering how the conservatively-minded rulers of this Christian ascendancy, both lay and ecclesiastical, reacted to the small challenge in their midst, it is best to refrain from moral judgments. The intolerance and cruelty shown by medieval Christians to men and women who failed to conform are shocking to their modern descendants. This is particularly so because heresy hunting combined with violence has been one of the vices most detested by the modern Christian liberal in his Communist, Nazi and Fascist opponents. But it does not help to inject contemporary feeling into the study of the past. The modern Christian liberal has little in common with a medieval heretic and there is even less point in drawing parallels between inquisitors and secret police. The events to be described took place seven hundred years ago.

As towards the end of the twelfth century a new order settled upon Europe, an order presided over by the Church, so nonconformists sprang up to contradict it. In Rome Arnold of Brescia came preaching religious reform, criticizing the clergy for corruption and setting in place of Emperor and Pope a revived Republic. When he fell the Emperor, at the behest of the Pope, had him hanged and his ashes scattered in the Tiber. In the suppression of the unorthodox in medieval times, the secular power was more active than the ecclesiastical. The two often quarrelled but against the third man, the outsider, they combined.

About 1170 a merchant of Lyons, Peter Waldo, gave his wealth to the poor and began to preach, at first with papal permission.

But the Poor Men of Lyons, as his followers were called, criticized the clergy for transgressing the Christian law of poverty. They taught the Scriptures which they translated into the vulgar tongue and their influence spread through Germany, Italy and Switzerland. More formidable than these were the Catharans who grew up in the French Midi and won much support among the provincial aristocracy. The elaborate heresy they propagated is of small concern; it is enough to say that it appeared to threaten all constituted authority. We see in them, as in the Waldensians, Patarines, Humiliati, and the other heretical groups, the true type of the Left, in line with some of the impulses of early Christianity. They rejected the world they saw around them, reformed though its spiritual organization had been by Gregory VII and his successors. Their tendency was to form small groups or associations dedicated to a purer way of life, one nearer that pointed out by Christ, than that lived by the generality of men, including the clergy. They found fault with the Church. It was not their wish to live a different and more ascetic life that procured their condemnation. Unlike the first Franciscans, who might almost have become themselves children of the same movement, they failed to make their peace with ecclesiastical orthodoxy. They flouted the medieval establishment; that was their crime.

In 1233 the Holy Office of the Inquisition was established to meet the dangerously spreading wave of heresy. It was staffed by the Franciscans, who might at one time have so easily qualified for its net, and the Dominicans. Independent of bishops and their own superiors, dependent only on the Papacy, the friar-inquisitors descended upon the heretical areas, set up their tribunals, called in the secular authorities to apply their penalties and acted as judges from whose sentences no appeal was allowed. They employed spies and encouraged informers. Report and rumour were enough to bring a man before them, and by their procedure he did not know who had accused him. Torture was used to extort confessions. The penances or punishments inflicted on those who recanted were to be sent on a pilgrimage, to be flogged in church, or more moderately to have to wear a saffron cross. Property was confiscated and passed to the Crown. It was a failure on the part of the Inquisition to have to turn a heretic over to the civil authorities for execution. The celebrated inquisitor Bernard Gui only sentenced to the stake 45 obdurate heretics of the 613 who came before him. Where mercy was shown it was by the ecclesiastical powers, and the zealots for pains, penalties and death were the lay rulers, Saint Louis IX of France himself among them. As always in processes which stir the blacker emotions, the careful rules drawn up to prevent abuse were broken. Once unleashed, ugly enthusiasms ran away with themselves and we find one prince insisting on burning heretics who had recanted and another who enlarged his own territories by the confiscation of their lands.

In one part of Europe, Provence and Languedoc, the heretics rose to power and influence; no longer confined to scattered groups, they won over rulers like Count Raymond VI of Toulouse. Pope Innocent III's first effort was to reclaim them by rational argument and he sent Cistercian monks into the area as missioners. They had small success and made a bad impression: the Catharan leaders were austere, the Cistercian abbots looked well off in the ways condemned by the heretics. The arrival of St. Dominic, who in his order's rules had returned to the practice of apostolic poverty and was able to match the heretics' severity, brought no change for the better. After persuasion had failed, the Pope sent legates into the country who, when diplomatic pressures brought no result, organized a holy war against the heretical rulers. In 1207 the spiritual benefits of a crusade were promised by the Pope to those who took part in this war, and lords and bishops from all France gathered at Lyons under Simon de Montfort, a distinguished soldier of fortune whose son was to play an important role in English history. In 1209 this orthodox army marched against the heretical towns and gained a first victory at Beziers, whose sacking has since been remembered for its remarkable brutality, heretics and good Catholics alike being massacred. The standards of cruelty and indifference to the sex or age of victims set here were on the whole maintained throughout the campaign. The objects of the military exercise lost some of their simplicity, because while the Pope sought only to persuade noble heretics to recant, and had no wish to dispossess them of their lands, the actual crusaders, including de Montfort, were anxious to enrich themselves with heretical properties. This naturally prolonged the bitter conflict which dragged on, through many unsuccessful efforts at compromise, until 1229, when the armies departed and the inquisitors returned to round off the task of restoring the French south to Christendom. The rather charming culture of the small Provençal courts, with its troubadour literature of secular love, was of course destroyed, or, more accurately, dispersed. The court poets fled to the north and east, and it must be suspected that beside their ballads and romances they carried with them some of that dislike of ecclesiastical pomp and authority, so cruel when crossed, which had inspired the heretics of the Midi and was not to die out of Europe before it flared up again in the Reformation.

The Jews fared ill at the hands of the medieval Christian. As money-lenders not governed by the Christian rules against usury, they were tolerated for their usefulness, but hatred for what their forefathers had done was always alive. The pogrom was never far away from the Jewish communities. They were expelled from England at one point and from France at another, bloody attacks on them were regular in Germany, and they were accused of having caused the Black Death, that terrible pestilence to which one-third of Europe's population may have succumbed in its first attack. The deeper the hold of Christianity upon a people the worse the Jews suffered; in Castille, towards the end of the Middle Ages, they were faced with the choice of conversion or expulsion and discrimination was made against them by race rather than belief, purity of blood being insisted upon for lay and ecclesiastical office.

Saint Louis IX of France was on many counts the most Christian ruler of these times, a medieval Gladstone who accepted arbitration even when it went against him, and was often called upon, so great was the trust placed in him, to act as arbiter himself between monarchs in dispute. He had a deep sense of justice, so keen that in days when the efficiency of royal administration was for the first time making itself felt, he was impelled to institute a system

E

for mitigating its rigours. No one can read the contemporary life of him by Joinville without coming away convinced that here was a brave and great man, a good king and a good Christian. That indeed was the common opinion of Europe, so clearly written into history that no one can doubt it. Yet St. Louis had a profound aversion for the Jews, as he had for heretics, and often proceeded against them harshly. His contemporary, Henry III of England, the rebuilder of Westminster Abbey, although of lesser stature, was still a deeply pious king. Financially he was much in need of the Jews, largely on account of religious enterprises, and off and on he tried to be fair to them. But as he meditated, a man constantly in mind of Our Lord, he became overwhelmed with the guilt towards Him of the Jewish people. A pilgrimage to Bromholm or Walsingham sharpened his sense of their wickedness and he returned even more hardened against them than before. He would determine upon fresh and entirely unjust means of extorting their money; he would order his justices to sell the Jews' sacred books so that with the proceeds he might purchase vestments and furniture for Christian shrines.

The attacks on heretics and Jews sprang out of deeply religious feeling and conviction, mixed in less spiritual minds with motives more mundane, and the same is true of the military attack on the infidel. The idea of the Crusade came to the surface as the means needed were for the first time ready. The Normans in Sicily and the Italian seaports of Genoa and Pisa had built navies for their Mediterranean wars upon the Moslems. It was possible to move fairly large bodies of men about the Mediterranean, and in Europe there were plenty of noblemen, whose occupation was war, eager to employ their talents in a spiritual cause which might bring material rewards. The Seljuk Turks in Asia Minor were driving back the Byzantine Christians, whose schism from the Roman allegiance was not at this time regarded as deep or final, and European pilgrims who went in large numbers to Jerusalem were suffering hardships and indignities at the hands of its Moorish rulers. In 1094 the Eastern Emperor appealed from Constantinople to Pope Urban II who at once seized the opportunity to win back the Holy Places by a joint effort of Christendom. At Clermont in 1095 Urban outlined his plan, urging kings and knights to cease from internecine strife at home and instead gain their souls' salvation by fighting in the cause of God. If they died on the Crusade, it would be penance enough for their sins; *Deus volt* (God wills it) would be their war cry and the cross on their battle dress would be their sign. So the great enterprise was launched. This first Crusade was successful; Jerusalem was recaptured and a Christian kingdom established there. But in this, as in the series of Crusades which followed, the ideal was stained by the frailties of those who pursued it. The most notorious episode was that of Count Emico of Leiningen who celebrated the start of a crusading journey he never completed by massacring and pillaging the Rhineland Jews, the first large-scale medieval pogrom. But many of the best-intentioned nobles who took part had strong subsidiary aims of winning princedoms for themselves in Palestine. In this some of them succeeded, but quarrels between themselves and with the Eastern Emperor reduced the strength that the Christians would have possessed if they had kept to their main task, and before many years were out the Moslems recaptured the Holy Places. The crusading spirit persisted throughout the thirteenth century, but the fervour and idealism which had marked the first three at least gradually waned. The crusade of 1271, for example, headed by St. Louis of France who died during its course, was diverted to Tunis largely because St. Louis's brother, Charles of Anjou, the King of Sicily, was more interested in gaining a valuable position in North Africa, opposite his Italian territories, than in any onslaught on Jerusalem. More and more the religious impulse of the Crusade was diverted into purely secular channels, a means by which Popes or princes advanced their statecraft or raised money. Before the idea finally died, a Pope was to preach a Crusade against the Holy Roman Emperor himself.

'It was in these wars', remarks Bryce of the Crusades, 'that the ideal of a Christian Commonwealth, embodied in the theory of the medieval Empire, was once for all and never again realized by the combined action of the great nations of Europe.' That was how they began, whatever they became later. But we must remember that if the one time in history the countries of Europe shared a common aim and pursued it practically together was when they sought to regain the Holy Places of their faith, there was always a large intrusion of worldly motives and selfish ambitions. Here was a Christian policy *par excellence* (if one grants, as all then did, that war is a just means), but the history of the Crusades is a lasting reminder of how much evil can become identified with the Cross, once it is raised above a political enterprise.

The Reformation was the first step in a radical transformation in the position and influence of the Christian Church in the world. The failure to reform from within cost Christianity dear. The Protestant breakaway did not at first bring any startling changes, except in radical sects like the Anabaptists, in Christian attitudes to politics. On the whole, the Protestants took over existing views, just as they inherited with approval the medieval Church's policy on usury and other economic matters. Inevitably Christian monarchs received an access of power and dignity wherever the Reformation broke the hold of the Catholic hierarchy, but Luther, for example, though accepting a sharp separation between the civil and spiritual authorities, still thought of religion as the dominating and directing influence in the State. The theocracy established by Calvin in Geneva, with its close supervision by the clergy of the life of the city, down to the smallest details of personal conduct, was a thoroughgoing subjection of the temporal to the spiritual and when his enemies styled him a 'Pope' they exactly hit off a similarity to his many medieval precursors.

Yet later Calvinism was to move sharply into the modern world. The separation of Church and State was unavoidable, for with the growth of the idea not only of a Free Church, but of several Free Churches in one community (it became accepted that as they in fact existed too great an emphasis on the claim to absolute truth of any one of them was inconvenient), the medieval conception of unity became logically untenable. The English solution — several churches but only one of them established — is typically illogical. It was originally made, of course, on the assumption that only one church was to be permitted and penal laws drove that point home for many years. The break between Church and State is a turning point in the relations of Christianity and politics. In the Middle Ages, there was no fundamental distinction between the two; each in its special ways represented a single spiritual authority. The notion that the State had the duty of furthering the Christian moral law hung about and is still not entirely dead in Protestant countries. But the essential fact of the Reformation in the political sphere is that the medieval alliance of Church and State disappeared. In spite of this, Christians who seek inspiration for political intervention tend to turn to the medieval example which is, as one can see, inapplicable to a modern world. Roman Catholics descending directly from the medieval Church do this most consistently, but Anglicans do so also; for the concern with politics has been most active in the Catholic wing of the Church of England. This looking back blinds them to the realities of a world in which Christians have become a minority.

If the political potential of Christians was profoundly weakened by the divisions among them which the Reformation caused, the so-called Enlightenment entailed a still greater reduction. The self-dependence of Renaissance man and the birth of the scientific spirit must be added to the effects of the many scandals of the Reformation and the unfortunate identification of the Roman Catholic Church with the cruelties and evils of corrupt régimes. Religion came under sharp and bitter criticism. 'The world', wrote one of the French *philosophes*, 'is not governed by an intelligent being.' It is not necessary to recount here the corrosive history of the free-thinking movement. The result, which is still mounting, is that it became a commonplace for large numbers of intelligent men and women to believe that religion was a superstition whose residual utility consisted in its power to keep the masses quiet. Man, they held, was essentially good and his reason, once freed and properly applied by himself, was sufficient to solve all problems. This was a revolution far more potent than the Reformation, for it amounted to the overthrow of the Christian view of man, and therefore of the Christian view of politics. As has been said, the object of the State in the Middle Ages was to support the

spiritual power in ensuring the salvation of men's souls. With
Locke the separation of temporal and spiritual authority has become complete. 'For the political society is instituted for no other
end, but only to secure every man's possession of the things of this
life.' But if Locke saw churches as mere associations of men pursuing purposes of their own, he retained suspicions and reservations
about political authority not entirely unlike those held by the
medieval Christian. Just as the medieval king was judged to rule
legitimately only for as long as he observed the laws of God, so for
Locke there existed natural human rights, established in the Law of
Nature, which no earthly authority might invade. But with the
fading under criticism of the idea of God, and the weakening of
the institution that testified to this idea, the way was open for a
plainer recognition of the rights of power where it actually existed.
The notion of State sovereignty, unchecked by any other force,
grew steadily. In every State, judged Blackstone, 'there is and
must be a supreme, irresistible, absolute uncontrolled authority,
in which the *jura summa imperii*, or the rights of sovereignty,
reside.' The Middle Ages had recognized no earthly absolutes,
neither in rulers, nor (if they could have conceived Rousseau's
idea) in the General Will of the people.

Man's outlook on himself and the world had been radically
changed by the end of the eighteenth century. Then and since
there have been Christians who live, one might say, in the shadow
of the Middle Ages, the world that in fact has gone, and fail to
grasp the limited possibilities for Christian action in a setting that
has lost most of its connexions with traditional Christianity. Other
Christians have become caught up in the still briskly moving river
of the Enlightenment and have adopted its outlook as their own.
They believe in the essential goodness of man and see in his reason
an instrument of perfectibility. They find it easy to share in those
hopes of this world which have animated the Left in politics from
the nineteenth century on and now find their present resting place
in Communism. They are natural fellow-travellers with those
secularists who have made their politics a substitute for religion.
As J. L. Talmon has shown in *The Origins of Totalitarian Democracy*, the old religious hopes, freed from the checks imposed by a

belief in the corruption of man's nature, have burst out demonically into the secular world, where the Messianism of the Jews and the Christian expectation of the Kingdom have become translated into fables of what lies round the corner of revolution. The hopes which medieval Christianity had placed beyond this world, because of its pessimism about man, the secularists have attempted to realize here and now, and in the French, Russian and Nazi revolutions we may see traces of Christian hope run riot, without the restraints imposed by the Christian teaching about man. John Strachey in two articles entitled 'The Strangled Cry' (*Encounter*, November and December, 1960) instances recanting Communists like Arthur Koestler and Whittaker Chambers who regard Soviet Communism as the logical end of the Enlightenment and recoil from its inhumanities into the old paths of religion, throwing aside pure reason as a broken reed. But what we see in Communism is not so much the triumph of reason as a refusal of reason to accept facts about human behaviour which history presents for consideration. While Marx and Engels in the *Communist Manifesto* are historically-minded enough to admit that 'the exploitation of one class by another has been a fact common to all past ages', they do not make the historically reasonable deduction that what has persisted up to now is likely to continue. They postulate a new man, the creation of changed social circumstances. 'In proportion as the exploitation of one individual by another comes to an end, the exploitation of one nation by another will come to an end.' Having taken men to be entirely moulded by their social environment, they necessarily ignore the obvious possibility that men have built into them a will to exploit each other which is ineradicable however much the social circumstances may be altered. This is the enduring flaw which is so much part of the Christian understanding of man that from it the doctrines of the Redemption and Atonement have been raised. Christian explanations of how the flaw arose may seem to others irrational and unsatisfying, but its existence would appear to be a fact obvious to empirical reason. Ignoring the flaw is the irrationality of the Enlightenment, for theories maintained in spite of contradictory facts are the reverse of scientific.

Our brief survey of Christianity in its beginnings and its medieval prime has brought out one point of cardinal importance. Classical Christian thought lays emphasis on order and justice and in a restricted but crucial sense it has underlined the equality of men before God, but it has never, in the periods so far reviewed, supported the hope that earthly societies may be perfected. And, as we have seen, when Christians had all the seats of power they fell no less short of ideal government than most of their successors. No doubt they will have learnt from their mistakes and if Christians were in power today, in the absolute sense which the effects of the Reformation and the Enlightenment now make impossible, they would not seek to re-establish the Inquisition or the Crusade. But, if past experience is any guide, something equally unfortunate would seem likely. This is realism, not pessimism, and it flows from the observation of men and societies in action. Christianity teaches that man is sinful by nature; sin mars all that men do; and sin is mixed into the lives of Christians and non-believers alike.

However, in leaving the medieval period, whose influence still radiates, it is necessary to remember the two points already emphasized which mark it off from our own. In the Middle Ages Christians were nominally united and today they are separated by divisions that have grown deep with the years. In our own times, the Ecumenical Movement has brought the Reformed churches closer together, especially in their consideration, often now shared between them, of the social and political matters here being discussed. But by and large the divisions between the churches, not so much in matters of faith, as in social tradition and outlook, are still sharp. No less important is the fact that the members of this divided faith are hardly anywhere in a majority. In Britain, the practising members of the several Christian communities are greatly outnumbered. It is true that the Conservative Party has traditional ties with the Established Church, the Labour Party regards the origins of its socialism as more Christian than Marxist, and the vestigial Liberal Party, especially in the north and west, is still coloured by nonconformity. But these surviving traces of Christian influence in politics must not be allowed to lead to an exaggerated estimate of possibilities. If Christians in their divisions were able to decide on principles which should be applied to politics, they would have to convince the majority of their fellow countrymen before they could move further, and there would be no point in addressing them in terms of a religion they no longer accepted. Possibilities now are far more restricted than they were in the days of Christian ascendancy.

4

Four Politicians in Action

IN politics men are as important as ideas, and practice as revealing as theory. It is to the Christian politician himself that we must now turn and if our few examples, all drawn from England, are insufficient for confident generalization, they will encourage the interested reader to go further for himself. In the many modern books in which Christians have sought to relate their religion to politics the tendency has been to establish principles and discuss how they should be applied. In the historical approach chosen here, however, it is necessary to review not only what Christians have thought and believed, but how they acted. If one is seeking to distinguish the convinced Christian in politics, his differences from others in the field of action, if they can be clearly made out, are specially valuable evidence. No great claims are made for the venture made in this and the next chapter. The tentative conclusions drawn from comparisons between Christian politicians would be stronger if they had been based on more examples and a closer analysis of each. Deeper study, however, if it yielded a fuller picture, could never produce an answer to all our questions. The precise effects of a man's religion upon his politics are probably not entirely clear to himself and even the most careful biographer will find his judgment baffled when he enters a region where the facts are so difficult to lay bare. Often the Christian politician himself is extremely reticent. No English statesman of recent years can have been more devout than the late Earl of Halifax. In his short autobiographical sketch, *Fulness of Days*, he thanks God for the knowledge of Him gained by his upbringing in a Christian home and for the 'countless opportunities' given him of making this knowledge 'my invariable guide and counsellor'. But nowhere in this brief account of his career as Viceroy in India, Foreign Secretary, and Ambassador in

Washington, does he give one example of how for him the path of duty had been illuminated by a Christian principle. We might assume from this — though there are no secure grounds for the assumption — that he did what seemed right, sensible and logical in the circumstances, and that for him the Christian religion, to which he had such constant personal recourse, did no more than sustain and confirm his endeavour as a politician to act according to the guidance of natural reason. It may again appear obvious to us, from other sources, that Lord Halifax's devoutness, and Christian respect for human persons who happened to differ from him, were of great help to him in his difficult negotiations with Gandhi. He himself makes no such claim, and if the politicians we are now to consider were more articulate about the connexions between their religion and their work than Lord Halifax, the precise nature of these links for all of them will remain impossible to determine exactly. It is however essential, in spite of the difficulties, that a discussion of Christianity in politics should include some investigation into practical activity.

William Wilberforce (1759–1834) is an admirable subject for our purposes for he had already entered Parliament when in 1785 his conversion to an intense form of evangelical Christianity took place. The rich son of a Baltic merchant, endowed with charm and all the social graces, brilliantly accomplished, the closest friend of his Cambridge contemporary, William Pitt, the young Prime Minister, Wilberforce tasted early all the delights of worldly success. Social pleasures he adored; if, like Pitt, he abandoned gambling, there were still the all-night sessions of lively talk, kept going by drink and outbursts of singing. Then came the conversion and a sudden increase of seriousness (Wilberforce mercifully never lost his charm). One of his first thoughts, as he examined himself in a new light, was that he was wasting his time in Parliament. 'The first years that I was in Parliament,' he once said, 'I did nothing. . . . My own distinction was my darling object.' His conversion made him feel he ought to have a purpose and a cause. It also sickened him of party politics and their eighteenth-century associations with interest and influence. As soon as his change of view was completed, Wilberforce wrote to Pitt announcing his intention of withdrawing from public life for a time and saying that he could no longer be 'so much of a party man' as before. In his immediate reply Pitt criticized this attitude, urging Wilberforce to remember that 'surely the principles as well as the practice of Christianity are simple, and lead not to meditation only but to action'. His conversion, then, had weakened Wilberforce's loyalty to the Tory Party and disturbed the old closeness of his relationship with Pitt. This friendship never broke down — in fact, they collaborated and corresponded throughout their lives — but the greater distance between them suggests, what must be a general rule, that intense piety will always fit badly into an environment as mundane as that of politics. For the day-to-day personal support which an overworked Prime Minister needs, Pitt now turned to Dundas, very much more of a man of the world than his older friend.

'The fact is', Wilberforce wrote of Pitt at this time, 'he was so absorbed in politics that he had never given himself time for due reflection on religion.' This criticism of a Prime Minister for being absorbed in politics may seem odd, but a dislike of politics is characteristic of some Christians engaged in it and, as we shall see, Shaftesbury was much the same. When he was converted, Wilberforce felt no calling to the art of government in general; the management of a nation made no appeal. What he sought was a good cause, which he could advance through Parliament, and he found it in the campaign for the Abolition of Slavery. Pitt too was an abolitionist — indeed he encouraged Wilberforce in his choice — and in their different contributions one can see the value of the two sorts of men, the general politician and the crusader in one good cause. Pitt could not afford to be as single-minded as Wilberforce; he had to hold together a government, some of whose members were opposed to abolition. He did not hide his sympathies; he forwarded the cause in many ways, but he refused to walk out of step with his Cabinet. Some people criticized Pitt for not casting off the restraints of politics and pursuing the ideals, but Wilberforce, who had done precisely this, never added himself to Pitt's critics on this issue. Much later in 1821, after Pitt's death, Wilberforce surveyed his career generally without special reference to abolition and regretted that so great a statesman had not at the opening of his life resolved 'to govern his country by *principle* rather than by *influence*'. By this he meant Christian principle, and by influence he meant the circumstances of the eighteenth-century party system — the votes bought by the offers of 'places' and votes procured by the Crown through its patronage. 'It was not the least of Wilberforce's tributes to Pitt's greatness', notes Sir Reginald Coupland, 'to conceive him thus, if once his eyes had been opened to the truth, initiating and directing that one experiment in aristocracy which mankind has never cared or dared to try — a government of saints — and bringing down to English earth the incredible dream of a Christian State.'

Pitt never had such a vision; if he had, he was too wise to think of attempting its realization. It is not, as Coupland suggested, that no one had dared to try. Cromwell's disastrous experiment through his major-generals was on record in England, and Calvin had dared at Geneva and not lacked imitators (Savonarola's brief ascendancy in Florence is a Catholic example). Ordinary men will take unkindly to the rule of saints, even if enough of them could ever be found at one time to form a government,[1] for their demands are set too high for weaker flesh.

Wilberforce lived long enough to see Abolition achieved, and his efforts (along with other Evangelicals, and with much help from the Quakers and other dissenters) bore fruit long afterwards, for there can be no doubt that his concern — which extended to oppressed native labourers in South Africa — settled into the conscience of the British people and left them with a permanent sense of duty, sharpening with the years, to the backward peoples of the world. He was inspired throughout by Christian motives. In his great speech in the Commons on 12 May 1789, after he had argued the case against slavery on every practical ground, and refuted in detail the case in expediency for retention, he showed his hand:

[1] Actually the so-called Clapham Sect of Evangelical Christians living near one another in the suburb of that name, with whom Wilberforce was associated, had almost enough talent among them for the job. Several were M.P.s; others rose to high rank in Government service. This brotherhood of Christian politicians has been without parallel since.

I have urged many things which are not my own leading motives for proposing [abolition], since I have wished to show every description of gentlemen and particularly the West Indian planters, who deserve every attention, that the abolition is politic upon their own principles. Policy, however, Sir, is not my principle, and I am not ashamed to say it. There is a principle above everything that is politic; and when I reflect on the command which says, 'Thou shalt do no murder', believing its authority to be divine, how can I dare to set up any reasonings of my own against it? And, Sir, when we think of Eternity, and of the future consequences of all human conduct, what is there in this life that should make any man contradict the dictates of his conscience, the principles of justice, and the laws of God?

Many have pointed out that Wilberforce and his friends who espoused the cause of black slaves abroad showed no similar concern at the exploitation of white labour at home under the impetus of the factory system. He himself was not unmoved by social distress, and he pressed Ministers during the rural depression of the 1790s to give public assistance to severe cases. But it is clear that he, like other Evangelicals of his time, felt that material hardships suffered in this world were only of secondary importance. He was a true child of the Conservative strain in Christian political outlook. In his best-selling book, *A Practical View of the Prevailing Religious System of Professed Christians in the Higher and Middle Classes in this Country Contrasted with Real Christianity*, published in 1797, he sets out his view of society:

In whatever class or order of society Christianity prevails, she sets herself to counteract the particular mode of selfishness to which that class is liable. Affluence she teaches to be liberal and beneficent; authority to bear its faculties with meekness and to consider the various cares and obligations belonging to its elevated station as being conditions on which that station is conferred. Thus, softening the glare of wealth and moderating the insolence of power, she renders the inequalities of the social state less galling to the lower orders, whom also she instructs, in their turn, to be diligent, humble, patient: reminding them that their more lowly path has been allotted to them by the hand of God; that it is their part faithfully to discharge its duties and contentedly to bear its inconveniences; that the present state of things is very short . . . that the peace of mind which religion offers indiscriminately to all ranks affords more true satisfaction than all the expensive pleasures which are beyond the poor man's reach . . . and finally that all human distinctions will soon be done away, and the true followers of Christ will all, as children of the same Father, be alike admitted to the possession of the same heavenly inheritance.

There is no change here from the twelfth-century attitude of St. Hildegard quoted in the last chapter. Wilberforce believed that the poorer classes should stay quietly in their lowly place within a hierarchically ordered society, though he combined with this a strong sense of the upper classes' obligations to the lower in case of need — a position more humane than that of the classical Liberal economists with their 'iron laws' of supply and demand. He was opposed to trade unions and supported the Combination Act of 1799 by which Pitt smothered trade unionism for a quarter of a century. His vote was given to all the repressive measures passed at the end of the Napoleonic wars, and, for his support for the Habeas Corpus Suspension Bill, modern opinion would suppose him to have more than merited the rebuke from Sir Francis Burdett, the radical: 'I confess I am astonished at the concurrence in this measure of an honourable and religious gentleman who lays claim to a superior piety.... Nothing could be more anti-Christian than to shut up persons in solitary confinement.'

There is one incident which shows the single-minded Christian in Parliament at a moment when the moral law clashed with party and personal loyalties. In 1805 a report was presented on corruption at the Admiralty. It showed that a Mr. Trotter, deputy treasurer of the Navy, had used £10,000 of public money for private speculation and that Dundas, as treasurer, could and should have prevented it. There was no suggestion that Dundas had profited himself in any way from such transactions. Pitt was devoted to Dundas and leant heavily upon him during war years of immense exertion, and it was natural for him to seek to refer the report to another committee and so preserve his friend. During the debate on the report Wilberforce rose at 4 a.m. and members noticed Pitt lean forward and cast him an appealing glance. 'It required no little effort', Wilberforce confessed afterwards, 'to resist the fascination of that penetrating eye' — the eye of a life-long friend. Nevertheless Wilberforce demanded that the full

rigour of the rules of ministerial responsibility be applied to
Dundas, lest the doors be opened to every species of corruption
and there be 'no security left for the faithful discharge of any
public trust'. When the vote was taken and went against him,
Pitt was seen to weep, and some used to maintain that his death a
year later could be dated back to that night. Wilberforce did not
believe that any injury was done to Pitt's health, but, as his biographer notes, if he had known that Pitt was to leave the House
for his death-bed, he would have felt distressed but would in no
way have held his hand or spoken differently. It is strange that to
the conversion of one of two friends may be traced the deepest
blow that ever befell the other in the course of his political life.

Antony Ashley Cooper (1801–85), seventh Earl of Shaftesbury,
came of the same religious stable as Wilberforce, though he
imbibed his Evangelical Anglicanism from his childhood nurse
and not from a mature conversion. 'After some thought,' he noted
in his diary, 'I see nothing but a political career, for everyone must
take that in which his various circumstances will give him the
best means of doing good. Where can I be so useful as in the public
service? This question could be easily answered did it require but
zeal, patriotism, honesty; but there is likewise a need of talent and
knowledge. Yet, perhaps, my success in earlier life has made me a
debtor, and I am bound to try what God has put into me for the
benefit of old England.' The cause he espoused was the reduction
of the hours of work in factories. He did not invent it, but on
being invited to assume its leadership in Parliament he did so,
'after meditation and prayer, and "divination" (as it were) by
the word of God'. Just as Wilberforce was moved by the in-
humanity of slavery, so was Shaftesbury by the heartlessness and
pitilessness of the factory system which failed to treat its employees,
the children especially, as human beings. It would appear, moreover, that one of his main objections to long hours of work, by
which we must understand often well over twelve hours a day,
was that no time was left for the religious education of the
young. 'It was a great religious question', he said in his first public
utterance in 1883 on taking over the campaign for the Ten Hour
Day, 'for it involved the means to thousands and tens of thousands

of being brought up in the faith and fear of the God that created them.'

Against him were the economists who held that the industrial world was governed by its own laws, that profit must be pursued where it led, and that only the industrial system, left to its own devices, could produce the wealth which in time would alleviate the sufferings of its employees. Shaftesbury's friend Peel, the Prime Minister, accepted these views. For Peel, Shaftesbury said, 'cotton is everything, man nothing'. Sir James Graham was another who accepted this doctrine of the times and resented even the exposure of social evils: 'Take, for example, the Poor Law Inquiry; it is often most embarrassing where it discloses the full extent of evils for which no remedy can be provided, as, for example, the inquiry into the condition of the hand-loom weavers. I might add Lord Ashley's[1] investigations into the sufferings of children employed in factories and mines.' Shaftesbury in his campaign against human misery rode full against the opinions of the intelligentsia of his day, and he provides a remarkable instance, which must be rare, of a man intervening in practical affairs on mainly humane and religious grounds and being proved right against the experts — for industry as well as its workers benefited from shorter hours. Wilberforce had had to cope with arguments that British trade would lose to France and other countries if slavery were abolished, and Shaftesbury met similar contentions not only from economists and their parliamentary followers but in the industrial north. When in 1835 Baines, M.P. for Leeds and editor of the *Leeds Mercury*, was asked to receive a petition he replied that 'he would prefer that petitions should not be forwarded by clergymen, and persons not connected with the trade, and who could not know what the required hours should be'. (Although Shaftesbury himself complained that he got too little help from the Church, and this charge was repeated by the Hammonds in their biography, this is not entirely borne out by the facts. If some parsons and perhaps more dissenting ministers were opposed or indifferent, at least sixty-eight clergymen were among those summoning a Yorkshire meeting in 1832 and they

---

[1] Shaftesbury's title from 1811, until he succeeded his father in 1851.

F

would have supported him when he took over the leadership.)[1]

Shaftesbury and his Evangelical precursors and followers in the Ten Hours campaign lacked any clearly thought-out Christian social philosophy, such as Gore and Temple would have been able to apply a century later. Prayers and pieties abound in his diary, but we shall not find any systematic attempt to justify the campaign on Christian principle. First, his pity is aroused by human suffering, and then he seems to reflect that this suffering rises from a failure to maintain the obligations — extremely close to those existing under medieval feudalism — of master to man:

> We cover the land with spectacles of misery; wealth is felt only by its oppressions. . . . No wonder that thousands of hearts should be against a system which establishes the relations, without calling forth the sympathies, of master and servant, landlord and tenant, employer and employed. . . . Sickness has no claim on the capitalist; a day's absence, however necessary, is a day's loss to the workman. . . .

His second thought is that the intolerable conditions of the poor threaten their salvation; they come to prefer the promises of Socialism to those of Christianity. 'Worst of all', he goes on in the same article, 'is when the ignorant and excitable multitudes are surrendered, almost without a struggle, to the "philosophy of infidels and democrats".'

Though such judgments are never certain, and properly belong to God alone, it could be hazarded that of the six politicians examined in this section Shaftesbury's faith was the most invincibly Christian. Doubt for him hardly seems to have existed. No more moving example of an absolute hold on the promises of God can be found than in the passage in Hodder's biography describing the death of his son Francis at Harrow School. Father and son were equally devoted, both desolate at their coming separation, and both certain that it was only to last for a short time. The incident is a beautiful memorial of Evangelical religion and family love — to be set against the gloomy puritanism into which this brand of churchmanship often degenerated.

But Shaftesbury, like Wilberforce, was a man who entered politics to support a single cause. When the Ten Hours campaign

[1] J. C. Gill, *The Ten Hours Parson*, p. 152.

was won, he turned to ragged schools and other good works among the poor, but he was uninterested in general politics and often showed little political acumen in advancing the causes he chose. *The Times* hit off his weakness exactly: 'We have no wish to be severe on Lord Ashley... we have the greatest possible respect for his humanity, his zeal, his industry, his abilities, his piety. But he is not a political leader; he is no statesman; neither is he capable, it seems, of extending the range of his vision beyond one object at a time.' He could not work beside other men in a party and the general business of politics he found distasteful. He would never subordinate his own views to the interest of his party. 'I am under a great infirmity,' he once wrote, 'an insuperable infirmity to public life, that I cannot ever speak unless on conviction. Now, I know that it is as just as it is necessary that, in the long range of policy, weak points must be defended, and, oftentimes, very questionable doings may be made to appear good. But such oratory is beyond me. I can say nothing but what I feel, and my feelings frequently get the better of me. So I should have proved an awkward and not seldom a dangerous Minister.' His conscience was disturbed by the expediencies of politics, as when the Whigs joined the Tory Government which he supported in 1827 — 'Can they have agreed to lay aside all their principles...? Oh, honesty, honesty, thou art indeed but a name...' — and he had no ambition for office. Invited by Palmerston to join the Cabinet in 1855, he stated his reasons for refusal as the impossibility of working in a Government which did not oppose the opening of museums on Sundays, countenanced the admission of Jews to Parliament and endowed the Roman Catholic College of Maynooth in Ireland — 'I could not satisfy myself that to accept office was a divine call.' As it happened he succeeded from outside, in 1856, in defeating the attempt to open the British Museum and Crystal Palace on Sundays and in persuading Palmerston to cancel permission for military bands to play in the parks.

He was a thorough Tory in attitude, a life-long opponent of a democratic franchise who regarded the 1867 Reform Bill as catastrophic. Recounting the conversation of an acquaintance he admired, Shaftesbury wrote, 'He stated beautifully and truly that the democratic principle is anti-Christian, being founded on a hostile and contradictory basis; the Christian Religion asserts man to be morally corrupt, Democracy assumes him to be perfect, or at least perfectible.' 'I dread, sadly dread,' he declared, 'these schemes of national education' — on the ground that they might take education out of the Church of England's control. On the other hand, when he had to address his mind to foreign affairs, which was not often, he frequently took a moderate and liberal line, as when in 1876 he opposed the Bill for adding the title Empress of India to the Queen; such a title, he said would have 'an air military, despotic, offensive and intolerable alike in the East and West of the Dominions of England'.

Shaftesbury achieved the victory of only one great cause, and he unhappily introduced into politics the sectarian demands of his narrow religion. He was so averse to the demands of office and incapable of working with men not exactly of one mind with himself that one sometimes feels that he is hardly to be described as a politician at all. Yet this severe evangelical Tory, for whom, it is said, the poor of London lined the streets at his funeral, released the forces of Christian compassion for the socially oppressed. His labours prevented the total estrangement of the factory employees from his own class and party, thus contributing to the unity of the nation, and it was his example, and its influence on Christian bodies, that made it possible for British Socialism to be so largely inspired by Christianity. It is worth giving the tribute paid to Shaftesbury by the Hammonds, themselves not believing Christians:

> The devil, with sad and sober sense on his grey face, tells the rulers of the world that the misery which disfigures the life of great societies is beyond the reach of human remedy. A voice is raised from time to time in answer; a challenge in the name of the mercy of God, or the justice of nature, or the dignity of man. Shaftesbury was such a voice. To the law of indifference and drift, taught by philosophers and accepted by politicians, he opposed the simple revelation of his Christian conscience. This was his service to England; not the service of a statesman with wide plan and commanding will, but the service of a prophet speaking truth to power in its selfishness and sloth. When

silence falls on such a voice, some everlasting echo still haunts the world, to break its sleep of habit or despair.

If Wilberforce and Shaftesbury were one-cause men, William Ewart Gladstone (1809–98) was a general politician. No statesman in modern times, as Sir Philip Magnus-Allcroft writes, 'has been in a position to dedicate such an extraordinary combination of qualities so unreservedly and effectively, on so grand a scale and for so long a period, to the task of giving effect in politics to the Christian religion'. Yet Gladstone too was not entirely at home in politics. He said in later life that he had never encouraged his sons to enter politics because it was a way of life that pandered to the passions and gave too much scope to the 'natural man'. He had been forced to recognize the truth that ideals in politics could never be realized. Politics were for him a duty. Towards the end he was always wishing to retire so that he could spend his days on the more important business of defending religion against the rising tide of unbelief. But he had more of politics in his little finger than Wilberforce and Shaftesbury had in their whole bodies. Shaftesbury could refuse, as has been already said, to join a Ministry on strict sabbatarian grounds, but Gladstone in 1871 forced through the Bill abolishing religious tests at the universities, although in his own view it was 'beyond anything odious'.

He set out his conception of the politician's task in *A Chapter of Autobiography*:

Honour and duty themselves require their loyal servant to take account of the state of facts in which he is to work, and, while ever labouring to elevate the standard of opinion and action around him, to remember that his business is not to construct, with self-chosen materials, an Utopia or a Republic of Plato but to conduct the affairs of a living and working community of men, who have self-government recognized as in the last resort the moving spring of their political life, and of the institutions which are its outward vesture.

This will to conduct the affairs of the community is the mark of a true politician and Gladstone possessed as well the sense of being an instrument. When he first became Prime Minister in 1868 he noted, 'The Almighty seems to sustain and spare me for some purpose of His Own, deeply unworthy as I know myself to be. Glory be to His Name!'

To his opponents, of course, his unvarying conviction that what he did was right was a temptation, not resisted, to accuse him of hypocrisy. Queen Victoria, as is well known, found him trying: 'No one can be sure for a moment what he may *persuade himself* to think right, and hence the impossibility to place confidence in him.' To the ordinary changes of course demanded by politics, he added over his long career a fundamental change of view. He began as a Tory holding to Burke and ended a Liberal disciple of Rousseau. As he remarked to Morley, 'I was brought up to distrust and dislike liberty, I learned to believe in it. That is the key to all my changes.' The Christian faith which sustained his early Toryism remained to give him absolute confidence that the Liberal way was right.

'Righteous indignation' as a political force was invented by Gladstone, and the national inclination to require foreign policy to be ethically sound dates from him. Fine though his moral rages were, it may be wondered whether as much evil as good has not flowed from them. Governments must act in the national interest abroad and it is not an unmixed blessing to have behind them a public which has been trained to expect such action to be always capable of being presented as morally respectable. The cloak of respectability is sometimes very thin, as Gladstone found for himself. The bombardment of Alexandria in 1882, admittedly under provocation, and the beginning of the British occupation of Egypt do not accord well with Midlothian morality. Gladstone tried to get the support of other Powers for his action, but failed, and finally presented their resentful non-co-operation in the Egyptian adventure in this light: 'We undertook it with the approval of the Powers of Europe — the highest and most authentic organ of modern Christian civilization.' The Powers had not approved — they had merely not interfered — and the bombardment, in no way Christian, was aimed at safeguarding British interests in the Middle East. An insistence on righteousness in policy is bound to introduce hypocrisy; that is the bad side. But the good must not be forgotten. Gladstone held before him a vision of a world — or rather a Europe, for that is where all the strength that mattered was concentrated then — where the political problems which inevitably arise would be solved by the great Powers in concert. This was no grandiose speculation, but the practical aim of his policy for the Balkans, then in a dangerous state of vacuum by reasons of Turkish weakness. Unlike Disraeli, who saw the whole question in terms of Anglo-Russian rivalry in the Mediterranean, Gladstone wished to settle the Balkans by a joint effort of the European powers. His reference of the *Alabama* dispute between Britain and the United States to arbitration is a more famous example of Gladstone's fairly consistent attempt to move towards a world where peace would be maintained under the rule of internationally accepted law. His righteousness was far more than an interior sense of self-justification. If Gladstone taught the British people the peculiarly objectionable habit of being morally censorious of other nations, he at least encouraged them to be critical of their own Governments' actions and also widened that stream of ethical feeling which made it possible for many of them to support the grant of independence to India when the day came.

Gladstone shared Wilberforce's indifference to social reform, but had none of Shaftesbury's concern for the poor (neither he nor Disraeli bothered to vote on the Ten Hours Bill). Nevertheless he has probably been the strongest moral and Christian influence in English political history. It was not so much what he did, but the manner in which he did it. He noted once what he considered to be his merit as a politician:

I am by no means sure, upon a calm review, that Providence has endowed me with anything which can be called a striking gift. But if there be such a thing entrusted to me, it has been shown, at certain political junctures, in what may be termed appreciation of the general situation and its result. To make good the idea, this must be considered as the simple acceptance of public opinion, founded upon a discernment that it has risen to a certain height needful for a given work, like a tide.

This picture of himself waiting on public opinion is not entirely accurate. Gladstone did much to create the public opinion with which he worked. He saw the path before his party as a series of moral challenges and he believed that the conscience of the electorate could be educated to overcome them one by one. Sometimes he failed to do enough of this education, as with his Irish policy. But he succeeded in spreading through wide sections of British society the idea that politics was an intensely moral business. As Desmond MacCarthy wrote of him: 'Gladstone's genius was a moral passion. His power over men, apart from his immense abilities, lay in the faculty of rousing in them a sense of responsibility.' And the surviving records of the man suggest personal power and ascendancy slowly built up during a life-time of laborious searching after God's will. How much of what Gladstone's Governments did was more God's will than what was accomplished by the other side is not to be unravelled. But in Gladstone people had before them a man, a great man, whom they knew assuredly sought to follow God and do His will. Such earnestness in a politician is naturally more to the taste of supporters than of opponents, but the strength of personal character that Gladstone had built up for himself through years of striving was clear to all, and is amusingly illustrated by a story told by Desmond MacCarthy in his *Portraits*.

Professor Blackie, another grand old man, was fond of narrating how, in the course of an argument with Mr. Gladstone, he was about to deliver a final and crushing rejoinder, when he found, to his astonishment, that the words were frozen on his lips; Gladstone had opened his eyes a shade wider and looked at him. The professor, on whom this experience had apparently made a great impression, repeated the story so often that it acquired a title among his acquaintance, and was always referred to as 'Blackie's peep into hell'.

Lord Salisbury (1830–1903), another great Christian politician, the leader on the other side, was thrown into intense irritation by Gladstone's constant appeals to religious feeling on behalf of policies which he, Salisbury, believed profoundly wrong. Gladstone's policy of Home Rule for Ireland he saw as a concession to violence and the idealistic campaign as no better than the encouragement of anarchy. Gladstone had much faith, Salisbury little, in human nature, and Salisbury's final tribute to his fellow

Christian and opponent is interesting for its careful qualifications.
He said in the Lords:

> What he sought were the attainments of great ideals; and, whether
> they were based on sound convictions or not, they could have issued
> from nothing but the greatest and the purest aspirations. . . . He will
> be long remembered, not so much for the causes in which he was
> engaged or the political projects which he favoured, but as a great
> example, to which history hardly furnishes a parallel, of a great
> Christian man.

Salisbury would have disputed the claims of many of Gladstone's policies to be sensible and good, let alone Christian, but
he would never have denied the force of Gladstone's example as a
Christian living out his life in politics.

Like Shaftesbury an aristocrat, like Gladstone a high churchman,
Salisbury, though several times at odds with the Conservative
Party, which he was to end by leading, never wavered in his
allegiance to Conservatism. He was as attached to the privileges
of his high rank as he was conscious of its duties. He opposed the
extension of the franchise, the admission of Jews into Parliament
and the removal of religious tests for university admission. He
was more articulate than Wilberforce and Shaftesbury about the
principle which has always been a chief concern of Christian
politics — the maintenance of the family. It was at the base of his
hatred of Communism, whose rise he foresaw. Communism, he
said, would 'thrust what we call politics into the background, in
favour of a social conflict the most critical and the most embittered
that has yet shaken the fabric of civilization'. He believed that as
natural affection and family feeling raised a barrier to Communist plans for destroying private property, Communists would
'find themselves forced to declare war against the family and as a
necessary consequence against religion altogether'. The uncer-
tainty of arguments from principle and theory is well illustrated
here, for in Soviet Russia today much emphasis is laid on the
need for family stability, and divorce is considerably more
frowned upon than it is in the countries of the West.

For some Christians there is a constant tension between the
claims of this world and the next. It is easy for one who meditates

long on the mysteries of religion to feel, at least at some moments, a strong sense of the insignificance of worldly activity in the infinite scheme of things. Salisbury had more of this sense than most Christian politicians. Sometimes at the Foreign Office he would startle an over-zealous official by remarking at the end of a discussion of some awkward point 'Nothing matters'. Men should exercise their reason to the utmost on the problems, political and other, which confronted them, but in great matters, like those of foreign affairs and the rise and fall of nations, there was another actor, God Himself, whose power was far greater and more effective than any held by the men engaged in these issues. In private talk once, he said of his political efforts — 'with the result, I have nothing to do'. A judgment of him by one of his biographers, A. L. Kennedy, expands this point: 'The belief in the over-ruling power of God gave him, then, the conviction that the course to choose in politics was that which had the most reason behind it. It might or might not produce an immediately favourable result; but it would, under God's Providence, benefit posterity even if it did not benefit his own generation.'

It may have been this persistent feeling of the superiority of other things which enabled Salisbury to ride rather loose to his party, though in those days party discipline had anyway not become as stiff as it is now. In his youth he was given to voting against his front bench on big issues — he voted against the conduct of the Crimean War — and in 1867 he resigned from the Government over Disraeli's Reform Bill. He had opposed Gladstone's lesser extension of the franchise the year before and found the volte face required by Disraeli's more generous measure too much for him. Later this resignation was to advance his popularity, for the electorate remembered his sacrifice of place to strongly held opinion. But it may be that deeply held religious faith is always of service to politicians, freeing them from that sense of strain which comes when work, career and ambitions so fill the whole of life that it contains nothing else of significance. No genuinely religious man can make a total stake on the matters of this world, and this underlying detachment is not without its bearing on political success. Disraeli, of course, was free with his compliments, but he remarked to Lady Gwendolen Cecil: 'Courage is the rarest of all qualities to be found in public men', and added: 'Your father is the only man of real courage that it has ever been my lot to work with.' It is perhaps easier to be courageous in politics when your life contains something of infinitely greater importance. Salisbury was not greatly convinced that politics could contribute much to what really mattered in this world — the stilling of hatred, malice, envy and mistrust — and he often maintained that clergymen were more useful than politicians for being at closer grips with these evils of man's nature.

Salisbury was no more interested in legislation for social improvement than Wilberforce, Shaftesbury and Gladstone. By his day any statesman, whatever his personal views, had to pay some attention to it, but Salisbury quickly allowed his to wander. In 1886 Lord Randolph Churchill resigned the Chancellorship in Salisbury's Government on the grounds that he wished to cut down on armaments and spend more on social amelioration. No great efforts were made to meet him, and it is interesting how little sympathy this Christian Prime Minister showed for the social conscience of his far less Christian Chancellor of the Exchequer. In 1898 Salisbury's Government was committed to Chamberlain's project for Old Age Pensions, but as soon as Chamberlain became occupied with the Boer War Salisbury's personal lack of interest in pensions made itself felt and nothing more was heard of them.

Salisbury's fame is in the sphere of foreign policy and here he certainly showed no inclination to find in Christianity some key for solving its innumerable problems — that was far more in Gladstone's line. Salisbury himself expressed the principle by which he worked: 'Our first duty is towards the people of this country, to maintain their interests and their rights; our second duty is to all humanity.' He considered that the electors had put him into power to look after their material interest and that no statesman should trifle with such a trust. Salisbury conceived it to be his national duty to use diplomacy as an instrument for maintaining British influence and power in Europe at the highest point possible. No consideration deflected him from this aim. When in 1898 the Turks were massacring Armenian Christians, Salisbury was pained but did nothing to stop them. Putting Turkey down would only raise Russia, and Salisbury held that anything which encouraged Russia to draw advantage from Turkish weakness must necessarily harm the British position in the Middle East.

As it is impossible to be in politics at all without being prepared to tell some lies, it will be worth referring to a notable deceit practised by Salisbury. In 1878 when Foreign Secretary he was negotiating with the Russian Ambassador in London about Bulgaria's frontiers. The whole Balkan situation at the time was tense and a war among the Great Powers rising out of it was entirely possible. Salisbury's discussions were successful and a secret treaty was signed. Almost immediately a version of the treaty, accurate save for one small point, was published in the *Globe* newspaper. Asked in the Lords by Lord Grey whether there was any truth in the press report, Salisbury replied, 'The statement to which the noble Earl refers, and other statements which I have seen, are wholly unauthentic and not deserving of the confidence of your Lordship's House.' Salisbury believed in secret diplomacy and his treaty was part of his effort towards the temporary pacification of Europe achieved in the Congress of Berlin. Salisbury was a scrupulously honest man but there are moments in politics when lies have to be told, as we shall see again when we come to Sir Stafford Cripps, and Christians cannot escape this professional hazard any more than their colleagues.

There is something very attractive in the figure of Salisbury. He governed Britain at one of her moments of greatest power and that power it was his constant endeavour to raise. But his methods were not those sometimes used by the powerful. In foreign affairs he thought it as contemptible to be arrogant with the weak as it was to be cringing to the strong. 'A policy of moderation', he wrote, 'is one to which no Christian man could raise an objection. . . . Courtesy of language, a willingness to concede, a reluctance to take offence, if they are impartially extended to all, will always, even when they are carried to excess, command respect and admiration.' He earnestly sought divine guidance in his work (though he conceived himself to be applying plain reason rather than any set of Christian principles to the movement of politics) and when he had done his best he was content to leave the upshot to God. If good came, it was God's work, not his. A young man once troubled Lord Salisbury very much by discussing the question of his future profession in the light of 'the good he might do'. Somebody suggested that it was surely a noble wish to get good done in the world. 'Yes,' replied Salisbury with intense earnestness, 'but not by you — never by you; never allow yourself to believe that for an instant.'

5

Two on the Left

SOCIALISM, the creed of George Lansbury (1859–1940), was
heartily feared and reprobated by all four of the Christian statesmen so far examined. But for Lansbury Socialism was not only
his politics but also in a deep sense, and he often proclaimed it,
his Christianity as well. 'Christ', he said, 'was the first Socialist.'
'Kneeling with others at the altar of the sacraments will and can
bring no real peace unless those who so kneel spend their lives
as brothers and sisters; and this is quite impossible within a system
of life which depends upon the ability of the children of God to
dispute, quarrel and fight for their daily bread.' Born of working-
class parents in the East End of London, he received little education compared with his predecessors in these pages and was far
behind them in intellectual ability. He did, however, share their
membership of the Church of England, which was unusual in a
working-class politician, for most of his colleagues who professed
religion had received it from one or other of the Free Churches.
Lansbury was much loved by all kinds of people — that is perhaps what should most be noticed. He was exasperating, sometimes
passionate, and often in general matters extremely stupid and
weak in judgment. One could say of him, perhaps, that in the
Middle Ages he might well have got mixed up with some wild
and ultimately cruel impracticality like leading a children's
crusade. But those who knew him recognized his goodness which
indeed shone out of him, with an outgoing affection for everyone.
He fought in his time, nevertheless, many battles for his class and
his son-in-law writes of him:

He was not even a saint in the conventional meaning of the phrase.
He was not meek, nor simple-minded, nor passionless. He was, indeed,
by nature a man of very strong, almost violent passions, held in check
and directed by a very firm will and by ardent Socialist and Christian

principles. . . . To the end of his life those who knew him well and could read his face would sometimes see flash in it the signs of impatience or anger, struck down at once by his ever-watching conscience.

Like Gladstone, whose leadership he was under at the beginning of his parliamentary career and whom he admired, Lansbury was often accused by opponents of dragging in God as a political instrument. He would maintain too easily perhaps that the next step in Socialist policy was God's will; more irritatingly still, in arguments within the Labour Party, he tended to suggest that the side he favoured had God's approval. Yet his whole life illustrated his dictum, 'A religious person, in my view, is one who shows his love of God through love of his neighbours.' He would call anyone Christian who lived up to this, whatever their faith. He described a life-long friend as 'a good Christian gentleman' although he had lived and died a Jew — 'it makes no difference — he loved his fellow men'. Lansbury put these principles into practice as M.P. for Bow, where he was always at home to anyone in any sort of difficulty — in those days the idea that an M.P. should be at the beck and call of his constituents was less widespread — and although a poor man he gave a good deal of money help. He was fifty-four when in 1913 he took over the editorship of the *Daily Herald*, then a Left-wing paper of savagery and bitterness. The strength of ill feeling was great in those days — Ben Tillett on Tower Hill could cheerfully say of an enemy of the working classes 'God strike Lord Devonport dead!' — but Lansbury had no taste for what he called 'the good old gospel of hatred'. When he became editor, he cut out the undertone of personal spite — along with racing tips. He too had courage. Lloyd George was a flatterer but there was truth in his words to Lansbury in the 1931 crisis: 'Your colleagues are too easily scared by obstacles and interests. Unless you can inoculate them with some of your faith and courage your party and ours will be landed in an overwhelming catastrophe.' The catastrophe was not averted, but with other leaders in the National Government and the rest defeated at the polls, Lansbury took command of the forty-nine Labour M.P.s remaining at Westminster.

In spite of his loyalty at this point, Lansbury was not a good party man. His conscience or conviction of righteousness was always facing him with the sort of difficulties which Wilberforce and Shaftesbury saw clearly were bound up with party membership. In 1911, for example, when Lloyd George introduced Health Insurance, the Labour Party as a whole supported the Bill, but Lansbury and some others opposed it on the odd score that when social reforms were needed the State ought to pay for them by taxing the rich, whereas Lloyd George's contributory scheme was a way of making the poor pay for their own relief. As Raymond Postgate says of him at this time, 'Lansbury alone behaved as if party discipline did not exist and party policy was what each Member considered right in his Socialist conscience.' Urged on by Mrs. Pankhurst, Lansbury held that the Labour Party ought to vote against every Government Bill until the introduction of an official measure for granting votes to women. He attempted to turn their own constituents against fellow Labour M.P.s who disagreed with him, and he was called to order by the Parliamentary Party. Finally, he resigned his seat and contested it again as a suffrage candidate. His loss of it taught him the dubious wisdom of indiscriminate resignation.

His main clash with the Party, as its leader, came on the issue of Christian pacifism. Sir Winston Churchill (in *The Second World War*, Vol. I, p. 251) well summed up the usual opinion of politicians on this issue.

> The Sermon on the Mount is the last word in Christian ethics. Everyone respects the Quakers. Still, it is not on these terms that Ministers assume their responsibilities of guiding States. . . . The safety of the State, the lives and freedom of their own fellow-countrymen, to whom they owe their positions, make it right and imperative in the last resort, or when a final and definite conviction has been reached, that the use of force should not be excluded.

Such an opinion is widely approved and the difficulty of any party disposed to pacifism in making headway with the electorate has been more than once experienced by Labour. For all the mounting dangers of the middle 1930s, with Hitler's increasing strength and Italy's attack on Abyssinia, Lansbury clung to his firm belief that nothing good could be achieved through force. The great question for Labour was whether support for the League of Nations should extend to military sanctions — to war, in simple terms. By 1935, the bulk of the Labour Party had come to believe that it should, though they had fairly consistently opposed the armaments required by such a policy. But at the Labour Party Conference of that year at Brighton Lansbury expounded the view that not even the League could justify the disaster of a modern war. He re-emphasized his opinion that Socialism could not be obtained by force: 'And why have I said that? I have said it, first, because One whose life I revere and who, I believe, is the greatest figure in history, has put it on record: "Those who take the sword shall perish by the sword." ' He said that God had intended us to live peaceably and quietly with one another and that if some people would not allow us to do so, he would stand as the early Christians did, and say: 'This is our faith, this is where we stand, and if necessary, this is where we will die.' It was all very well, but the majority, including the T.U.C., had slowly swung to that determination upon national survival which belongs more to the order of creation than that of love. Ernest Bevin spoke for them in an excoriating personal attack. 'It is placing the executive', he shouted at Lansbury, 'in an absolutely wrong position to take your conscience round from body to body asking to be told what to do with it.' Twenty-five years later, Lord Attlee made the acidulous and not entirely fair comment that 'Bevin despised leaders who wanted to cling on to their conscience with one hand and to power with the other'. (*Observer*, 20 March 1960.) In his old age Lansbury was far more concerned with what was right than keeping control of the Labour Party. 'Stand by your beliefs, George,' Herbert Morrison said as Lansbury left the platform that day. If those beliefs had become the basis of Western policy, Europe at least would have been entirely subjugated by Nazism, but Lansbury stood by them and resigned. Writing to Cripps (who was on his side in 1935, though for different reasons), he told him, 'I think my work for the Party, as a Party, is finished. I see life ever so much broader than in the days gone by. . . . The Party nearly chokes me; I want to shout out *against* them.'

The demands of party are often galling to a Christian. We

G

remember Shaftesbury's saying that he could not argue in favour
of any matter which he did not believe in though his party did.
Lansbury was rather more able to accept this demand of political
life. In the early days of the second Labour Government, for
example, he was with Oswald Mosley on a small committee
which presciently recommended that unemployment should be
attacked by creating credit to revive home purchasing power.
Lansbury had warmly espoused these views, but once they had
been rejected by the orthodox free traders in the Cabinet, he
found himself called upon to denounce them on behalf of the
Government to the Party Conference. Party membership is
bound to put a strain from time to time upon the individual conscience. A long, rather muddled letter from Lansbury to Cripps
is worth quoting because it illustrates so well the frustrations and
doubts which beset a devout Christian who tries sincerely to live
out his religion in politics:

> Everything gets so mixed; persons, causes, tumble into each other
> and form such a hotch-potch of ideas that truth or what seems like
> truth gets just smothered. . . . One day the party seems all important,
> the next day quite unimportant because its interests seem to conflict
> with truth. Then I find myself smothering my own mind and thoughts
> because others think a certain way better than mine. . . . But my chief
> thought is of the multitudes outside who *trust* us, those thousands
> who pin their faith to our assurance that given power big things will
> be attempted. . . . Somehow, in ways it is impossible to describe, I
> get bewildered by the fact that though we cannot live without bread
> is true, it is equally, if not more, true we *cannot* live by it alone. . . .
> I believe the world, and our people especially, need a purely religious
> message, not theological. In fact the world needs this more than any-
> thing else. Is the House a place where such a message can be given? . . .
> Yet there come days when the jealousies (*my own*, as well as other
> people's), and want of faith both in our actions and our courage and
> discretion, worry me to distraction. I laugh and keep as stout a heart to
> the hills of difficulty as is possible, but often my heart fails and my soul
> seems to cry out within me whether I am spending my old age in the
> way that is best. At the start I felt God had given me a task to do. It
> may be He has; my doubt is whether I am good enough to do it or
> whether the way is right. . . . You know the saying: 'God is waiting
> for the people who are good enough to enter and enjoy the Promised
> Land.' The daily question which hits me in the face is: Are we teaching

and living our lives in the way best calculated to produce such people? It is me and my own faults, shortcomings and misgivings which perplex and baffle me and make me so tiresome in thought and action. DON'T answer. Always, G. LANSBURY.

If one may expect one thing more than another from Christian politicians, it is perhaps that they will take the lead in attempting to reconcile conflicting groups and to restore conditions of friendship with other nations after conflict. Lansbury showed the same will towards reconciliation with Germany after the First World War as Sir Stafford Cripps and one or two other Christian politicians did after the second. He was much opposed to the harshness of Versailles. On the other hand, his overflow of Christian charity led him into some dangerously mistaken judgments of people. In the series of mediatory visits he made in 1936-7 with the aim of removing the threat of war, he ludicrously mistook Hitler's character and intentions. 'He *will not* go to war', he wrote of him, 'unless pushed into it by others', and he described Hitler as 'one of the greatest men of our time'. It is fair to recall that Lansbury was only a year or two short of eighty when he made these visits and his gullibility was no doubt fostered by his pacifism. It is strange however that he paid so little attention to the evidence of Hitler's actions.

What did Lansbury achieve? No great reform lies to his credit and his period as party leader was undistinguished. What remains still with those who knew him is a memory of his warm heart and Christian goodness. His mistakes and miscalculations were many, but about this man there was a touch of saintliness which his fellows saw and respected. It is good for institutions like Parliament to have examples of Christian living before them, and Conservative views of Socialism in Britain must have been tempered by the spectacle of George Lansbury on the opposite benches.

This section is concerned with sketches of politicians in action, but as Sir Stafford Cripps (1889-1952) is the only one of our subjects to have worked out a regular if unorthodox theory of the relation of Christianity to politics it seems right first to pay some attention to his views. For Cripps the mistake the Church had made was to concentrate too much on the hereafter. On the contrary, he saw the Church 'as the active protagonist of the Kingdom of Heaven, or the rule of God here on earth, as the pioneer of social salvation, more concerned with creating the greatest sum of human good and happiness here and now, than with encouraging individual merit as a means to personal salvation hereafter'. 'We are not primarily concerned with individual preparation, in a hopeless world of evil, for an ideal world to come hereafter. We are concerned with the creation, out of the present drab unhappiness, of a new and joyous life for the people in "our green and pleasant land".' 'Our Christianity must form the everyday basis for our actions because, as a nation or as a community, it will pay us better in the return of happiness, prosperity and safety to be enjoyed here on earth as apart from the hereafter.' Cripps's obliviousness of evil as a dangerous and permanent force and his tremendous faith in human capacities are attitudes borrowed from humanitarian Liberalism, which sometimes make his Christianity seem a recipe for making the world run properly.

This stands out in his view of the Church. 'It is for the Church', he says, 'to provide *the moral force and the driving power* for social and economic development.' It had failed in the past by tolerating injustice and not championing the poor; it had come to accept 'society-as-it-is', and in consequence its spiritual life was low. A Church living up to God's command had two main ethical duties. The first was to condemn existing social and economic conditions not in accordance with Christian principle. The second was to work out and proclaim, in line with that same Christian principle, 'the juster social and economic arrangements of the future'. Cripps did not believe it necessary for the bishops and other church leaders to enter politics — here we may see the influence of Temple, whose close friend he was. What he wanted from them was that 'they should be prepared quite fearlessly to lay down the Christian principles which are to be followed, leaving it to the lay-men and women to interpret those principles in terms of political action'.

Cripps had no doubts in his own mind that the discovery and interpretation of these principles in the Gospels was a matter of the utmost simplicity. He would select a concept like 'the brother-hood of man' and proceed to develop a string of principles from it:

We insist upon the dignity of human life and the right of all persons — whatever their class, creed or colour — to contribute equally to the orderly development of their and our civilization. This must follow from the basic Christian teaching of the brotherhood of all peoples. . . . Second on our positive list of Christian advocacy, we declare for a democratic way of life, because only in that can we give value to Christian brotherhood in our national life. The very idea of dictatorship is wholly contrary to that equality which brotherhood implies; nor can we acknowledge any human being as supreme or as fit to control and order the destinies of others, whether in the political, social or economic spheres of our life.

Refining the matter still further, he goes on:

We might well adopt as our Christian objectives the list of the five simple desires of the people of America, as expressed by President Roosevelt:

1. Equality of opportunity for youth and others.
2. Jobs for those who can work.
3. Security for those who need it.
4. The ending of privilege for the few.
5. The preservation of civil liberties for all.

These arguments and deductions which were entirely satisfactory to Cripps, an inspiring and sustaining power to him in his work, will not fail to convince equally some Christians who read them, but there will be others more in doubt. Can the good news of the Gospels, the message Christ came to earth to bring, be summed up, in modern times, in Roosevelt's five points?

Cripps did not fail to see that love lay at the heart of Christianity: 'The Kingdom of God upon earth is to be achieved, and it will be accomplished through this divine power of love.' He referred this power to the affairs of industry for which as President of the Board of Trade and Chancellor he was closely responsible. 'The problem of industry is the problem of industry and human relationships. Directly this fact is realized, it becomes abundantly clear that our religion, which is so intimately concerned with the

whole range of our human relationship, has a very close bearing
upon our industrial efficiency and so upon our standard of life.'
It is odd to hear industrial efficiency and a high living standard
classed among the fruits of the spirit, but in seizing upon human
relationships as the key to industry's troubles most sensible people,
let alone Christians, would agree that Cripps was right. A
Christian faith with its emphasis on love should give the politician a specially keen understanding of difficulties caused by
failures in relationships and possibly a particular facility in dealing
with them. Cripps was also impressed with the far-reaching effects
of the Christian idea of the equality of men before God. He
believed, and he was right, that industrial negotiations would go
more smoothly, as would dealings between white men and
coloured men, if there was a deeply felt sense in those holding the
stronger position that the men on the other side of the table were
ultimately as important as they were.

As a Socialist, Cripps necessarily had high regard for the State.
It is an interesting example of how strongly held secular opinions
can break in upon traditional Christian attitudes. As we have seen,
at no period have Western Christians been for long greatly
enamoured of the State. They have seen its power as unavoidable
but always associated with the sinfulness of man. Many would say
that the impersonality of the State makes it a difficult setting for
Christian activity. Cripps, however, turned all this upside down.
The idea of the amoral State he firmly rejected and believed that
the conduct of the State was likely to be more humane than that of
individuals. He is here, admittedly, referring to questions of
property, public and private:

> It is perhaps worth discovering the reason for our reliance upon the
> State's protection. The basic assumption is that the community as a
> whole is more likely to be Christian-minded in these matters than the
> individual. The community, unlike the individual, is not tempted by
> profit or by the desire to gain personal power, and so we can examine
> the relationships in an impartial manner, and with an eye to justice
> and equity rather than to individual advantage.

This trust in the 'Christian-mindedness' of the State is a rarity in
political writing. Perhaps it could only have come from someone

nurtured in the extraordinarily fair and reasonable environment of British public opinion.

A man as sure of the right application of Christian principle to political practice as he was tended towards the doctrinaire approach in general. The combination of strong religious views, personal austerity, and the intellectual ability of a leading advocate did not make Cripps a popular figure with everyone even in his own party. He was Chancellor at a time of severe restriction after the war and sheer circumstance built up for him a skinflint reputation. His readiness to talk publicly about religion — he often accepted invitations to preach in churches and published his sermons — gave more ordinary men of the world a peg for criticism. Herbert Morrison said of him that 'he was not actuated by careerist motives; but perhaps his subconscious belief that he was a political Messiah sometimes made his actions as inconsiderate as if he had been a careerist'. He often showed a proud indifference to arguments not his own. Lansbury, to whom he was devoted, would say to him, 'Stafford, you have not heard a word that I have been saying, listen.'

Cripps was yet another whose party relationships were stormy. When war began to threaten in the middle 1930s we have already seen Lansbury clinging tightly to pacifism while the Labour Party in general inclined to a policy of military support for the League of Nations. Cripps took neither of these positions. He believed, on formal Socialist lines, that war was caused by the economic conflicts of capitalist systems and that the League of Nations was itself the creation of those systems. His view was close to the line of criticism developed against the United Nations by Mr. Khruschev during the Congo troubles in 1960 — that it had become a club of capitalist and 'imperialist' states. Cripps, who founded the Socialist League to further his opinions, argued that the Labour Party should throw over its League policy and instead develop close relations with the U.S.S.R. and other countries where Socialist governments were in control. In 1935 he resigned from the Labour Party executive and campaigned in the country for a popular anti-Conservative front of all Left-wing bodies including the Communists. Throughout this course, clearly

dictated by his habit of following arguments logically through
(not always a rewarding practice in politics), Cripps fell more and
more out of touch with majority opinion in the Party and gave
every appearance of paying no attention to its existence. He even
got as far as saying, in November 1936, that he did not believe it
would be a bad thing for the British working classes if Germany
defeated Britain. It was all too much for steadier members of the
Labour Party like Ernest Bevin, and in January 1939, Cripps was
expelled from the party on the popular front issue. As Mr. Colin
Cooke says of him in his biography:

> If, as he believed, the majority decision of the Party was wrong, no
> consideration of party loyalty should tempt him either to conceal that
> belief or to refrain from using his full power and energy to work for the
> later acceptance of that belief by the Party and his countrymen. To
> conform to the official party line was, to him, an act of mere political
> expediency.

Such an attitude did not endear him to the trade unions, who set
great store by loyalty. Cripps, especially before the war, leant
more on principle and theory than almost any other successful
English politician.

Cripps possessed in high degree that spirit of reconciliation
which is a special property of good Christian politicians. (That is
to say, if Christian politicians were allowed — as some would not
allow them — to have special properties by reason of their religious
outlook, a will to reconciliation would be high on the list.) Like
his father, Lord Parmoor, he had a keen international sense and it
may well be that his membership of the World Alliance for
Promoting International Friendship through the Churches
wakened interests in him which in war-time bore fruit in his
missions to Moscow and India. He made it clear that he believed
the Churches should point the way in international affairs, as they
had done in national life, and should band together as champions
of peace. A good practical test of such an attitude came with the
question of how to treat Germany after the war. The official
Government line was severe — the policy of 'non-fraternization'
for the occupying troops was one expression of it — but Cripps
took a leading part in the Cabinet and outside in pressing for a

more moderate line. On 3 January 1945, he had told the Baptist
Board:

There must be no revenge against the people of Germany, but protection for their frightened neighbours. The Germans are equally
brothers in the human family and sharing the fatherhood of God. . . .
To the German people we, as Christians, would say 'We desire to
treat you as brothers and with friendship, but we must insist on taking
measures to protect and comfort our other European brothers upon
whom you and your leaders have inflicted such untold suffering. We
are not your judges — God alone can judge of human actions and
motives.'

Another opportunity for reconciliation came at the Board of
Trade where his keen interest in better industrial relationships led
him to work hard as a mediator between the two sides. Here, as
President of the Board, Cripps's material and spiritual concerns
ran close together: the unkind would say that they often became
confused. He had two important policies to foster — greater
industrial productivity and greater exports — and he made both
sound as though they were a branch of Christian ethics. Into
arguments for increasing productivity he would weave a Christian
appeal, 'There is in it [i.e. our skill at our job] part of your own
soul, of that divine aspect of our being which is directly linked
with God, and it is that part we pour out for his service and for
our own fulfilment.' The main purpose of the increased productivity and exports policy, which has continued to this day, was to
raise Britain's standard of living, and it was necessarily pursued in
competition with other countries aiming at the same object. It was
in this context that Cripps would strike the Christian note, as in
1947, in a broadcast designed as propaganda for the export drive,
he said: 'Faith in the divine purpose and guidance which comes to
us through the things of the spirit can, as has been said, move
mountains, mountains of material difficulties.'

It is not surprising that such a man aroused some irritation in
spirits less fervent, and the remark of a later Conservative Minister
of Education, that Cripps seemed to think he possessed a 'private
line to the Almighty', expressed the feelings of more worldly men.
There are dangers in a too open profession of Christianity.

Politicians are bound to err and sometimes to resort to subterfuges, and opponents are not slow to seize on such opportunities for persecuting those who have professed overmuch virtue. One came in 1949. On 6 July that year, Sir Stafford Cripps, as Chancellor of the Exchequer, told the Commons that the Government 'have not the slightest intention of devaluing the pound sterling'. He no doubt had hoped to hold the position, but events developed fast. By 19 August, after he had returned from a cure in Switzerland, he found the decision to devalue had already been taken. In September it was announced.

In defending his policy in the Commons on 27 September, Cripps said that his statement of 6 July 'was a completely accurate and deliberate statement', but added that 'even if we had then had some future intention of altering the rate of exchange, which in fact we had not, no responsible Minister could possibly have done otherwise than deny such intentions. To admit it would have been to have invited the speculators and profiteers to destroy our reserves.'

Churchill's attack, we may be sure, was all the more relished for being delivered against a man like Cripps who had perhaps succeeded in giving 'holier-than-thou' impressions to his fellow politicians. Churchill said:

The question is much discussed in the country of the Chancellor's political honesty. Ordinary people find it difficult to understand how a Minister, with all his knowledge and reputation for integrity, should have felt it right to turn completely round, abandon his former convictions and do what he repeatedly said he would never do, and, moreover, enforce upon his party and his most faithful followers the humiliating tergiversation which we have witnessed. I am surprised, I must say, that the Chancellor's own self-respect did not make him feel that, however honest and necessary was his change of view, his was not the hand that should carry forward the opposite policy.

He added that he knew currency changes could not be announced beforehand, but he congratulated Cripps and the Foreign Secretary on the high art which they displayed in 'the necessary process of deception'. He said Cripps's personal honour was not to be impugned but added: 'It will be impossible in the future for anyone to believe or accept with confidence any statements which he may make as Chancellor of the Exchequer.'

Cripps was bitterly upset by this rough handling and carried it as far as refusing to receive an honorary degree from Bristol University because Churchill was its Chancellor. He felt, no doubt, that as Churchill knew as well as he did that no Finance Minister would dare to announce a devaluation beforehand and must always deny the possibility, it was disgraceful to try to use the incident to besmirch his reputation for integrity. He was justified up to a point. Churchill was merely making the most of the spectacle of the austere and Christian Cripps caught out in what at least seemed a lie. The Socialist Chancellor had been caught in one of the inescapable necessities of politics, and his declared high principles ensured that he would not be spared.

If we look back over these six Christian politicians, we shall be struck at once by profound and fundamental differences of view between them. One of Shaftesbury's arguments for the Ten Hours Bill was that it would counteract the evils of socialism and the philosophy of 'infidels and democrats' whom he classed together. For Lansbury Socialism was practical Christianity, while Cripps preferred to a League of Nations policy an alliance with Communism which Salisbury regarded as the main threat to Christian civilization. Wilberforce was a sincere apologist for 'society-as-it-is', which Cripps blamed the Church for supporting, and the notion of equality which Lansbury and Cripps derived from Christian brotherhood would have been totally rejected by Wilberforce, Shaftesbury, Gladstone and Salisbury.

A large part of this division in view may be ascribed merely to the passage of time. Between the birth of Wilberforce and the death of Cripps is a period of nearly two hundred years, and men's views of themselves and hence of the ends of politics changed more in that time than they had done in the twenty previous centuries. When Wilberforce was a child the forces of democracy and industrialization were hardly yet loosed. The more senior of our six politicians may not be accused for failing to respond to claims and challenges which in their days had scarcely arisen. If the Early Church showed little awareness of the arguments for equality and social justice which Cripps believed to be implicit in the Gospels, he and Christians who agreed with him had had their attentions sharpened by the philosophical prophets of the French Revolution and the powerful analysis of Marx. We must allow that the sensitivity of clerics like Gore and Temple and of politicians like Lansbury and Cripps to the needs of the poorer and labouring classes had been aroused by secular as well as Christian influences. But these strong and pervasive influences were hardly alive when Wilberforce and Shaftesbury were at work, and the chief reason for the breadth of difference between them and Cripps is historical. In fact, the division between Salisbury and a modern Conservative like Mr. R. A. Butler is hardly less.

There are, however, differences in outlook and attitude which descend directly from those sharp contrasts in early Christianity discussed in an earlier chapter. In varying degrees, the first four of these men, including Gladstone, were strongly affected in their views of society by Pauline conservatism. They accepted and felt no urge to change a settled, hierarchical community in which all ranks could find what was most necessary to them, the means of salvation in the world to come. But even among these conservatives there are streaks of world-rejection. Wilberforce's retreat from party, after his conversion, may be interpreted as a partial rejection of the world as being too evil. Shaftesbury's behaviour indicated much the same, while even Gladstone had uneasy calls to lay down office to take up more important religious business. Lansbury, of course, if only in respect of his pacifism, must be taken as an example of the world- and State-rejecting politicians. He is a natural descendant of those early Christians who, unwilling to make the Pauline compromise, wished to establish separated communities, outside the common stream of a too sinful world.

If we now turn to look for similarities between these men, to see whether they share characteristics which might be held to be the typical marks of Christian politicians, we must remember the cautions with which this section began. On the basis of a quick review of six men, nothing firm can be established. If they should have certain points in common, the lives of many more Christian politicians would need to be investigated to see if these points applied to them too, before any claims about 'typical characteristics' were made. It would be necessary also to investigate as many non-Christian politicians as a check on any generalization. All that can be done at this stage is to touch on a few points of similarity between our six subjects, with the suggestion that any larger and more thorough inquiry into the nature of the Christian politician in action should pay particular attention to them.

All six men at one stage or another sat extremely loose to their parties. If Gladstone appears an exception, it might be argued that his precipitate adoption of Home Rule for Ireland, which caused the secession of the Unionists from the Liberal Party, showed the same conscientious refusal to compromise with principle for the sake of party unity which is so clear in Wilberforce and Shaftesbury. Wilberforce withdrew from party on conversion, Shaftesbury refused to work as a party man, Salisbury, Lansbury and Cripps had experienced either resignation or expulsion. Not only Christians resign, of course, but there are plausible reasons why we should expect them to resign more often than other people. They should have — and the six great men here considered certainly did have — a set of religious beliefs, related to life, which are more important to them than any secular party concerns. These men had sharp views of right and wrong and some of them had also that sense of spiritual justification and righteousness which makes of its possessors somewhat restless team-mates.

A second rather obvious point is that these men had in their lives a matter of great concern which was beyond politics. It could be argued that this introduces into the life of a politician a sanity and sense of proportion which is lacking when his career or even a worthy temporal aim is the sole absorbing interest. This outside point of reference is still usefully supplied in quite other ways. Disraeli was doubtless the better for his old ladies, Lord Rosebery for his horses, and Lord Grey for the birds whose study gave him delight. But religion, when it is held to as strongly as it was by our six examples, is the greatest counterweight to worldly interest. The desire to rise in his career is natural to a politician, and, since that career depends more than others on the friends he makes and the impression he gives, he is tempted, for one thing, to modify his own thinking for the sake of toning in with the general background of his party. This is one of the many ways in which hacks and insincere machine-like ministers are made. They have lost all spur save ambition. For Wilberforce and Shaftesbury the counter-pull of religion was so strong that as well as draining them of ambition, it made them incapable of party activity. If it is difficult to suppose that a man who held party leadership for as long as Gladstone did not enjoy the use of power, yet one does not think of him as an ambitious man, and in his private writings there are many signs of unusual humility. Salisbury could ask himself whether the issues he handled mattered much in the total scheme of things. No man could have done more than Cripps to flout and irritate the party on which his political career depended, for the sake of pressing opinions which he believed to be right. It may be that religion, by reminding a politician that his career and party are far from all-important, enlarges his freedom of action.

To move on, it is natural to expect the Gospel emphasis on love for all men and forgiveness to find some reflection in the public conduct of Christian politicians. Both Wilberforce and Shaftesbury of course were unconscious reconcilers, for the espousal of the slave's cause kept open the lines of understanding between white and black, and the fight for the factory children, with other humanitarian campaigns, helped to moderate in Britain the bitterness between classes which has vexed the history of some other countries. It is doubtful, however, whether either of them clearly recognized a reconciling duty in the field of public affairs and certainly Shaftesbury's hatred of the Tractarians, against whom he readily sought political sanctions, exhibited the *odium theologicum* in an unpleasant form. The whole bearing of Gladstone's foreign policy at a time of great British power showed, in spite of the foray into Egypt, a steadily reconciling aim. It animated his policy towards Ireland, which cost him so many of his supporters, and his willingness to accept arbitration, in cases involving British interests, reveals a constant preoccupation with the art of coming to agreement by peaceful means. We have noted in Lansbury and Cripps the tendency to outpace their colleagues in restoring relations with defeated foreign enemies. Lansbury in editing the *Daily Herald* toned down the violence of polemic against the class enemy. Cripps spent much of his political life in violent controversy and suffered for it, as we have seen, by expulsion from his party, but he appears to have been a man who held few personal grudges. When war broke out, many were surprised at the extremely easy and efficient way in which he entered into co-operation with Conservatives for whom no denunciation had been too severe a few months before.

Several warnings to the Christian in politics stand out of our brief review. A reputation for piety, as distinct from more sociable virtues like sincerity, can be a hindrance. If a politician has talked too much of his religious beliefs, he may arouse enmities which he would have escaped if they had been kept hidden. Cripps set up this kind of dislike in many. Wilberforce, for all his charm, had his beliefs quoted against him more than once. Gladstone raised the moral temper of the nation, but his appeal to righteousness often so exacerbated his opponents, some no less Christian than himself, that no one can be surprised to find in the lower Tory propaganda of the period a line of argument which presented him as the devil in angel's clothing. Salisbury, whose religion was more private to himself, perhaps took a wiser course. The politician who labels himself a Christian runs into the same hazards as those parties on the Continent which style themselves 'Christian' in their titles. Politics is a devious activity and sooner or later all politicians will be forced by its necessities into some course or expedient which can hardly be defended on the strictest moral grounds. Not one of our subjects but has found himself in this sort of difficulty. It is at such moments that more worldly opponents will seize upon a politician's known religiousness as a stick to beat him with. No doubt the politician himself will easily survive this buffeting, but he should consider whether some of the punishment is not borne, quite unfairly, by the religion to which he belongs.

This brief and inadequate excursion into practical politics may

now be concluded. In a book over-given to theory, it will have
served its purpose if it has reminded readers that no full understanding of Christianity and politics may be reached without a
study, far fuller than made here, of the political conduct of
Christians. If Christianity has something of its own to contribute
to politics, it is in actions that it will be chiefly discovered. But a
political success is hardly ever the work of one man, and there are
serious defects in concentrating on six men untypical alike in the
strength of their faith and, in general, in the outstanding character
of their abilities. With Wilberforce laboured many Quakers and
Anglicans; Shaftesbury was himself no more than the figurehead
of a large group of reforming Christians; Gladstone had behind
him the whole force of Victorian nonconformity, while as we
come down to Salisbury, Lansbury and Cripps we shall note that
many accepting their leadership in good causes were not Christians at all. It is enough to suggest that the unravelling of the
motives for large-scale human activity is a task hardly likely to
be satisfactorily completed.

6

Politics and Religion in England

AFTER our look at some Christian politicians in action, the next step is a return to theory, to the views on politics held not by practising laymen but by the clergy, mainly, who became concerned about the subject in the nineteenth and twentieth centuries. As far as policy goes, one could start there without much loss, for the eighteenth century is the dark night of Christian political initiatives. But as we are also interested in deep-rooted political attitudes, it is necessary to start farther back, for, as G. M. Trevelyan maintained, the opposition of churchman and dissenter — in itself mirroring the Early Church's two attitudes to the world — constitutes the historical basis of the English party system.

The intellectual origins of the conservative colour of the Church of England are to be found in Richard Hooker's *Ecclesiastical Polity*, the first books of which were published in 1594. He wrote in full conservative reaction against the Puritan sectaries of Elizabeth's reign. 'When they and their Bibles were alone together,' he said of them, 'what strange fantastical opinion soever at any time entered into their heads, their use was to think the spirit taught it to them.' Hooker looked back to the settled order of the Middle Ages, and extolled the authority of traditional institutions like the monarchy and episcopacy. His conception of society (still largely held by Wilberforce, it is worth noting) was of a closely-knit community whose graded classes fulfilled the functions of their various stations, the lesser serving dutifully and the greater protecting them as they served. Religion was a preservative of order, checking the ambition or acquisitiveness that might destroy it, and the State, holding all together, was the temporal expression of spiritual obligations.

Hooker's conservatism demanded from the great of this world a sense of obligation towards the poor, a survival of old feudal

H

responsibilities, which Archbishop Laud in his day and Lord Shaftesbury in his bewailed the lack of in the men of their times. Laud did his best through the Star Chamber to save the common people from those who 'engrossed' corn and by other means to check the enclosers of the poor man's common land. The idea that Christians were not called to intervene in social and political affairs was certainly not held in the court of the first two English Stuart kings. But this right of intervention rested ultimately on the authority of the Church, maintained by its bishops, and it was this authority that Puritanism, in the many guises it displayed during the Civil War and after, slowly and steadily undermined. Puritanism sprang from the anti-conservative, radical stream of Christianity, which refused the temporary composition with the world that St. Paul advised and sought instead to withdraw from it into perfect groups and societies, and had deep suspicions of all authority, particularly ecclesiastical. 'Christ has made all men free.' That was their text. It was not that the Puritans, unlike many of their predecessors in this stream, felt called to flee the market-place. 'God', wrote one of their divines, 'doth call every man and woman . . . to serve Him in some peculiar employment in this world, both for their own and the common good.' It was not economic entanglement they feared, but spiritual. They could worship God more purely outside the fence of ecclesiastical organization and authority. They withdrew from the hierarchical church into independent congregations. Sometimes, in pursuit of their greater freedom, they invented eccentric social schemes. In 1647 the 'Levellers' under John Lilburne proposed the dissolution of Parliament and a purer democratic rule. Two years later Gerrard Winstanley gathered together a company, called 'Diggers', who sought to found a communist society by taking over Crown lands and cultivating them with their spades. But the significant invention of this period, the real basis of Dissent, was the doctrine of the Inner Light. Its extreme form was found in a sect called the Ranters, who denied the authority of Scripture, Christ, the creeds and the ministry, and accepted guidance only from the individual conscience. The Ranters, of course, were a *reductio ad absurdum* of the Inner Light theory. Its intellectually respectable presentation (though it was not admitted to be that even by the Dissenters of his day) was made by George Fox. The chief apostle of the Inner Light in England, he did not entirely repudiate a doctrine of the Church. In 1668 he published his *Rule for the Management of Meetings* and so advanced the purely individual principle of the Inner Light into a sustaining bulwark of church order. Nevertheless, the elevation of private conscience into ultimate authority was a denial to the organized churches of any competence to pronounce upon the affairs of the world. All Protestants, and not only Quakers, came to repudiate the whole medieval tradition of ecclesiastical surveillance and intervention. As Tawney shows, the common lawyers were as eager on their own account to prune the jurisdiction of the Church as the Puritans, and before long the growth of the natural sciences, coupled with Locke's worldly common-sense, encouraged men to view the political and economic sphere as a machine of divine manufacture with which it would be impious to interfere. A late Nonconformist version of this belief was declared in the *British Quarterly Review*, in 1846:

Economical truth is not less divine than astronomical truth. The laws which govern the phenomena of production and exchange are as truly laws of God, as those which govern the phenomena of day and night. To ascertain by inductive inquiry the natural condition of commercial and industrial prosperity, is to ascertain the will of the Deity in regard to a certain department of human conduct: to act in conformity with those conditions, so ascertained, is to act religiously.

Such were the Christian arguments put in the way of Shaftesbury as he struggled to reduce the working hours of factory children.

We see then in the seventeenth and eighteenth centuries in English religion a fascinating reproduction of the cleavage of attitude which existed in the Early Church and Middle Ages: the feeling for order and authority was deeply ingrained in Anglicanism; the feeling for movement and freedom animated Dissent. Both branches came to regard religion as largely a matter of personal piety, and all thought of its having a prescriptive right to interfere in politics would have been judged ridiculous. All the same, these Anglicans and Dissenters took distinctive political positions, which were largely determined for them by their religious outlook and experience. In fact, the origins of the English two-party system may be traced back to a difference of opinion between two sets of men over whether bishops were necessary.

⅄ The aim of Elizabeth was to comprehend all Englishmen in one church, and it was pursued with varying degrees of insistence by the Stuart kings. The Puritan dissenters passionately rejected this policy and demanded full religious freedom for themselves. Persecuted under Tudors and Stuarts, gaining a tumultuous freedom in the Civil War, persecuted again in the Restoration, the dissenters finally won toleration in the Whig revolutionary settlement of 1688. It was not complete, this toleration; they were to labour for more than a century under disabilities, political and other. But broadly they had gained the right to worship as they pleased and to ply their trades as citizens, and in this considerable result their allies had been the great Whiggish interests. Episcopacy and kingship had gone together, and if the Whigs were largely indifferent to bishops, yet they were the traditional opponents of royal power. It was as natural for the dissenters to shelter under their wing as it was for Anglicans to gravitate towards the king's party. From the start of our modern political history one brand of churchmen enrolled under the banner of liberty while the other took up position behind the ramparts of authority. Thus those forces, whose interplay creates the tension and life of politics, became intimately bound up in England with two bodies of religion.

If a survey of the eighteenth century hardly illustrates the cleansing effects on public life of religious allegiance, one must admit, with gratitude, the harmonizing influence on British society of the peculiarly religious way in which its politics were organized. In France, for example, where dissent was stamped out in the seventeenth century, there was no refuge for the man who quarrelled with the Church except outside the confines of religion. On the Continent the cause of liberty or liberalism, everywhere attacking oppressive régimes, invariably found those régimes buttressed by institutional religion and it was natural for Continental liberalism to grow up as an anti-religious force. In England, on the contrary, a man who quarrelled with his church might find a home in dissent and the party which became the mainspring of liberalizing activity was deeply anchored in Christian belief.

It did not occur to either Whig or Tory to devise a political policy based on their religion. Politics was a humdrum, everyday thing, something separate from the concerns of a man's heart. But both parties used politics, and the balance of power it offered, as a means of ensuring for themselves the pursuance of religious beliefs they held important. They were both in greater or lesser degree Christian, and for this reason there never grew up in England that political antipathy to religion, springing largely from the fact that in its organized form it was tied to oppressive and conservative forces, which fed the socially divisive movement of anti-clericalism on the Continent. It was less easy in England to feel that not only were your opponents badly wrong politically, but godless and wicked as well. Although the division between Anglicanism and Dissent took social forms of which their members were intensely conscious — the change from chapel to church of the rising and ambitious man was a spectacle much seen and commented on in industrial Lancashire, for instance — the barriers were not felt to be impassable. Nonconformity found nothing incongruous in banding itself behind the political leadership of the High Anglican Gladstone. The political affiliations of Methodism are instructive. The latest and largest of the dissenting movements, Methodism's strong authoritarian government under John Wesley himself gave its members natural inclinations towards Toryism. Although dissenters, they came late on the scene, toleration had been won, and the urgency of the Whig connexion no longer seemed apparent. Further, Wesley's emphasis on personal piety and his wish to keep his following respectable led him to institute a 'no politics' rule. As is well known, in England those who proclaim neutrality tend to be hidden Conservatives. In spite of these Conservative beginnings, as Mr. E. R. Taylor shows in his *Methodism and Politics*, the movement between 1797 and 1837 worked its way slowly from right to left, ending as a solid factor in the Liberal Party's support. It is not so much the reasons for this changeover that concern us as that it happened quite naturally and with so little upheaval. Not only had religion done much to shape the English two-party system, but, as time went on, it came to have a moderating effect on party warfare. The Methodists' switch in allegiance over fifty years is significant. If they ended in Liberalism, they had begun, without any sense of strain, in Toryism. In the nineteenth century, the antagonism between Anglicanism and dissent grew less, and a sense of common Christianity harmonized the relationships of the political parties, keeping them in a certain general accord, despite their clashes over franchise, Ireland, and imperial policy. Neither Tory Anglican nor Whig dissenter tried to find in the Gospels a key to the proper ordering of terrestrial affairs. They did, however, come to require politicians to set a moral example. It was Hugh Price Hughes, the Methodist and Liberal leader, who, in demanding from the platform of the West London Mission the adulterous Parnell's resignation, cried, 'We love Ireland, but our first obedience and our highest devotion must be to God. . . . We stand immovably on this eternal rock; what is morally wrong can never be politically right.'

We reach the nineteenth century then with British politics still divided partly on religious lines, but with Anglicans and Nonconformists agreed that churches had neither right nor capacity to interfere in political matters. A change of view on this point came first in the Church of England, but it affected only a few, and only by the twentieth century with Gore and Temple did politically concerned Christians appear to gain much of a hearing from their fellows. There are three periods of active interest. F. D. Maurice, J. M. F. Ludlow and Charles Kingsley were founders of a Christian social movement in the years 1846–54. The next wave of activity came under men like Samuel Barrett, Arnold Toynbee, Stewart Headlam and Scott Holland from 1873 to 1890 and the third and final period of thought and protest came after the First World War, with Archbishop Temple as its leader. What caused these outbursts of Christian interest in politics? In each case it was undoubtedly the condition of the poorer people. Interest rose and fell according to the prosperity of the nation. Maurice and Kingsley spoke out during a period of bad trade when many public inquiries were for the first time revealing the wretchedness to which the Industrial Revolution had reduced many of the working class. As prosperity returned and the condition of the people improved, the Christian protest died away. It was the same in 1875-89, which were years of trade slump relieved only by a short burst of greater activity in 1881, and, of course, the strikes and unemployed of the nineteen twenties and thirties are still deeply imprinted on the British memory. Archbishop Temple has had no successor since the end of the Second War and the conferences and books on Christian politics have died away. It seems clear that a Christian concern for politics in England has waned in prosperous periods and waxed in times of depression. There is little evidence of it now under the Welfare State and full employment. No signs exist in the Church of England or the Free Churches of any persisting conviction that Christianity has a perennial concern with the day-to-day course of politics. The interest, when it comes, seems practical and ad hoc. It is stirred by the spectacle of suffering and by that, it would seem, alone. Compassion for the afflictions of the poor and weak would appear to be the mainspring of Christian political action in England.

Even so, it cannot be maintained that churchmen played a large part in the rise of the working-class movement. Poets like Coleridge, Wordsworth and Southey did more to alert the public mind to social evils and political opportunities than did the bishops. A practical idealist like Owen was far more discussed at home and abroad than any Christian writer, and, of course, the various branches of secular Socialism gained vastly more adherents than any of the few nineteenth-century Christian initiatives in England which were on a small scale. What can be said is that the Christian stirring was at least large enough to provide links with the secular advance guard. There were sufficient interested Christians to convince the progressive members of the working class that the Church was not throughout and by nature unfriendly to their cause. This was a valuable achievement for it kept communications open, so that, for example, a Christian might find himself entirely at home in the infant Labour Party, among free-thinking colleagues who regarded him without dislike or suspicion. The man who rescued the Church from a charge of complete indifference, the father of that always small wing of the Church of England with a keen concern for social and political affairs, was F. D. Maurice. Of Unitarian stock, he became an Anglican clergyman, and professor of theology at King's College, London, and Cambridge. A man of the study and the pulpit, he knew most of the notabilities of his day, and from our point of view his work — he was above all a theologian — was to provide intellectual foundations for the idea that Christians had a duty in the political sphere. His breakaway from the eighteenth-century tradition of complete withdrawal was a turning point of great significance and his extension of the range of the Christian conscience has never afterwards been wholly forgotten.

Maurice did not suppose that a careful study of the Bible or Christian tradition would reveal a neatly consistent political policy on any necessary subject. His theology kept the divine order of the universe firmly in mind, and his political thought was anchored in Natural Law conceptions. God was the creator of the world, which was his world, and there was a way, discoverable by reason, in which its affairs could be well managed. The principle of that way was the brotherhood of men founded on their common childhood. This for Maurice meant socialism — though he was as far as anyone could be from accepting State socialism. He established with his small group of supporters some co-operative societies, which failed, and some educational projects that, like the Working Men's College, were more successful. But these were merely illustrations of his thought. 'The Christian Socialists', as Dr. H. G. Wood remarked, 'were not committed to any particular scheme of economic organization. They thought things should be subordinate to persons and that wealth should subserve welfare, and they looked to the working classes to bring this to pass.' Maurice's achievement was to re-establish inside the Church of England the belief that the Church was the means by which the redemptive love of God was to be brought to bear on human society. The Church was not for him a withdrawn pietistic society; it had a duty in the world of everyday affairs, a concern which included politics and economics.

No one can say that the seed sown by Maurice in the mid-nineteenth century had produced a striking harvest by its end. No really powerful mind developed his line of thought and the main characteristic of the next phase of Christian activity, from 1875 to 1890, was a somewhat facile identification of Christianity with the working-class movement and Socialism. By some clergy, in the little Guild of St. Matthew founded in 1877, Socialism was adopted almost as a means of expressing sympathy and keeping in touch with working men. 'Christianity', it was said some years later, 'is the religion of which Socialism is the practice.' Stewart Headlam was the leader of this mainly Anglo-Catholic group, but there were many in that section of the Church, including the *Church Times*, who were emphasizing the dangers of equating Christianity with the provision of material welfare. 'Too many Christian Socialists', wrote Egerton Swann in 1914, 'think of the Kingdom of God as merely a human society in which perfect justice rules and whose members are bound together by perfect human love. It is simply the apotheosis of humanitarianism. . . . God for them remains quite in the background.' Maurice, whose whole philosophy flowed from his conception of God, would have disapproved of these of his children.

Charles Gore (1853–1932) is the next name of intellectual consequence after Maurice and is in some sense the bridge between him and Temple. Son of a distinguished Anglo-Irish family, founder of the Community of the Resurrection, Bishop of Oxford, Gore gave a high place in his scholarly mind to the proper duty of a Christian towards society. He played an important part in the Christian Social Union, founded in 1889 by a body of men who, while believing in Christian Socialism, by which they meant the application of Christian law to social practice, did not subscribe to the political Socialism preached by the Guild of St. Matthew. As Gore was to write later of the Christian Social Union:

Its motive was the sense that Christianity, and especially the Church of England, had lamentably failed to bear its social witness — its witness to the principles of divine justice and human brotherhood which lie at its heart. It had left the economic and industrial world to build itself up on quite fundamentally unchristian premises, as if Christianity had got nothing to do with the matter.

The Union's aims were:

(1) To claim for the Christian law the ultimate authority to rule social practice.

(2) To study in common how to apply the moral truths and principles of Christianity to the social and economic difficulties of the present time.

(3) To present Christ in practical life as the living Master and King, the enemy of wrong and selfishness, the power of righteousness and love.

If the C.S.U. was open to the criticism made by Mr. G. C. Binyon in *The Christian Socialist Movement in England* — it 'had claimed for the Christian law the ultimate authority to rule social practice; but it had omitted to explain what the Christian law was' — it was none the less a lively centre for propagandizing the duty of Christian social witness and its many meetings and discussions must have helped Gore in forming his own views. To these we shall give now rather more detailed attention, for he was a churchman of great standing and influence and, in so far as the Church of England has a mind on the matters discussed in this book, Gore and Temple did more than any other men to form it.

In his book *Christ and Society* (1928) Gore does examine the Gospels to discover from the teaching of Jesus what the Church, as a visible organization of the Kingdom of God on earth, is meant to stand for. The first point in that teaching is that God is the Father of all and so each member of the human family possesses an equal and eternal spiritual value. As in spiritual value all are equal, anything that exalts a man in his own eyes above his fellows is condemned. At the same time, Jesus's teaching is to be distinguished from the spirit of modern democracy, because there is a flavour of spiritual aristocracy about it. Although He proclaims the fatherhood of God and the brotherhood of man He never speaks of men *as they stand* as already sons of God, nor is the word 'brother' used in apostolic times of any except members of the regenerated community of the Church. The community, as Jesus proclaimed it, was open to all, but on the condition of surrender to God and faith in His way.

Gore notes that Christ is plainly on the side of the humble and poor, has no regard for conventions, such as that women are of less value than men, and has a particular hatred of the respectable sins like hypocrisy. He had not come into the world, as Gore sees it, primarily to save the individual soul. His message had a social sense. He called all men who were ready to surrender their wills to God to enter a community — in the world but not of it — based on the fullest recognition of brotherhood, to the exclusion of any selfish claim for a privileged position, and on the acknowledgment in every single soul of an equal and infinite worth.

It cannot be said that Gore found in the original deposit a wealth of guidance useful to the Christian in politics. With reservations, however, he believed that the Gospels were on the side of human equality, and when he goes on to apply the Gospel principles to national affairs it is of this he appears to think chiefly. 'The present condition of our society, our industry, and our international relations . . . ought to inspire in our minds a deep sense of dissatisfaction and alarm, and a demand for reform so thorough as to amount to a revolution.' Gore was not a Socialist — 'I do not hold with the Socialistic theory myself,' he told the House of Lords in 1908 — but if he was, generally speaking, a Liberal in politics, he had sympathy with the Labour Party and the workers it represented. In industry, therefore, he held that the claims of human dignity and equality required a closer association of workpeople in the ownership and control of the places where they worked. (He quotes with approval a New Zealand scheme of industrial co-partnership.)

The industrial system of his time in his view denied justice, and people should heed 'the demand that social arrangements should be so re-moulded and re-directed as that everyone born into citizenship should have a fair chance of making the best of himself'. He noted that schooling ended too soon and argued for bridging the gap between fourteen and eighteen and for secondary education for all. His concern for greater equality came out again in proposals for the reform of the law of property because it was more given to maintaining the rights of the propertied classes than the good of the general public. 'Nothing seems to me at this moment more alarming than the concentration of capital, and the vast power which capital gives, in few hands.' 'If the prospect of making great fortunes were reduced', the momentum of industry would not be less, because there would be a liberation of workers' energies in 'an enterprise which they could feel to be their own'.

When we examine the implications of Christ's teaching, he says, 'We find how accurately and deeply they correspond with the ideal of modern democracy, not as we often see it but at its best.' He notes also that the fundamental idea of spiritual equality and democracy had seized upon the consciences of almost all men, of all colours and races. We must either answer its demands, in our attitude to race relations, or fall under the divine judgment 'which works in the slow process of history and occasionally breaks out in catastrophe and cataclysm'.

Finally, one of Gore's main points, at a time when Fascism had settled on Italy but five years before Hitler's advent to power, was that the State was an association of associations. This, as we shall see, is a favourite conception of Christian political theorists. 'We have to stand up', he wrote, 'for the natural liberty of free association within the unity of the state.' Men should primarily be attracted to matters of their immediate concern, their villages, their city districts, their factories. These departments of the common life should each have their own governments and be relatively free.

'It is of course true', Gore agreed, 'that "you cannot make men moral by act of Parliament"; yet the laws and institutions of a country do make it, to a degree which it is difficult to exaggerate, either easier or harder for men to walk in the right way.' He wished to see an inter-denominational association re-asserting the social meaning of Christianity. It would be political but would not tie itself to any party. Certainly it ought not to suppose that 'mere political changes can of themselves bring us nearer the Kingdom of God'. Gore knew that men must be changed before they can change their politics. A critic would doubtless say that changing men was the proper, endless and seldom accomplished task of the Church, and that if it could gain more success in its own sphere, it could safely leave the political to others. But Gore could have replied that the English Church for a century had concentrated on personal religion, without startling result, while during that time its lack of interest in the sufferings of the poor had alienated many who saw in it a wicked failure in Christian compassion.

Gore, as already said, was not a Labour man, but the tribute paid to him after his death and to his colleagues of the Christian Social Union in the *New Statesman* is worth repeating:

Charles Gore did more than any one man, except perhaps West-cott, to change the official attitude of the Church to the problem of Labour; it is due to him, and to men like Stanton, Dolling, Headlam and Scott Holland, that the assumption usually made on the Continent that Christianity and Socialism are incompatible has never been accepted in England.

The organizations within the Church with which these names were associated were small. The Guild of St. Matthew never numbered more than 400 members and the more moderate Christian Social Union had 6,000 at its height in 1910. But during the First World War, as a result of the National Mission — an enterprise responsive in 1916 to the wave of moral earnestness and desires to do better which rose in Britain during both major conflicts — the social movement was drawn into the main stream of the Church of England. Committees were set up after the Mission and one reporting on 'Christianity and Industrial Problems' in the sanguine days of 1918 gained much attention. If a Christian political concern was not even now widespread, it had become respectable; a group of bishops from now on were there to express it, and through the twenties and thirties a series of conferences and publications drove home to churchmen their political and social responsibilities. One of the most famous of the conferences was held at Birmingham in 1924 — the Conference on Christian Politics, Economics and Citizenship known as COPEC. Both Gore and Temple attended, Gore as an honoured veteran and Temple as the moving spirit; it was here, one can say, that the older man passed his mantle to the younger. Copec's reports, of which there were twelve, each running to the length of a short book, are a fair sample of how Christians at that time believed their religion should affect the world.

The report on Politics and Citizenship is typical, and its mixture of liberal idealism and common sense creates a certain impatience. After expounding the Christian doctrine of the State, with lesser associations ranged freely beneath it, the report remarks that democracy is the constitution *par excellence* because the end of social life is the development of personality in fellowship. It is a normal Christian duty to take a share in political affairs. Men tend to separate into groups according to their temperaments; some welcome change, some resent it. All such groups are good and Christians may join any. The report then throws in a suggestion that it would be good for inter-party discussion groups to exist in each parliamentary constituency. Differences between parties should be about means not ends and they should all have the common good of the community before them. Politicians may find themselves in a difficulty when they cannot agree with the whole programme of their party. They must beware of the besetting sin of mere advocacy and not be ready to argue any brief that is put into their hands; they are responsible for their arguments in a way the barrister is not.

There is a discussion of how much the Church may lead in politics and agreement that while the Church can say there is a case for State action, she can hardly claim to be a judge of the methods to be used. She can call attention to the sin of the slums, but she has no competence to decide how best they may be abolished. The report ends with a series of recommendations which may be summarized:

1. The State is ordained by God for the purpose of binding men together in a justly ordered social life and its authority ought to be loyally accepted by Christians: the State should be challenged only in the name of God, and Christians must not take that name in vain.

2. There can be no class distinctions in the Church. Christians must use their influence against any class distinctions which are an obstacle to true social communion.

3. The Church recognizes the call to Christian service in national and local politics and in social work. The need for a high standard of preparation for such work should be urged and the formation of inter-party groups to study subjects of current political

discussion from a Christian standpoint should be encouraged.

4. Christians should use their influence in favour of a Press which not only presents accurate news, unbiased by editorial policy, but also provides all the materials necessary to enable the public to arrive at well informed opinion on public policy.

5. Christians must do all they can to foster the growth of a more healthy public opinion which will no longer tolerate the sensational details of the divorce courts and of sordid vice, incentives to wholesale betting and gambling, the vulgarity of much advertisement and the exaltation of false values which distort modern journalism.

It is always easier to declare general principles than to apply them. How, for example, do Christians exert influence over newspapers? We might at this point notice an attempted application of a general principle to the troubled economy of the 1920s. The Church had espoused the trade unions' claim for a 'Living Wage'. The 1918 report 'Christianity and Industrial Problems', which the Lambeth Conference of 1920 more or less explicitly adopted, stated firmly:

> The first change upon every industry should be the payment of a sufficient wage to enable the worker to maintain himself and his family in health and honour, with such margin of leisure as will permit reasonable recreation and development of mind and spirit.

The demand seemed moderate and unexceptionable. But the early 1920s were a period of severe deflation caused by economic assumptions and financial policies which most Christian leaders were ill-equipped to criticize or even comprehend. They were without an answer when the Federation of British Industries told them in 1921 that 'the real and ultimate test must always be what industry can bear' and that 'it may be necessary... for the workers to be prepared to accept a money wage which may, till trade revives, give them a lower standard of living . . . even than their pre-war standard'. Sound or unsound, it was an argument the bishops found themselves unable to refute. When the controversy over the 'Living Wage' took practical shape in the General and Miners' Strike of 1926, the Church, under Archbishop Davidson of Canterbury, attempted mediation, much to the dislike of the

Government, who excluded the Archbishop's proposals from their newspaper, the only one appearing.

The miners stayed out after the collapse of the General Strike and a group of churchmen including ten bishops, among whom Temple, then Bishop of Manchester, was prominent, tried to bring the two sides to terms on the basis of the 1926 Royal Commission's report on the coalmining industry. The coalowners said they could not adopt the report, but the miners expressed willingness to drop their slogan — 'Not a penny off the pay, not a minute on the day' — and to accept some of the report's proposals. However, they did not go far enough for the owners. The proposals the churchmen took to the Prime Minister came to nothing, the strike continued and the miners' defeat when it came was all the more bitter for having been delayed. The churchmen's intervention was well meant; it showed a genuine concern. As Maurice Reckitt remarks in his *Maurice to Temple*:

Here was evidence of two things of which organized religion, in its more official aspects at any rate, had been thought incapable since the Industrial Revolution — sympathy for the claims of a proletariat in revolt, and independence in face of the great ones of the earth.

In spite of these good effects in general, there are grounds for supposing that as far as the miners' strike went at the time, the episcopal mediation did more harm than good. Mr. B. Seebohm Rowntree certainly thought so. ('I find it hard to control my language', he writes in a letter quoted by Professor Asa Briggs in his biography, 'when I think of those blank! blank! blank! Bishops and the harm they have done.') Unknown to the churchmen, he with a few helpers, after long practice in industrial conciliation, had been trying to find the basis for a settlement with the miners' leader, A. J. Cook. They had covered a lot of ground and Cook was about to lay before the Miners' Federation a compromise proposal that would have ended the strike. In later years, Seebohm Rowntree wrote to Temple:

There is no doubt at all that the memorandum would have been laid before the Federation, had it not been for the intervention of the Churches' committee. . . . What convinces me that the strike would have ended in July rather than in December but for the intervention of the Churches is that up to the date on which that intervention took place we were steadily succeeding in bringing the two parties closer together and everything pointed to the fact that we were rapidly approaching a successful issue of the effort in which we were engaged. *But from the moment that the Churches intervened the atmosphere changed completely.* The miners thought they had the whole of the Christian Churches behind them, and they were no longer prepared to consider making any concessions beyond those which were contained in the terms they had offered to the Church delegation.

The incident illustrates well the difficulties and pitfalls of political action. The churchmen had been moved to sympathy by the miners' sufferings, but a main effect of their intervention was that the miners suffered longer and worse. On the other hand, the Church of England had shown once again that in modern times she was no longer bound to the owning classes or blind to the workers' needs.

Temple, the prime mover in these events, had an enthusiasm, a brilliance and a lucidity which marked him out among the high ecclesiastics of England since the Reformation. In turn don, headmaster, bishop and archbishop, he had a mind which astonished, and a sense of humour which endeared him to the men of his day. He had, however, some of the defects of the intellectual; in life he was held to be a bad judge of men, and when we now read his writings there is a certain absence of warmth and emotion. Nevertheless, on the question which occupies us now, he had no peer; on the part the Church and churchmen should play in politics, he is the master, and if one should wish to determine this particular Anglican attitude it is hardly necessary to look elsewhere. In 1920 he undertook the editorship of a monthly magazine called *The Pilgrim*, a 'review of Christian Politics and Religion'. In it he stated, after a ruinous war, that 'a religion which offers no solution to world problems fails to satisfy; a scheme of reconstruction, apart from religion, strikes cold and academic'. To this a very different sort of Anglican, Dean Inge, replied in a note, 'I think you must admit that "Christian politics" in *The Pilgrim* and elsewhere, are tinged with the roseate hues of early dawn. I should never call my brand of Whiggery Christian Politics, though they are the politics of one Christian.'

I

In 1918 Temple joined the Labour Party and gave his reasons in the *Daily News*:

Now the Labour Movement is essentially an effort to organize society on the basis of freedom and fellowship. As such it has a right to claim the sympathy of the Church. The Labour Party is a different thing: that is a political organization, and the Church as a whole must not be attached to any political party — not even to the Tory Party. But churchmen ought to consider very carefully the formulated programme of the Labour Party, and whether they should individually subscribe to it. Here is a party which has at least put forward an outline scheme of reconstruction in national and international life. It is a scheme based on moral ideals. We must not support it simply because we sympathize with the motives behind it: but if we believe that these motives are, on the whole, applied with wisdom, we have no right to stand aside. We must go in and help.

By about 1925 Temple had come to the conclusion that party membership was unsuitable to a bishop — he would never have thought it was for a layman — and resigned. He noted that 'we must be very careful that we do not give the impression that the Church is an agency for supporting left-wing politics which are often based on presuppositions entirely un-Christian'. In 1941 he was writing to a friend:

Christianity has something quite specific of its own to say about these things, and it seems to me immensely important that we should say it and challenge consciences with it rather than look round for that proposal in the political field which we think at the moment most likely to help in the right direction. This latter has got to be done but it is the job of the Christian politician rather than of the Church or its agencies themselves, and there is a great deal of course in the Left wing movement which is no more Christian than that of the diehard Right.

In 1942, he sets out his attitude to Labour still more specifically:

I find the Labour Party generally has conspicuous difficulty in realizing that our first job is with the Gospel, and that we can only commit the Church as a whole to what indubitably follows from the Gospel. They see so clearly what seems to them both the justice and the expediency of the Labour Party programme that it seems to them we ought to support that straightway. In fact, they often want us to give up being specifically a Church, i.e. the Household of our Lord, and become a political party. They do not really want this when it is nakedly presented to them, but they often want a line of action which in fact involves this; and then they become more irritated with a person like myself who actually sympathizes and agrees with them in most of their programme than they do with open opponents, because they think we are hedging for some discreditable reason.

Before examining more closely Temple's views on the Christian duty in politics, we might note his attitude to national enemies, as it is in line with that of Lansbury and Cripps. He was writing, as Archbishop of Canterbury, to Dr. Garbett, the Archbishop of York, explaining the difficulties he had in ordering prayers to be said for victory in the war:

But I have tried always to draw up prayers which do not range us over against any of our fellow-Christians in Germany or elsewhere, because it seems to me that the primary concern in prayer — and I mean 'primary' quite seriously — must be the approach to the Father of all men, with recognition that all His other children have the same right of approach, and that if we pray as our Lord taught us, we are never praying against each other, because we are always praying not that what we want shall be done, but that what God wants shall be done, and that we may be used for doing it. I regard this as really fundamental, and while it may lead one to be perhaps excessively sensitive about some kind of petition, I believe that sensitiveness is a pretty sound guide.

I am very much encouraged by knowing that on this point I am in agreement with Abraham Lincoln, who seems to me to have lead his people in war more Christianly than pretty well anybody in history.

Temple's political philosophy was set out in *Christianity and Social Order*, published as a war-time Penguin Special and widely read. The basis of the Christian concern he saw to rest on four points. First, it should be stirred by the claims of sympathy for those who suffer. (It is interesting that he put this first; we saw on page 109 that Christian political activity as such in England rose and fell in accord with the condition of the people.) Second, as men's social and economic environment can powerfully affect their characters (e.g. Sparta and Nazi Germany), so that environment becomes important to the Church, which seeks to develop in men Christian characters. His third point is more individual to himself: Christians should be drawn to right the injustice of the present system. For Temple, injustice rises from the denial of that equality proper to the sons of God. 'Why', he asks, 'should some of God's children have full opportunity to develop their capacities in freely chosen occupations, while others are confined to a stunted form of existence . . . ?' The fourth point demanding action is the Christian duty of conformity to the Natural Order in which is to be found the purpose of God — the Natural Law conception we have met several times on earlier pages.

Having established reasons for Christian interest and intervention in the political and social sphere, he raises the question of how this intervention should be made and lays down three rules. Members of the Church must fulfil their moral responsibilities and functions in a Christian spirit: they must exercise their purely civic rights in a Christian spirit; the Church must supply them with a systematic statement of principles to aid them in doing these two things, and this will carry with it a denunciation of customs or institutions in contemporary life and practice which offend against those principles. (Cripps describes the Church's duty in almost the same words in *Towards Christian Democracy*, published in 1945; it is an example of Temple's influence.)

What then are these principles? All Christian thinking must begin not with man but with God. Man is made in His image and the dignity of man comes from his being a child of God. In spite of the evil in his nature, which caused man's tragedy, he is made for God and moves towards His perfection; this is man's destiny 'and his social life . . . should be ordered with that destiny in view'. Temple in this passage, on the fundamental Christian principle, brings in the family, which is the only form of social unit essential to man. 'To ignore the family, as much in the organization of contemporary life ignores it, is to ignore both citizen and society.'

As we have touched often on the Kingdom of God, Temple's orthodox view may be given — quite different from Stafford Cripps's, who parted from him in this:

> The divine purpose to 'sum up all things in Christ', will not be effected till the end of history; and the fellowship of love which it is the divine plan to establish cannot come into being in its completeness within history at all, for it must be more than a fellowship of contemporaries.

The Kingdom of God is a reality here and now, but can be perfect only in the eternal order.

In some ways, orthodox or unorthodox interpretations of the idea of the Kingdom underlie the main differences in Christian attitudes to politics. It is extremely easy, however, for a man who believes he has the secret of making the Kingdom of God on earth to overlook God altogether.

Having founded his Christian politics on the relations between God and man, Temple derives from this fundamental some guiding principles. 'The primary principle', he writes, 'of Christian ethics and Christian politics must be respect for every person simply as a person. If each man and woman is a child of God, whom God loves and for whom Christ died, then there is in each a worth absolutely independent of all usefulness to society. The person is primary, not the society; the State exists for the citizen, not the citizen for the State.' Therefore a first consideration must be the spread of personal responsibility, with as many free choices reserved to the person as possible. 'Freedom', for the Christian, 'is the goal of politics.' After freedom, Temple places fellowship. Personality can be realized only in social life. It is wrong to confine attention to individual and State. Between them are many intermediate groupings — school, college, trade union, professional association, city, county, nation, Church. Revolutionaries are often impatient of these lesser associations, but they are of vital importance to the Christian politician because it is in them that the ordinary citizen exercises his freedom. Service completes Temple's trinity of principles. The greater part of the voluntary social work done in Britain is supplied by Christian people. But this is in leisure time. A man's job is service. 'We must recognize that the source of my vocation is in God and not in me. It is His call to me.' We have to create or restore a sense of vocation in relation to all the activities of men.

After this statement of his principles, Temple proceeds to consider their application under an order of priority regulated by justice. 'It is axiomatic that Love should be the predominant Christian impulse, and that the primary form of love in social organization is Justice.' What justice is in any particular instance, we must decide by the exercise of reason, in accordance with Natural Law; e.g. production is clearly for consumption, and so, if 'a system comes into being in which production is regulated more by the profit obtainable for the producer than by the needs of the consumer, that system is defying the Natural Law'. Temple winds up his argument by discussing the practical needs of the family, the maintenance of the sanctity of personality, and the principle of fellowship, and, as its climax, puts forward some objectives which Christians should require their Government to aim at:

1. Every child should find itself a member of a family housed with decency and dignity, so that it may grow up as a member of that basic community in a happy fellowship unspoilt by underfeeding or overcrowding, by dirty and drab surroundings or by mechanical monotony of environment.

2. Every child should have the opportunity of an education till years of maturity, so planned as to allow for his peculiar aptitudes and make possible their full development. This education should throughout be inspired by faith in God and find its focus in worship.

3. Every citizen should be secure in possession of such income as will enable him to maintain a home and bring up children in such conditions as are described in paragraph 1 above.

4. Every citizen should have a voice in the conduct of the business or industry which is carried on by means of his labour, and the satisfaction of knowing that his labour is directed to the well-being of the community.

5. Every citizen should have sufficient daily leisure, with two days of rest in seven, and, if an employee, an annual holiday with pay, to enable him to enjoy a full personal life with such interests and activities as his tasks and talents may direct.

6. Every citizen should have assured liberty in the forms of freedom of worship, of speech, of assembly, and of association for special purposes.

In the opinions of Gore and Temple there was much with which all Christian churches agreed; and the Ecumenical movement, starting from the International Missionary Conference at Edinburgh in 1910, gave its attention to political and social matters through its wing known as 'Life and Work'. Nathan Soderblöm (1868–1931), Archbishop of Uppsala, was the leader in this international field, and several conferences were launched at his instigation; that held in 1937, after his death, in Oxford, considered Church and State, the Church and education, the Church and the economic order, and the account of it by J. H. Oldham, *The Churches Survey their Task*, shows how wide was the area held in common. The Roman Catholic Church has maintained a certain aloofness even from the 'Life and Work' side of the Ecumenical movement, but between the principles established by Gore and Temple and the teaching of the papal encyclicals there is a remarkable affinity. *Rerum Novarum* in 1891 justifies trade unions on the argument for the freedom of associations beneath the State — 'to enter into a society of this kind is the natural right of man.' There is in this encyclical and in the *Quadragesimo Anno* of 1931 the same insistence on the priority of the family and the same immemorial opposition of the Church to the all-powerful State. In 1931, too, the Pope made it clear that while Socialism of the Communist kind, atheistic and denying the right of property, was wholly to be condemned, Socialism of a moderate, constitutional sort was not. The right of property is closely allied in Catholic thought to personal development, and if the Malvern Conference under Temple's chairmanship in 1941 recommended the nationalization of major resources, it too declared 'It is a traditional doctrine of Christendom that property is necessary to fulness of personal life', only allowing the rights of private property to be set aside where they stood in the way of social justice and welfare. Apart from papal pronouncements, no one has set out more compellingly in modern form the importance of personal freedom and the rights of associations beneath the State than the Catholic philosopher, Jacques Maritain, the most striking thinker in a large body of modern Thomists who have treated political matters. Temple often paid high tribute to him as to the official social thought of the Roman Church. In fact, divided though Christians are ecclesiastically, they draw in their political thought on a common inheritance. All of them, Roman Catholics included, fell into a lethargy in the eighteenth century and when they woke up it is noteworthy that even Protestants found their inspiration in the Middle Ages. The State as a 'community of communities' is an idea based on the guilds, orders and associations which flourished within the weaker medieval state structure. The modern Christian notion of freedom, founded on the pre-eminence of the person, carries too a medieval hall-mark. 'A person in medieval thought', writes Maritain, 'is a unity of a spiritual nature endowed with freedom of choice and so forming a whole which is independent of the world, for neither nature nor the State may invade this unity without permission.' Continental Protestantism, it is true, shows less trace than is found in the Church of England of the medieval connexion. But the Tractarians taught the socially minded Anglican to look back and between his political philosophy, and that of the Roman Church, as far as fundamental principle goes, there is much in common.

The difficulty lies in applying these principles convincingly to day-to-day politics, a task which was far from easy in the Middle Ages when Christianity was everywhere professed, and which has become harder now the hold of the faith is weaker. The nature of this difficulty must now be examined.

7

'Christian' Politics Examined

THE question is how far Christianity applies to day-to-day politics, the business of governing a society. We must distinguish this from what might be styled partial politics — an entry into the political arena for the purpose of pursuing a single cause. Shaftesbury, as we have seen, practised politics in this partial and limited way. He had no interest in the general business of government and no wish to undertake its responsibilities. This is not to criticize Shaftesbury — no Christian is required to be a professional politician — but we shall leave such one-cause men outside our discussion as not engaged in general politics. We shall omit also any consideration of those special concerns of churches, like the law of marriage or arrangements for religious education. From any government's viewpoint in these days, when churches are associations of minorities, such matters, however important, belong to the special interests of pressure groups. We are not considering here how Christian temperance campaigners, for instance, set about presenting their case to Members of Parliament. It is political activity but again of a limited sort. Our present interests are the applicability of Christian principles to politics as such, politics as a whole, and those Christians who enter politics with a thorough-going will to run the affairs of their society — men like Gladstone and Salisbury. We shall consider again the views outlined in the last chapter when, as in the Christian Social Union, men and women have come together 'to study in common how to apply the moral truths and principles of Christianity to the social and economic difficulties of the present time'.

Government is only in small degree the fulfilment of political programmes. Mr. Brendan Bracken liked to maintain that the major public appointments made by a government in the course

of its life were of greater significance to the country's well-being
than any of its legislation. Certainly there is far more to politics
than platforms and programmes. Yet it is with this side of things
that we must deal, for much of our evidence comes from Christians outside party politics and they necessarily deal in principles
and programmes.

If we look again at two typical Christian statements of policy,
that of Copec on pages 116–17 and of William Temple on page
124, the immediate impression is of how closely they reflect the
sound, liberal-minded opinion of their different periods. They are
Christian documents and yet they might well have been drawn up,
in their essentials, by liberal freethinkers. In a democratic society,
of course, it is natural that in any particular year certain aspirations
should be held by people as a whole and all political parties promise
to fulfil them in one shape or another. It is often surprising how
close opposing contemporary programmes are to each other.
There can then be no surprise that a Christian statement of political
aims should have secular parallels, for realism requires that any
political programme should address itself to the demands of
people at the time. Yet this necessity tends to rule out the possibility
of any specially Christian insight. It might indeed be asked why
Christians, as Christians, should feel the need to publish demands
which were being competently advanced by other bodies of
opinion. The answer would be that Christians ought to lend their
weight to and associate themselves with the better opinion of their
age. Re-reading Temple's war-time statement now, one can see
how clearly it foretold some of the main features of social advance
after the war. It helped to create the opinion that made these
changes possible.

On the other hand, Christians should not wish merely to en-
dorse current political commonplaces of one party or another, for,
if they do no more, their intervention hardly seems worth while.
There is a difficulty here. A Christian political document which
runs against the grain of contemporary political assumptions is
not likely to gain much of a hearing, but one that accepts them is
apt to water down its Christianity with the prevailing humanitarian fashions. An example is the renewed emphasis on social

equality, made strongly in the Labour Party and certainly not ignored by the Conservatives. Gore, as we have seen, believed that we should move towards a greater equality and that justification for this was to be found in the Gospels. In this he was more in the current of his times than in Christian tradition for, while it is true that a few Christians in most periods have professed equalitarian views, the great majority of them from the beginnings to Gore's own day had regarded a social hierarchy as written into the scheme of things. In this instance, it is easy to see how there is always a danger that instead of religion raising politics, politics will end in corrupting, or at least blinding, religion. For the future promises to be far less favourable to equality than the last century, and the problem is less how to spread it than how to make bearable the insistence on inequalities which technological society requires. It is becoming plain that an important function of the educational system of a modern society is through careful selection in the early stages to direct children to their positions in life: unskilled worker, craftsman, technician and technologist are the grades in their industrial form. This selection is virtually complete in Britain by sixteen and if anyone supposes that the ability and perseverance on which success in it is based are owed to merit, the educationists will assure him at once that they spring almost entirely from heredity and family environment. It is one of history's ironies that education, through which Rousseau, Helvétius and others hoped to realize the equality in human potentiality at birth in which they believed, should in the end be the agent of the idea's scientific disproof. Selection is not an English disease; it develops in one form or another (e.g. job selection in America) in any country where the industrial use of complicated techniques is widespread. It is a necessary part of industrial efficiency that children should be chosen early for the after-school training of which they are capable, so that, to put it simply, square pegs find square holes. Careers which not long ago were open to any youngster with the will or the luck or the influence to get a start in them are now hedged about with demands for educational certificates. In fact, the certificates a child carries largely determine his station in life and it is not fanciful to say that income ceilings are broadly decided in the class room, on the basis of what children were endowed with at birth and the years immediately afterwards within their families.

Social stratification by educational means was in its early stages when Copec produced its report in 1924. On the other hand, stratification of the old-fashioned kind, based on birth and wealth, was still in obvious existence. To the sceptical Christian critic, there must have appeared to be traces of the hypocritical or the absurd in Copec's declaration that 'Christians must use their influence against any class distinctions which are an obstacle to true social communion'. Where there are large disparities in wealth, as in 1924, or elaborate selection procedures for a hierarchy of jobs, as today, class distinctions are inevitable. It is idle to exert 'influence' against them, if there is no intention of striking at the social framework which gives rise to them.

This is not the place, however, for an elaborate discussion of equality and social grading. Enough has been said to show how Gore and his followers in Copec, by heeding contemporary attitudes and currents of opinion — as, indeed, practical politicians or even the politically interested must — abandoned the traditional Christian indifference to the issue of human equality. No lasting advantage was gained from this change of view, because only a few years later it became established that the former Christian attitude was more in accordance with the facts of human difference than the loose ideas of equality borrowed by Gore and others, rather late, from Rousseau and his French Revolutionary successors. If one wishes to communicate with those in the political swim at any period, it is important to deal with them in their own terms. But the adoption of those terms, or fashionable emphases, carries the danger of bad mistakes. It is easier for the politician or journalist to adjust his outlook to the movements of opinion than it should be for the churchman, from whom longer views tend to be expected.

Even Temple's outline of the coming Welfare State recalls a story told of Baron von Hügel by Sir Alfred Zimmern. The baron was being shown round a factory by its enlightened owner who believed that he had Christianized it. He was shown the ventilating system, the educational and welfare services, the clinics, canteen, swimming pool and playing grounds, and all the time he grew more impatient. Finally he turned to the factory owner and said, 'You haven't begun to understand what Christianity is: Christianity is not refreshment bars and swimming pools — it is a soul in the presence of God.' Baron von Hügel would have administered no such reproof to Temple who constantly showed himself aware of the dangers of confusing religion with purely secular objectives. Nevertheless, someone who did not know Temple, and had before him only the six points of his political programme, might have been excused for reacting much as the baron did on being shown the so-called Christian factory.

Middleton Murry in his later years, although as a kind of Marxist far more in sympathy with Gore and Temple than with the rest of the Church of England, criticizes the Church in terms which might be applied to the policy statements we have been discussing. The Church, he writes in *The Betrayal of Christ by the Churches*, 'has nothing to offer men beyond the pattern of behaviour that is current in existing society . . . the influences that are dominant in the world are dominant in the Church also.' Some who seek a Christian policy are disappointed when they receive only an amalgam of the more humane Liberal-Labour objectives in contemporary currency. Nevertheless other Christians, taking the point made in preceding paragraphs that any realistic political initiative must tie up with contemporary attitudes and desires, would repel the implied censure which accompanied it. They would say that the demand (which has been implied so far in this chapter) that Christian politics should be specifically and distinguishably Christian is naive and unnecessary. They would maintain that the implied distinction between Natural Law politics, at which the best men of their time can arrive by the use of their reason only, and Christian politics as such is a prejudicial invention of the writer's. While the classical Christian authors have drawn lines between natural and Christian principles for the purpose of maintaining clarity in philosophical discussion, there is no significant distinction when it comes to practice. The Natural Law is that laid down by the Creator to be discovered by man's reason and the Creator is the God of the Christians. Temple's political demands — a social minimum in health, housing and wages, educational opportunity, joint consultation in industry — were the objectives of enlightened and progressive people in his day, many of whom did not profess Christianity. This does not matter. The use of their reason had indicated to sincere and humane people what the next necessary and practicable steps ought to be. Any Christian who respects and accepts the society in which he lives must respect also the best opinions of its leading people, for however muddled and distorted these opinions may at times become they spring from men and women purposefully created by God in an order established by him in time before the advent of His Son. It is, of course, important, in view of the errors to which human thinking is prone, for the Christian to test secular political objectives against the full corpus of his faith. But Temple had done this extremely carefully. Not only did he find in the secular objectives he chose to back nothing incompatible with Christianity, but he believed that they were part, if not all, of what Christianity itself required as the next step inside his national society.

If Temple went too far towards socialism for many Christian members of the Conservative Party in his day, he did not go far enough for other Christians who tended to reject compromises with the world, believing that with Christianity came a new command of love which required an entirely new and different response from that made by ordinarily worldly and reasonable men to the claims of Natural Law. Temple was not, for example, a pacifist. Certainly in the popular mind, when people yearn for politics to become more Christian, the real underlying demand is that they should be conducted in the Gospel light, according to the high and supernatural ethics of the Sermon on the Mount. It is surely our duty to make human behaviour more Christian, but if the Christian in modern politics selects for his support only what seems best in the flow of secular opinion, how may the world be christianized? There is here a problem for those who doubt the applicability of the Gospel ethic of love to everyday human activity. The clash between Christ's commands and human

practice has occupied many minds. A notable example is Dos-
toievsky's passage on 'The Grand Inquisitor'. Nevertheless, for
our purposes, the matter may be settled pragmatically. It is only
necessary to regard history since the foundation of Christianity to
see clearly that the high counsels of the Sermon on the Mount are
beyond men's capacity in their common affairs. At no time, even
for a short number of years, has any successful relation of them
been made to life in general, and the disparity between Christ's
teaching and the few attempts to live it out publicly, as in Calvin's
Geneva, is so remarkable as to rule out any future hope in similar
enterprises of this sort. The lesson is plainly that those who wish to
follow the higher commandments of Christian love in human
community must withdraw from the world into small like-
minded enclaves, monastic or otherwise. If the life of withdrawn
perfection has its triumphs, it has also its failures, as the history of
medieval monasticism amply shows. Sin, the fatal flaw, is all-
pervasive; no shelter of human device can keep it out. In the
general world, in the realm of common activities, it is always
present as a major factor. Here it is not a question of men being
willing to aim high and then falling short; the great majority will
not wish to take aim. As the Gospel ethic, even in ages when
Christianity was wholly accepted in Europe, has been manifestly
beyond the capacity of human societies, it is wrong to present that
ethic as a desirable norm in politics. What most men singly fail
to carry out in their private lives, they will assuredly fail to honour
corporately. For any politician therefore to attempt to persuade
men in a state of emotional excitement that they may transcend
those moral capacities which history shows are all that belong to
them, is an error whose consequences will be suffered not only by
himself but by those he has misled. Only a few may seek to live
the life of perfection, and the saints will confess how much falling
short there has been in the attempt. Pacifism is a case in point.
'If someone slaps you on the right cheek, turn and offer him your
left.' Some few persons may attain this attitude and persist in it.
But those who would persuade whole nations to this outlook may
seem to gain some temporary success but fail in the end; they are
setting the standards too high. British pacifism in the thirties did

not prevent war and probably encouraged its outbreak; certainly it made it harder to win.

It is safer to see politics as belonging to the natural order. Its morality is that currently accepted by society at large. As Emil Brunner notes: 'It is not necessary to be a Christian to see that a certain order is unjust. Even though we may not believe in a *lex naturae* in the old sense of the word, we do know that there is a very far-reaching *sensus communis moralis*.' Every society which wishes to exist has to enforce a moral code, and in civilized politics a readiness to fulfil undertakings and promises is expected, as well as a proper respect for the rights of opponents. 'Always treat others as you would like them to treat you.' If that precept from the Sermon on the Mount appears easier to follow than most of the others, its practice is far from general. At the same time, it is accepted as a rough norm in political relationships. As Soviet Russia moves farther away from the revolution, the liquidation of her fallen statesmen becomes rarer and they tend to be found obscure but respectable employment. Any stable politics gravitates to the golden rule. But it is important to recognize that political standards are always and inevitably average standards, those set in the minds of ordinary men by many generations of experience of how men act. Government is in the sphere of the average. Its ethics are a social mean, reflected from the society beneath. It is hardly possible for a society with high standards, as ours developed in the last century, to have a corrupt government, and *vice versa*. On this score, however, it is extremely unlikely that Christian standards, markedly higher than those generally accepted in society, can be applied in the sphere of politics and government, where average standards prevail. The more representative the government, the truer this is. If Christians object to it, they should not enter active politics. The divergence between Gospel and average standards stands out most nakedly when Governments are conducting war. Lord Hankey, whom Asquith styled 'the organizer of victory' in the First World War, was a churchman and at the same time a strong and unwavering advocate of economic blockade. At the end of his book of memoirs, *The Supreme Command*, he congratulates himself on the success of this indiscriminate weapon against the German population and abuses President Wilson who with his doctrine of the freedom of the seas was seeking to strike it from Britain's hands. He quotes with satisfaction Prince Max of Baden:

The misery in the towns about the middle of October was indescribable. No coal, no adequate clothing, a ceaseless hunger. The influenza epidemic was striding over Europe. In Berlin alone on October 15 its victims numbered 1,722.

In the Second World War, the British Cabinet put its main effort over eighteen months into strategic bombing and its carefully determined aim, although not disclosed to the British people, was the destruction of German working-class homes. Their calculations of this bombing's effects proved to be less well-founded than Lord Hankey's for the blockade, but both Cabinets shared a common intention of making life unendurable for German civilians. As C. P. Snow commented in 1960:

It is possible, I suppose, that some time in the future people living in a more benevolent age than ours may turn over the official records and notice that men like us, men well-educated by the standards of the day, and often possessed of strong human feelings, made the kind of calculation I have been describing. Such calculations, on a much larger scale, are going on at this moment in the most advanced societies we know.

This may be taken by some readers as proof that the average standards of politics cannot be tolerated by a Christian. The truth is that no others exist. The Christian can reject them and stay outside politics, but if he enters he must accept the common coin. A leading critic of bombing policy in the last war was Dr. G. K. A. Bell, the Bishop of Chichester. He was heard with respect but made not the slightest impression. His political ineffectiveness was owed to the fact that he was appealing to standards higher than those of which average people were capable at the time. No doubt the average sinks to its lowest during war, but the principle holds. The courses of action open to politicians, including Christian politicians, are restricted by the need to convince and carry with them the bulk of ordinary men. To overestimate their moral capacity is a sure route to political suicide.

On the other hand, if no sensible person will enter politics with

K

the aim of applying the Gospel ethic, to say that its supernatural standards are totally without bearing on politics would be wrong. If it is not easy to disentangle and describe, nevertheless the conflict between the two standards of nature and super-nature is always present in men's minds, and what is in mind must have an influence. A whole host of prophets, denouncers and satirists have lain on the fringes of politics since it began — early hermits, medieval perfectionist sects, Puritan communities, and in our own age writers like Tolstoy and Middleton Murry who have maintained the possibility of the impossible ethic. Even Moral Rearmament with its four absolutes — as though men could govern their public life with absolutes! — contributes to the atmosphere in which politics is carried on. The effect of ideal Christianity, flying loose as it were in history, is hard to track down. Distorted, wrenched out of context though they be, the Messianic hope and the expectation of the Kingdom have had some part in creating the secular hopes of Communism. When we are confronted with inhuman crimes of the sort committed by the Nazis (and some would add the atomic bombing of Japan, and the massacre of Poles at Katyn), what part of our judgment of these affairs — and judgments made presently are not without effect on attitudes held later — springs not from natural but from the super-natural standards we carry in our minds? It cannot be said. In general, it is obvious, the ordinary Natural Law of reason is far above our heads. Yet there is still a shame-faced reference to the Gospel scheme so much higher still. There is an image of the Kingdom, of the Kingdom that cannot come on earth, glimpsed by many millions more of men than lie within the bounds of Christianity. The mixing of the ideal into the mundane is constantly happening; but it is not an operation that may be consciously attempted by the politician in his office. The ideal is in the air, it is not in the hand to apply. All a politician may know for certain is that these high standards, impossible to relate satisfactorily to the tasks before him, will usually be referred to, vaguely and distantly, by his contemporaries when they judge him and his actions. They will judge him also even more vigorously by natural standards, and woe betide him if some act of his has seemed to lower the prestige of his nation.

Men commonly want the best of both worlds; it is unfair to politicians.

It is worth remembering at this point that much of what most affects personal and family life, the realm that has always been of most concern to Christians, is outside political control. Two present tendencies may be taken as examples. The one is the trend towards large industrial units and the second is the increasing employment of married women. It has often been noticed, and supported by some sociological evidence, that the quality of personal relationships and of the personal contributions to a common enterprise suffers where the work-place grows large. The old intimacy has disappeared; the relationships inside a large organization tend to become more impersonal; responsibility has passed from a group of identifiable men to an institution. It is unnecessary to go farther, for the human dangers of this development have been given much attention. Temple rightly declared that 'the primary principle of Christian ethics and Christian politics must be respect for every person simply as a person'. Yet the direction in which scientific industry is moving is away from a working environment favourable to human personality. Awareness of Temple's principle will ensure that steps are taken to moderate the human evils of large-scale organization, but second best is not first best and its acceptance is partial surrender of a principle. Yet the large unit is as inevitable as the process of automation. It is in the stream of things that are not to be withstood.

The same kind of irresistible force dictates the growing employment of married women. One does not want to make too much of a *casus belli* out of this. Women have worked in the fields since time immemorial, and in the past house-keeping, without machines and pre-cooked food, was more a full-time labour in itself. The leisured middle-class lady of Victorian times was largely a passing phenomenon. All the same, the pressures exerted by a fully employed society ever chasing the target of increased production are something new in kind. The consumer demands it establishes lay down the desirability of two incomes and economy encourages what the Government urges — the return, to choose a relatively minor instance, of the married teacher to the school.

We can pass over the mother with time on her hands and her children grown up who rejoices in a job, but it is plain that many mothers (whose children are not grown up and suffer from her tiredness in the evenings) are drawn into full-time outside occupation. It is not perhaps a great matter but it does relate to the Christian concern for the health of family life. As before, palliatives are suggested — day nurseries, special arrangements for working mothers — but they do not remove the social dangers rising from strong inducements to married women to take up work. Is not this again one of those matters which politics, Christian or other, cannot greatly affect? It seems rather a shift in the given circumstances, the result of a social and industrial revolution.

Constrained to accept an existing average level of political behaviour, caught in an economic environment which might almost be held determined, what powers does Christianity possess? How, for example, is the 'average level' raised, for history demonstrates that this is possible? The answer here is almost certainly that Christianity may do most to raise the standards of politics by attending to the purely religious sphere. It is not possible, as we have argued, for Christian politicians singly or in groups to raise the prevailing average standards of political conduct or aims from inside. The more promising course is to change society by changing individuals, for a change in the social climate is reflected immediately in the political. As Emil Brunner wisely observed: 'All direct civil action is short-lived and changes nothing under the surface; the really shattering changes of the social structure take place as changes in the system of values, which, for its part, depends on faith and unbelief.' Nothing is more likely to change the standards of a country's politics than for religious belief to increase its hold upon people at large. For religion in the last fifty years to have emphasized the importance of a political concern is good, but we may feel less happy about this proper extension of interest if we recall that it has coincided with a rather dry period in the religious life of the nation.

Few periods better illustrate the raising by purely religious means of that 'average level' which determines the ethical possibilities of politics than the transition from the eighteenth to the nineteenth century in England. The age of Whig oligarchy, great victories abroad and some high thinking at home, with the establishment of important political liberties, will never lack defenders. There was a sinewy, worldly proficiency about this England, a splendour founded on small resources bravely used. But vice reigned publicly, sports were brutal and politics corrupt. Most men had their price. The Church of England had lost sense of any supernatural mission and its clergy with few exceptions believed in little more than a benevolent Creator and a certain moral standard. A religious apathy spread over the country. The universities and grammar schools, closely associated with the established religion, sank to their lowest. Churches, ill-attended, were allowed to decay. In many country parishes the Holy Communion was said no more than four times a year and large sections of the poorer population in the growing northern towns were left without Christian ministration.

No doubt can exist that it was the ending of this religious lethargy which mainly raised the standards of public life in England. The two wings of the Evangelical Movement, in Wesleyanism and the Church of England, insisted on the depravity of human nature, the need of personal conversion and the redeeming power of the Cross of Christ. Personal piety and devotion to our Lord were the marks of this movement. That Christianity ought to be applied to politics never occupied its leaders' minds, important politicians though some of them were. The Oxford Movement saw a further growth of the nation's religion. If the Evangelicals brought individual souls to God, the Tractarians taught them they belonged to the Church, the mystical body of Christ, of which the Church of England was part. There were differences in churchmanship between these two movements which led to some competitiveness and enmity, but between them they created a religious revolution in England and a social and moral one as well. Religious life was restored, churches and chapels were built and filled at once with crowded congregations. There were marked changes in the character of public life, summed up in the story on page 69 of Wilberforce's condemnation of Dundas for a financial misdemeanour in his department. For good or ill, the intense religious feeling out of which the Nonconformist conscience was to rise had come into existence.

Caution is needed lest unwarranted claims are made for the influence of this revival on politics and manners. As has been said, few nineteenth-century churchmen thought about relating their religion to politics and as far as can be seen national aims went unchanged. Lord Salisbury at the end of the nineteenth century regarded the increase of British power as the aim of foreign policy, as Lord Chatham had done 150 years before him. The changes in politics produced by the religious movements lay less in subject-matter than in the spirit in which public business was conducted. It is doubtful whether Christianity contributed to new policies or ideals, but it certainly increased seriousness of approach. There were many more who believed deeply that what they did in life, in or outside politics, mattered eternally. Shaftesbury did not work out, like Gore, for example, a list of Christian political principles, but he did not enter politics at all until, after earnest prayer and thought, he had convinced himself that God's work would be done. Now this general effect of Evangelical religion upon Shaftesbury was to be discovered in many other men of his time, who prayed long and weighed all their decisions with the utmost seriousness. This result, it must be noted, did not come from any campaign to make politics more Christian. It came out of a movement which in ways rather emotional — 'enthusiastic' as they were styled — sought to bring men to know and love their Saviour more deeply. Modern Christians, much concerned about political and social activities, are inclined to criticize a religion which concentrates on personal piety as neglecting wider duties towards the neighbour and community. But if Evangelicalism was largely personal piety it profoundly affected the character of men engaged in politics and it certainly sharpened the moral climate. If the average level of opinion of what is right and wrong, what sensible, what silly, what splendid, what ignoble, creates the standards of politics which all politicians must accept, Evangelicalism raised that average level a little. Many will still maintain that this is the way and that to bring Christianity to bear on politics requires no wrestling with programmes and applied principles but only the spread of a deeper personal religion among individuals.

It now remains to ask whether in spite of the many difficulties so far raised there are any specifically Christian attitudes for which politics is the better. We shall not talk at this point of the effect of Christian living within the personal relationships of parties and parliaments. Our aim is to take a final view of the field of modern government and to note briefly what Christianity may bring to it. The most important and most ancient contribution is a firm sense that the sphere of the State, the realm of Caesar, is bounded. When states make total demands, the good Christian is bound to refuse, if only because his religion requires freedom. He is a man with his feet in two camps, a citizen of the spiritual Kingdom as well as the one of this earth. He will never commit himself soul and body to any of the kingdoms of this world, and so he insists upon having from each of them his corner of freedom. In a sense which is general, Christianity is an ultimate safeguard of freedom in politics. It may well be that from time to time Christians, as in Soviet Russia, will find themselves citizens of states requiring total commitment. In Russia this will come the more easily, because of the historical quietism of the Eastern Orthodox Church as far as politics is concerned. But even in such states, where the very claim made for Christianity as a safeguard of freedom seems belied by the conformity of Christians, it is in fact confirmed by the settled enmity of the authorities towards religious allegiance. The core of German resistance to Hitler was found in the Roman Catholic and Protestant Churches. It was weaker than might have been wished, but it was there, and provided a basis for a new start when the tyranny was overthrown.

It may be noted in passing that those Christians criticized earlier who set so little store by tradition as to speak of building the Kingdom of God on earth are in danger of abolishing the beneficent division between God's realm and Caesar's with the freedom that rises from it. Christians who conceived themselves to be building the Kingdom on earth, if they should anywhere gain power, would be much tempted to require total commitment to the enterprise. It would merit it no more than any other human activity, for it would suffer from the inevitable mixing in of sin and failure. Christianity is a bastion of freedom only when it preaches that God's Kingdom is not of this world. We have considered earlier, at the end of Chapter 5, the practical and personal value to Christian politicians of their second citizenship; and we need not refer to it again here, important though it is.

To claim for Christians a monopoly of compassion would be offensive and untrue. At the same time, we have seen that the main interventions of Christians in politics in England came when the conditions of the poorer people were at their worst. Throughout its history Christianity has shown a striking ambivalence in its attitude to suffering, now seeing it as something to be endured and profited from, now as something to be removed. In recent history, as we have seen, some leading Christian politicians have displayed a striking indifference to social reform, while others have devoted themselves to it. Yet today, it would seem fair to allow that a social conscience is something the Christian politician cannot be without. In fact, one might feel that in England the Gospel references to poverty seem to Christians those that have most relevance to politics. Poverty in the old sense, of course, hardly exists, but in the voluntary sections of the social services many Christians are found at work and their activity is reflected in a special concern for these subjects among Christian politicians. Rising out of this same impulse, Christians in many countries, not least in Britain, have in these days played a part in the relief of refugees. A widespread humanitarian sentiment brings multitudes of non-Christians into this sort of work. What may be said, perhaps, is that its appeal is not one the modern Christian politician is likely to ignore.

We have mentioned how the Gospel emphasis on forgiveness was applied by Lansbury and Cripps to their dealings with national enemies and to their handling of domestic conflict. This impulse too would seem to be necessarily in the forefront of a Christian mind. The exact manner of its application is seldom clear, and no one can say that Christian intervention in the aftermath of the General Strike in 1926 was wholly successful. Nevertheless, it illustrated a consistent readiness to reconcile which is not without importance. It is useless to search the New Testament for a code of industrial relations, nor is one to be built out of deductions from its texts. Yet it is remarkable how often in industrial disputes up and down the country deadlock has been resolved by the neutral offices of bishops and priests. Within industry itself, if Christianity offers no code, its teaching about personal relationships has a particular relevance. Between management and men differences are bound to occur, but their settlement is eased when leaders on both sides can approach each other with that outgoing warmth and mutual respect of man for man which Christianity requires. It is futile to suppose that any religious principles exist for an acceptable distribution of an industry's rising profits, a matter which lies at the bottom of most wage disputes. On the other hand, the issues are regularly complicated by the attitudes of the negotiators to each other, by their purely human treatment of one another as persons, and in this field Christians on each side have much to add. Moral Rearmament is a movement suspect to many, but its campaign for Christian relationships in industry is right in principle.

There are other Christian emphases which have political usefulness. Professor H. Butterfield is one who shares the general opinion of this book. In *Christianity and History*, for example, he notes:

I cannot say that in history statesmanship works under entirely different laws if a politician happens to be a Christian or even a clergyman — if politics are influenced, say, by a Wolsey or a Laud. I cannot say, looking over the centuries, that the clergy seem to me to have been always right against the laity, at any rate in the conflicts that pertain to mundane affairs. I think that in modern centuries the unbeliever has sometimes even fought the churchman for what we today would regard as the higher ethical end, the one which most corresponds with the deeper influences of Christianity.

He thinks, nevertheless, that of all the influences playing on politics, Christianity alone attacks self-righteousness and, he goes on, 'though conflict might still be inevitable in history if this particular evil did not exist, there can be no doubt that its presence multiplies the deadlocks and gravely deepens all the tragedies of all the centuries.' One can see what he means. The contemporary power conflict between the United States and Soviet Russia is exacerbated by a moralizing insistence by both sides on the rightness of all they do in a competition which is less for freedom on one side and for Communism on the other, than for world supremacy on both. It would be pleasant to be able to claim with Professor Butterfield that Christianity supplies an infallible critique of self-righteousness. Certainly it does so in the ideal, and Christians who have grasped this can loose a stream of valuable wisdom, but self-righteousness, alas, is too often a Christian vice for regular attack on it to be claimed as a Christian virtue. The sense of self-righteousness with which Gladstone imbued the nation has found many unfortunate outlets since and in the very conflict between Christianity and Communism, which stiffens the antagonism between America and Russia, its notes may be detected often in the utterances of Christian spokesmen.

There is a theme in modern politics, of great significance to the world, on which Christianity has spoken with a fairly consistent clarity, whatever the behaviour of individual Christians. When Gore spoke of the spiritual equality of all men and all races, and said that to ignore it in our day was to invite cataclysmic retribution, he was within a long tradition. A classical example of its working was at the time of the Spanish discovery and development of Central America. It was convenient to treat the Indians as sub-human savages, as cheap beasts of burden to whom no responsibility was owed. There were Spanish Christians indeed who argued that the Indians were natural slaves, in the Aristotelian definition, and, as has been seen, slavery was long tolerated in Christian countries. But Christian counter-arguments prevailed in the Spanish Council of the Indies. In the bull *Sublimis Deus* of 1537 Pope Paul III declared that the Indians were not to be treated as 'dumb brutes created for our service' but 'as truly men ... capable of understanding the Catholic faith'. 'The said Indians', the bull continued, 'and all other people who may later be discovered by Christians, are by no means to be deprived of their liberty or the possession of their property, even though they may be outside the faith of Jesus Christ ... nor should they be in any way enslaved.' Las Casas, the Dominican apostle of the Indies, insisted that 'mankind is one — all the peoples of the world are men', and it was on this principle, after some debate, that the Spanish conquest was developed. Many Spaniards ignored it and their history is scarred by torture and massacre. Yet if one considers today the areas of Spanish and Portuguese settlement in the Americas, having regard to their present independence and to their earlier winning of it, and to the fusion of races which exists in all these countries, one must surely allow that the doctrine of the spiritual equality of men has not been unavailing. If in South Africa the principle of *apartheid* is defended on religious grounds by the Dutch Reformed Church — a notorious instance of the application of Christianity to politics — it is the voice of an insignificant minority, a breach in the general tradition. Race prejudice, and its underlying fear of miscegenation, will vex the world for many years yet, particularly in its African setting, and there can be no doubt that true Christians, knowing and accepting their tradition on this matter, have here something of their own to say and do.

Non-believers may question this short list of qualities and attitudes which are claimed here to be specifically Christian and politically relevant. Do you have to be a Christian before you can forgive? they may ask, or, is it necessary to invoke a Catholic tradition to prevent men from judging each other by the colour of their skins? Some answer to these questions may be made by suggesting how greatly over the centuries Christianity has influenced the common stock of morality which the modern non-believer has inherited. Nevertheless, there is some force in his questions, which the Christian will have to admit. It is a further reason for modesty when it comes to making claims on behalf of the specific Christian contribution. Politics is a sphere where the Christian and the non-Christian must work together amicably and trustingly. Does it help this co-operation for the Christian to be over-zealous in underlining his special share? In general, the work of government and the shaping of society are concerns of human reason and are subject to the natural morality open to all men. His faith calls the Christian to take part, because as God has used the world for the revelation of Himself, so He requires us to use the world. It is possible that sometimes a Christian in whom ability is joined to a deep religiousness may have a keener sense of injustice and work more resolutely for its removal — because he is a Christian. But it must be admitted that the average Christian and the average man are not easily distinguished. And even the good Christian, as he marks down the social injustice and seeks to remove its evil, can work only as a member of his society, along with his co-citizens, and the language in which he will speak to them is that of ordinary human reason. In fact the Christian cannot lift himself out of the everyday world, least of all in politics, and it is a mistake for him to assume that he can devise policies and ways of action different from those of non-Christians and more in accordance with the divine purpose (to which he has some special key). The thought itself of such a course suggests an attitude over against the world — the world on one side and the Christian Kingdom on the other. But in politics it is in this world that one seeks to govern and to begin by an implied rejection of it would be absurd. In taking our place in the world, beside men of other beliefs and of none, our tasks which are wholly secular in one sense are in another sanctified, for the Christian must believe that the work of the world, no matter how streaked through with sin, is related to God's own work in the world, to this divine purpose, to this coming Kingdom.

Nor must it be forgotten that politics has its own realm of personal relations, where the Christian may show love for his neighbour. Brunner writes of this:

. . . the individual will seek a 'private' way of working behind the established institutions of public life. The distinction between an 'official' or 'vocational' sphere and a 'personal' sphere of action cannot, it is true, be absolute; for even the most public form of action has its private aspect — in witness, and even the most private form of activity in so far as it is operative has its public aspect, in the use of effective means . . . but this distinction is certainly necessary. . . . It is an essential part of the Christian life that we should seek our *real* work in this *personal* sphere, in the personal relation between one human being and another. It is here that love applies as a law. . . .

One does not enter upon personal relations with a principle in mind; one seeks mainly to establish sympathy with the other person. In politics, as in every walk of life, decisions depend often on the play of personal relationship, even in its ridiculous detail. Lord Hankey tells a story of how an interview between Lloyd George and our Commander-in-Chief in France foundered because the one relished talk after breakfast while the general's digestion required other things to come first. When a Prime Minister chooses his advisers personal compatibility enters into it more often than the outsider would suppose. Work is made the harder when it has to be done with a man whose abilities you respect but whose nature is antipathetic. It is in the personal exchanges within parties, within committees and cabinets, that the Christian becomes known as a man and is judged as a man. At these close quarters what faith he has is seen and felt without his need to say a word. Here it is, where men are angry, tired, depressed, exultant, ambitious, in all the changing emotions of the political life, which is one where man is pitched against man, that some men may move as Christians. Here in the circle of personal exchange, where eye meets eye and *cor ad cor loquitur*, is perhaps the true outlet of Christianity in politics.

8

Christianity and Foreign Affairs

IF difficulties are met in applying Christian principles to home affairs, they are greater when it comes to foreign policy. To point the problem, it will help to take a practical example, and no excuse is offered for rehearsing at some length the events leading up to the Munich agreement of 1938, and asking some questions at the end of the narrative. The principal actors on the British side were the Prime Minister, Neville Chamberlain, a man of stronger fibre and ethical character than is sometimes allowed, who might be religiously described as a lapsed Unitarian, and Lord Halifax, Foreign Secretary, and the austere lay leader of the Anglo-Catholic party in the Church of England.

Hitler came to power in Germany in 1933 and began immediately to rearm. In 1936 he felt strong enough to move his forces into the Rhineland, whose demilitarization at Versailles had been confirmed by Germany in the Treaty of Locarno. If his violation of the treaties had been met by armed force at this point, he would have been repulsed and possibly have fallen, but the fear of war in England and a lack of spirit in France, coupled with some guilt about the Versailles treaty in both countries, led to his being left in possession. The uselessness of the League of Nations had been exposed by Italy's successful invasion of Abyssinia in the previous year and Hitler's Rhineland stroke was followed a few months later by Franco's rising against the Spanish Republic, which enterprise was soon to be supported by German and Italian arms and men. Hitler did not hide his ambitions for Germany and the apprehension these aroused spread far wider than the small group round Churchill who busily advertised Nazi preparations and prophesied general war. Chamberlain, as Chancellor of the Exchequer, was laying the basis for rearmament in 1934 and it was in full course well before the Rhineland was invaded. He believed passionately, his biographer Keith Feiling related, that 'policy must depend on power' and he had a proper contempt for those — and in that period they included many Christians — who declaimed in favour of collective security through the League of Nations but rejected the rearmament necessary to give that institution backbone. In only one matter was he agreed with them; he too desired peace. War, he said, 'wins nothing, cures nothing, ends nothing'. The loss of life in the First World War appalled him. He devoted himself then to the 'appeasement of Europe'. 'I believe the double policy of rearmament and better relations with Germany and Italy will carry us safely through the danger period, if only the Foreign Office will play up.' He tended to believe in German promises and in the reasonableness of some of the German claims. 'I don't see why', he noted, in November, 1937, 'we shouldn't say to Germany, "Give us satisfactory assurances that you won't use force to deal with the Austrians and the Czechoslovakians, and we will give you similar assurances that we won't use force to prevent the changes you want, if you can get them by peaceful means." ' He discussed with the French the possibility of providing Germany again with colonial territories in Africa. Hitler's attitude to these friendlier approaches was illustrated by his invasion of Austria on 12 March 1938. 'It is perfectly evident, surely, now', Chamberlain remarked in a letter the next day, 'that force is the only argument Germany understands, and that collective security cannot offer any prospect of preventing such events, until it can show a visible force of overwhelming strength, backed by determination to use it.'

Maintaining his initiative and that sheer rapidity of action which bewilders hesitant opponents, Hitler now turned his attention to Czechoslovakia, one of the weaker creations of Versailles. Czech-dominated, the State included $3\frac{1}{4}$ million Germans, $2\frac{1}{4}$ million Slovaks, $\frac{1}{2}$ million Hungarians, $\frac{1}{2}$ million Ruthenes, and 80,000 Poles. It was a good instance of the difficulties of applying to the real world an over-riding principle like self-determination, which has attracted much Christian support in our time. None of the minorities was satisfied with its place in the new State, and certainly more Germans were incorporated in it than the British

Foreign Office thought wise or right at the time of its foundation. This German minority, with encouragement from over the frontier, and with the German army threatening Czechoslovakia on a new front, began a tumultuous agitation, beginning with demands for more freedom and going on to press for reunion with the Reich.

Enough was now known of Hitler's methods for the likelihood of an outright attack on Czechoslovakia to be obvious to all. France was bound by treaty to go to the Czechs' support; we were bound only to France. Russia was also bound to the Czechs, and several times acknowledged the existence of these obligations, but neither Britain nor France had great confidence in her, a doubt which must have been shared by the Czechs themselves, for they made no appeal in her direction. The chief responsibility for taking the lead in Czechoslovakia's defence belonged to France, but Chamberlain had throughout serious anxieties over her willingness or capacity to act. Anyhow his main concern was not with organizing a successful war, but with pacification, and to this end both Britain and France pressed the Czechs to make concessions to their minorities. In August 1938, Lord Runciman was sent out to mediate between the Czech Government and the Sudeten Germans and to discover some form of settlement to which Hitler would agree. He, of course, was unsympathetic to this whole method of approach, and, looking back, there was indeed no reason to expect a dictator-leader to accept the round-table procedures of democracy. The train of events leading to Munich exemplifies one of the constantly recurring obstacles to applying principles, Christian or other, to relationships between States. Principles are of no value whatsoever in the settlement of disputes unless both sides accept them. That peace was a prize worth sacrifice was obvious to Chamberlain, as it must be to all Christians. His mistake was to assume that Hitler also saw it in this light.

By September matters were moving to a head. Blood had been shed in the Sudeten areas, German troops were on the march, and war was near. On the 9th we called up mine-layers and mine-sweepers; on the 11th Chamberlain announced the probability of our support for France. But he was still not convinced that France would fight and it was doubtful whether the Dominions would join in.

Winston Churchill maintains in his history of *The Second World War* that what might have stopped Hitler was a plain declaration jointly by Britain, France and Russia that any invasion of Czechoslovakia would lead to general war. It is possible that this might have been effective, for the German generals were alarmed at the prospect of an attack from France, with something like 8 to 1 superiority, while the bulk of their divisions were engaged in the east. Yet any such declarations involved a risk of general war and this Chamberlain was still hoping to avoid. 'I would never take', he said, 'that awful responsibility upon my shoulders unless it were forced upon me by the madness of others.' So on 15 September he flew to meet Hitler at Berchtesgaden and agreed there to arrangements for transferring the chief Sudeten areas to Germany. He made no mistake about Hitler — a 'wild beast' was how he described him — but his hopes to some extent led him astray. 'I got the impression', he wrote after this first meeting, 'that here was a man who could be relied upon when he had given his word.' This judgment was almost at once to be disproved. Chamberlain took the plan for the dismemberment of Czechoslovakia back to London for discussion with the French. Once it had been accepted and the Czechs had yielded under pressure, Chamberlain found on his second visit to Hitler at Godesberg that the terms had been raised. Germany insisted on a show of force and immediate occupation. On hearing of this the Czech Government mobilized, and on the 25th and 26th Britain and France rejected the new terms. Orders for the mobilization of the British fleet were issued on the 27th. 'It seemed', Mr. Churchill wrote, 'that the moment of clash had arrived and that the opposing forces were aligned.'

But he reckoned without Chamberlain's perseverance. On the night of the fleet mobilization he made a broadcast in which he said, 'I am myself a man of peace to the depths of my soul. Armed conflict between nations is a nightmare to me; but if I were convinced that any nation had made up its mind to dominate the

L

world by fear of its force, I should feel that it must be resisted.' He had come to that point and now, on the brink of war, Hitler made him the gesture he needed by sending a letter modifying the Godesberg ultimatum and offering to guarantee the new Czech frontiers. Flying out for the third time, Chamberlain signed the Munich agreement — a document which differed from Hitler's Godesberg terms only in including certain German pledges about the time-table of occupying the Sudeten areas, international supervision, and safeguards for Czech interests. These pledges were what Chamberlain gained by his third journey and in fact they were never fulfilled. Czechoslovakia retained a shadowy independence for only a few months more; in March the Germans overran the entire country. It was an odd commentary on a sentence in a letter Chamberlain wrote to the Archbishop of Canterbury a day or so after Munich: 'I am sure that some day the Czechs will see that what we did was to save them for a happier future.'

Was Chamberlain pursuing in these months what might be called a Christian foreign policy? Churchill clearly thought it could be described as such, for he notes in his summing up of Munich that 'religion and virtue alike lend their sanctions to meekness and humility, not only between men but between nations'. He clearly, in his simple way, supposed Chamberlain to have been assiduously seeking to turn the other cheek. He contrasts with Chamberlain's supposedly Christian policy an alternative course:

There is however one helpful guide, namely, for a nation to keep its word and to act in accordance with its treaty obligations to allies. This guide is called honour. It is baffling to reflect that what men call honour does not correspond always to Christian ethics. Honour is often influenced by that element of pride which plays so large a part in its inspiration. An exaggerated code of honour leading to the performance of utterly vain and unreasonable deeds could not be defended, however fine it might look. Here however the moment came when honour pointed the path of duty, and when also the right judgment of the facts at that time would have reinforced its dictates.

For the French Government to leave her faithful ally Czechoslovakia to her fate was a melancholy lapse from which flowed terrible consequences. Not only wise and fair policy, but chivalry, honour, and sympathy for a small threatened people made an overwhelming concentration. Great Britain, who would certainly have fought if bound by treaty obligations, was nevertheless now deeply involved, and it must be recorded with regret that the British Government not only acquiesced but encouraged the French Government in a fatal course.

Duff Cooper, First Lord of the Admiralty, who resigned after Munich, explained his decision in these words: 'The Prime Minister has believed in addressing Herr Hitler through the language of sweet reasonableness. I have believed that he was more open to the language of the mailed fist.'

It is not here our business to make a judgment on the efficacy of Chamberlain's policy in procuring advantages for Britain. A year of time was gained and in his testament Hitler reproached himself for it. But if the thought of gaining time was not unconsidered by Chamberlain, it was not his chief aim. That was to avoid the war which immediately threatened and to create a basis for lasting peace. He failed, but what we have to ask ourselves, after turning to those fuller accounts here presented in summary, is whether he was pursuing a policy which might be styled Christian, and if we judge that he was not, what would have been a Christian policy in these circumstances. It may well be that every honest Christian, when confronted with this question, will confess himself bewildered, and in this bewilderment will be discovered the cardinal difficulty of applying Christianity to the relationships of nations.

Chamberlain held no power when the situation with which he was to be faced was being shaped. If the League of Nations was not the instrument which many wished, if our arms were not what they might have been, he had no main share of responsibility. The past had been in the hands of others and the hand that was dealt him he had to play. During the war the Bishop of Chichester wrote a popular book called *Christianity and World Order*. 'Men', he wrote, 'are searching for order.' So was Neville Chamberlain. We were, he said, on the outbreak of war, fighting against evil things — 'brute force, bad faith, injustice, oppression and persecution'. These were what he had had thrown in his face when he had sought for peace. He had been willing, and so had the French, to make great concessions — unhappily out of another country — to bring Hitler to accept the restraints of order, to make his gains at least through rational negotiations towards agreements which would be observed. If there was nothing specifically Christian about this endeavour it was, in its appeal to reason, well within the bounds of that Natural Law which has an honoured place in Christian philosophy.

It is, however, not within the power of a Christian statesman to choose his opponents or to command that the contents of their minds shall be much like his own. If Hitler had possessed the usual share of common reason, let alone any part in the Christian inheritance, Chamberlain might have moved him. As it was, there existed no common understanding between them. This absence of any shared language of argument, save that of force, is not rare in history. We may note that the adversaries of today, whether Russian or Chinese, neither confess Christianity nor claim any part in its tradition. It is with them that Christians must do business and maintain peace, if possible.

In the end, Chamberlain found himself with the bare bones of what foreign relations so often are — the play of one self-interest against the other, with force the sole effective arbiter. There was no court of justice to which he might appeal, and no judge. World opinion, of which he was careful, was no substitute. The opinion of the world was largely set against Hitler's Germany, but that nation held out for years, destroying many lives and cities, and any taking the same path in the future will achieve far greater devastation.

Some readers may feel that Munich, the last link in a chain of disasters, is not a fair example to choose. If Christianity seems not to apply in the moment when two powers clash, it may be asked, surely its spirit, properly exerted, could slowly eradicate the causes of war and inclinations to it. Christianity is love, and justice is the public face of love. Justice should be the aim of international affairs, and through an orderly growth of relationship between nations the brotherhood of man may be realized. At no time did Christians in Britain believe this more firmly than in the twenty years after 1918. In the Copec report on *International Relations* drawn up in 1924, the early failures of the League of Nations were duly noted, but the naïve faith in the institution's powers to promote international justice and avert war, which was later to rise to an astonishing height of credulity, had already seized on churchmen. 'In a world in which the supreme power is love,' the report noted, 'we believe it is impossible to advance human happiness and develop human character by armies and navies. True civilisation does not go forward on a powder cask, but by the growth of love.' The moral principle accepted by Christians as binding between individuals in their political, economic and social relations, the report asserted, should be no less obligatory on nations in their dealings with each other. Such facile assumptions on the part of Christians helped to create that weakness of public opinion which made possible the humiliation of Munich. In his *Spiritual Values and World Affairs* Sir Alfred Zimmern, himself a Christian, in 1939 when the full effects of these disastrous illusions had become apparent, showed how completely the nature of the League had been misunderstood. The League was no more than a piece of machinery, and its vocal supporters failed to grasp the point that member nations had reserved their sovereignty. The League of Nations Union in Britain, to which the churches in the main gave an intensely emotional support, speedily identified the policy the League ought to pursue at any given moment with the interests of Great Britain, as seen either by the Government or by a section of opinion. The interests of other nations, equally members, were overlooked. This muddled view led, as Zimmern points out, 'to a confusion between the sphere of religion and the sphere of politics, to the intrusion of religion, in a crude and wholesale fashion, into the discussion of a problem on which religion *by itself* could offer no safe guidance.' It led in the long run to a foolish trust in a collective security which did not exist. Far from helping, the uninformed Christian clamour for international justice actually hindered what small possibility of it there was. Zimmern may be quoted again:

One reason — not indeed the only reason, but an important reason — for this chronic deadlock at Geneva, for the utter ineffectiveness of the technique of international co-operation in the very place where it might have been expected to win its greatest triumphs, was the intrusion of religious and pseudo-religious sentiment into the diplomatic Council chamber. There were moments when, in listening to speeches in the League Assembly, one felt that one was in the presence, not of statesmen representing different policies, but of the devotees of contending Churches. For our continental friends who, though they do not always admire our intelligence, maintain under all circumstances a very real respect for our practical ability, were not slow to perceive the value of religious emotion as an ally in their various causes.

The Christian conscience was disturbed often by wrong reasons when it meditated upon the manifold injustices presented to its attention. That wrongs were done to Germany in the Treaty of Versailles was obvious, but the concentration upon those wrongs in much Christian polemic, which served to create among some Christians even an initial sympathy with the rise of Nazism, was owed to feelings less respectable than a concern for justice. Germany was near, and she was growing more powerful. Behind conscientious objections to the Treaty of Versailles lay fear of war. On the other hand, injustice to smaller nations, for which we carried large responsibility, passed almost unnoticed because the stimulus of fear was lacking. The Armenian people fought with the Allies in the war of 1914–18, and suffered more than any of them, losing one million out of a nation of four and a half million. In war and after the war the British Prime Minister gave them the strongest pledges for their liberation from Turkey. But in the end, in spite of their gallantry and trust, they were left to their fate and appeals against their barbarous maltreatment by the Turks who still ruled them were ignored in both London and Geneva. To put it shortly, Christian consciences missed the far worse wrongs of a small people and became obsessed with the lesser grievances of Germany, a country powerful enough to cause trouble.

Part of these inconsistencies which marked the moralizing on foreign affairs of the twenties and thirties sprang from sheer ignorance. Foreign relations are a vast and complicated net and the amateur lacks the training and the information to see them as a whole. He tends to single out a particular aspect which engages his sympathies — the Spanish Civil War is a good instance — and to make specific demands on the policy-makers for action in this one direction, without considering, because he does not know, the repercussions his recommended line of action must have on the intricate array of other problems facing his Government in the foreign field. He reasons inevitably on too small a scale and the engagement of his emotions means that even here his reason often functions badly. He indulges easily in a whole string of pathetic fallacies. He personalizes entities like the 'United Nations' or 'Germany' without heeding the fact that they are bundles of influences and factions, now pulling this way, now that. And by personalizing these large bodies, he slips into the illusion, as Copec did, of assuming that the moral principles binding on relations between individuals can apply to relations between States.

By now, Reinhold Niebuhr's influence has injected a needed astringency into Christian thought on this subject. He himself was not being wise after the event, for his *Moral Man and Immoral Society* was written in 1932, when Christian commentary on foreign affairs was at its most idealistic and impractical. He drew attention to the underlying realities of human nature and emphasized the facts of power in the relationship of States. The obviousness of many of the points he sought to establish is itself a measure of the illusions to which his fellow Christians had succumbed. He had to point out that groups behave differently from individuals; he felt it necessary to say that two nations in a quarrel were never face to face like two men, and that the relationships of nations were different in kind. He examined patriotism and loyalty and showed how they made claim on human virtue, changing a personal unselfishness, a readiness of men to sacrifice themselves on behalf of their community, into national egoism of an aggressive kind. Thus what was goodness in the individual became badness in his State. He dwelt upon the immense difficulties of the leap from loyalty to the nation, 'the most absolute of all human associations,' to loyalty to mankind or humanity, a concept too vague for most men to hold long or firmly. His realism has lost none of its value to Christians today. The short history of the United Nations, which mercifully has never drawn to itself extravagant hopes like the old League, has illustrated once more

the rock-like endurance of nationalism. Over and over again in
its debates we may discern how cases are not decided on their
merits, but by how the greater nations consider their interests to
be affected, the weaker client nations casting their votes according
to the wishes of the Great Powers their leaders. This is a poor substitute for anything that might be called international justice.

The root of the difficulty in foreign relations, for Christians
and not for them only but for all men, is the permanent tension
between freedom and order. As we have seen, these two principles have caught Christian minds since the earliest days of the
Church, some Christians being more drawn to the one and some
to the other. Today it is correct to say that among Christians, in
the western world at least, freedom is felt to be the principle more
characteristic of their religion's message. This is, however, a
temporary attitude — one might almost say a fashion — born of
recent experience. We have lived for so long in conditions of
order that their real benefit fails to be valued. Two great wars
have disturbed order, but for most of their course trains ran to
time, the health services functioned, people were fed moderately
well, and in the courts of law justice was done. Even in those
countries most affected, where the destruction and loss of life
were greatest — Germany, Poland and western Russia — order
was soon completely restored. The interruption was short-lived
and its damage easily recoverable. The slow breakdown of the
Roman Empire was more catastrophic in its effect. For centuries
the amenity of living disappeared from the face of Europe; the
law ceased to offer protection; the rule of the stronger prevailed
and for families to be extinguished, separated or enslaved was the
common lot. It was natural for men emerging from such times to
set infinitely more store by the principle of order than by that of
freedom, and we may say that down to the eighteenth century
order was the fashion. But out of a comparatively prolonged
stability, to which technological invention contributed, rose confidence and a new taste for freedom. We cannot rest sure that this
attitude will never alter. A world nuclear war might plunge mankind back into ways of life not wholly unlike those which
existed after the fall of Rome.

But even at present successful management of the world's affairs depends upon a delicate balance of the two principles. Necessarily they are in perpetual conflict. Freedom engenders change and change unsettles order. Both principles must be pursued at once and yet they are not easy to reconcile. If freedom is the watchword in domestic affairs and in formerly subject territories, most idealists seek strenuously to establish order in international affairs. The fear of nuclear war leads many to desire the establishment of some form of world government. One is doubtful whether this end, if ever gained, would be much relished. There is no reason why a world government, monopolizing the possession of nuclear and all other heavy arms — if it did not have this monopoly, it would not be a government — should not be able to remove all threat of large-scale war. For some, this might be considered a sufficient result. For others, the concentration of world authority in a few hands fortified by all the world's power seems to threaten a tyranny of such proportions that it would be a price too high to pay even for peace.

It is always a question of striking a balance between freedom and order. Now Christianity, while out of its faith and history it can establish freedom and order as twin needs of man, equal in importance, has less to offer at the succession of critical points when some balance between them has to be struck. Take the principle of national self-determination which was warmly espoused by many Christians during and immediately after the First World War. The old corrupt empires of Austro-Hungary and Turkey had not only been on the losing side, but for many years before the war the various nations under their rule had been demanding their independence. With the peace they received it, the principle of self-determination being honoured. We saw, in the course of the passage on Munich, an example of how difficult it is to apply any general principle like national self-determination to the actual world — for Czechoslovakia was a packet of peoples too many of whom had received no benefit at all from the principle. But if we look nowadays at the successor states of the Austro-Hungarian and Turkish Empires, it is not altogether easy to maintain that the principle of freedom as enshrined in self-determination has conferred the hoped for benefits. In eastern Europe, Soviet Russia is a severer taskmaster than Austria ever was, while in place of the lax Turkish rule in the Middle East lie a series of small, weak States so torn by hatred and jealousy that they are a perennial threat to peace. Dean Acheson, an American Secretary of State who took his religion seriously, remarked in the *Yale Review* in 1958 on the effects of self-determination: 'As one looks back upon the results in Eastern Europe and the Middle East, one has more difficulty in seeing the moral or ideal achievement than in recognizing the immediate and, perhaps, irrevocable disaster.'

Freedom, again in the shape of self-determination, largely governs Christian and liberal attitudes towards the aspirations of the colonial peoples in Africa. Their case for independence is not to be seen as the same as India's. India was a civilized nation with a large educated class, whose members had shared with the British for many years before independence the work of administration. The grant of independence was owed to no sudden change of heart; the justice and the sense of it, one day, had been plain to early nineteenth-century Englishmen like Lord Hastings, Henry Lawrence and Macaulay. In Africa, on the other hand, the resources of tradition, of administrative and technical skill, and of educational background are much less. If freedom argues for granting self-determination quickly, order counsels that it would be wise to wait. Yet it is not wholly a matter between ourselves and the Africans. At the time of writing important powers outside Africa — Russia, China, India — have declared against 'colonialism'. Their means of fomenting unrest where they will it are by now so well known, that we must admit we should find it difficult to maintain our rule in Africa, against local revolts backed by a hostile world opinion, even if we happened to judge that it was in the best interest of the Africans for us to do so. In other words, we are not free to strike our own balance between freedom and order in our African territories, because our judgment must take account of powerful pressures from outside. Nor need we suppose that these pressures are applied out of humanitarian regard for the rights of the people of Africa. They spring from the oldest impulse met with in foreign affairs, the wish of one nation, or set of nations, to extend their power and influence at another's expense. Russia's intervention in the Congo, professedly made with the highest motives, brought more misery to that region than the miscalculations of Belgium and the petulant inexperience of its own peoples combined.

Enough has been said to suggest that policy in Africa has perforce to take account of other concerns besides the future welfare of Africans. But if that were the sole matter, and it were a question merely of balancing the African wish for independence against our own interest in ensuring stability after our departure, the issue would remain extremely difficult and not one, it must appear, which the application of Christian principles, if relevant ones were discovered, could resolve. In very general terms, men need reminding, for they tend to neglect one or the other, that freedom and order have an equal importance at all times, and for churches to proclaim that truth is salutary. It is not, of course, a truth peculiar to Christianity, though Christian freedom and Christian order may be distinguished from other forms. But when churchmen descend from the general to the particular and hold meetings concerned with the pace of colonial advance they enter a field where principles are of less use than commonsense, skill in negotiation, and knowledge of the facts of each case and the personalities involved. Burke was a man who dealt in principles, but he was sufficiently a politician to know that complicated disputes could not be settled *a priori* from afar, as he made clear to a member of the French National Assembly in 1791:

Permit me to say that, if I were as confident as I ought to be diffident in my own loose general ideas, I should never venture to broach them, if but at twenty leagues' distance from the centre of your affairs. I must see with my own eyes, I must, in a manner, touch with my own hands, not only the fixed but the momentary circumstances, before I could venture to suggest any political project whatsoever. I must know the power and disposition to accept, to execute, to persevere. I must see all the aids and all the obstacles. I must see the means of correcting the plan where corrections would be wanted. I must see the things; I must see the men.

If in 1961 Lord Salisbury thought Mr. Macleod, the Colonial

Secretary, was moving too quickly towards African self-government in the Federation of Rhodesia and Nyasaland, this was not a difference on which Christianity could have anything useful to say. In Burke's phrase, everything hangs upon judgments of things and men, and no key exists to the making of such hazardous judgments rightly for certain.

Mr. George F. Kennan, a Presbyterian, an American ambassador for many years and a distinguished authority on foreign affairs, noted in an article in *The Atlantic Monthly* in 1959 how it had become assumed by many Christians today that any form of foreign rule was oppressive and worse than any form of indigenous rule and that any anti-colonial effort was therefore good in the Christian sense. 'I am confident', he said, 'that for such assumption there is not a shred of justification.' The colonial era was coming to an end as the impulses which had given rise to it no longer existed. The resolution of this period, with the immensely difficult task of transferring power at the right time to the right people, called for laborious statesmanship. He adds:

This process could not fail to give rise to tensions of tragic bitterness and difficulty. In the anatomy of these tensions, one will look in vain, as a rule, for any Christian meaning. The resistance to change on the part of the mother country has sometimes reflected selfishness and shortsightedness, and it has also reflected in many cases a genuine sense of responsibility. Conversely, the demand for change on the part of the colonial people has sometimes reflected a real love of liberty, and it has often been borne by a spirit fiercely chauvinistic, full of hatred, undemocratic, and irresponsible.

If the emancipation of former colonies must be admitted a complex affair to which Christianity is not directly relevant, it is worth making a similar point about foreign aid, financial support for undeveloped countries and the like. Such schemes are specially attractive to Christians, because they seem related to doctrines of Christian charity, the helping hand and cheerful giving. Here again it is important to keep in mind the differences between the relationships of human persons and of States. If in purely personal exchanges the feeding hand is sometimes bitten, this is an experience far commoner between nations, and with more reason, for generosity on the international scale is seldom pure. The massive outpouring of American money and aid throughout the globe, great though some of its benefits have been, not least to this country, has not been a gesture of complete altruism. It is part of America's effort to counter the spread of Russian influence and we see already, as a result of Russia's technological revolution, a competition to give aid developing. If the West refuses to build Egypt's dam, Russia speeds to do it instead, and the pattern is being many times repeated. This competitive charity, with its political implications, is far removed from what it signifies in Christian feeling. Even the reception of foreign aid, as it enters the beneficiary's economy, has intricate effects, some of them far removed from what might be expected to result from an act of personal Christian charity. However much it may advantage the receiving nation as a whole, it is likely to work to the disadvantage of at least some of its citizens. The aid will enrich some factions and areas in its competitive internal economy more than others. Some will rise in the world through the effects of this help from outside and some will sink. This side-effect provides no reason for not proffering the aid, which anyway is no doubt well justified in the giving nation's conception of its own self-interest, but it supplies one more cause for doubting whether Christian ethical principles translate well into the relationships of States. It might seem admirable, for example, that Britain should supply valuable text-books at much below cost price to developing nations like Pakistan which lack the foreign exchange to buy them on the ordinary market. It could be a simple act of generosity towards a country, once ruled by us, which needs to master modern scientific knowledge to make its way in the world. In fact, our decision here was dictated by the knowledge that American text-books were being distributed cheaply in Pakistan and other countries, while Russia was supplying many free. There is held to be a connexion between the books a student engineer studies and the orders he will one day place for heavy equipment. 'Trade follows the book,' declared our publishers, and the Government accepted their slogan. There is nothing at all disgraceful in such a transaction, which does all involved more good than harm. But it is not something that can be brought under the general heading of Christian charity.

It is not cynical to take the world as it is. In foreign affairs every nation moves out of the area under its own control and meets principles and policies which are not its own. It is not even an axiom that all nations wish for peace; what can be said is that some have more need of it than others. In 1961 it was plain, from the recent confrontation of the Chinese and Russian leaders in Moscow, that the Russians were more inclined to think that Communism might gain the world without war than the Chinese (whose widespread territories suggest to them that they might come better out of nuclear war than anyone else). The one certain thing nations have in common is self-interest, and the greatest disservice Christians can do to the cause of humanity is to seek to give their own nation's self-interest a moral covering. There are enough sound reasons in economics and politics for well-directed aid to undeveloped countries for the voice of the moralist to be silent on the matter. When Britain invests money in a hydro-electric power plant for some African territory, this act does not appear to the Russians as altruistic but as the snatching of a certain advantage in the region, and in the broad terms of the cold war, in which both East and West think at this moment, the Russians are right. Certainly there is benefit to the Africans, and men of goodwill can be glad at this and keenly support further schemes of the kind, but in the present world context generosity is the wrong word to apply to such undertakings. When doing good becomes competitive the virtue has gone out of it.

It is right for all men, Christians especially, to examine their motives and to consider also how they might appear to others. When Lord Salisbury said in 1896 'Our first duty is towards the people of this country . . . our second duty is to all humanity' he was not laying down some absurdly outmoded, jingoistic principle. He was declaring the rule that guides all national statesmen, in a world divided into nations, to this day — a rule of which the majority of their peoples approve so strongly that no moralizing will shake them out of it. It may well be that slowly mankind will move forward from the nationalist era and Christians, whose faith antedates modern nationalism, may help to point the way. But that way forward, which cannot by any historical measure be rapid, can only be from where man stands now. It is possible to argue, for example, that all aid to undeveloped countries should be administered by the United Nations. This would be a great advance. But at present this is not to the taste of Russia, which regards the United Nations as being an adjunct of Western diplomacy. Nevertheless, the aim is good, and may be achieved if some kind of agreement, gained out of the old processes of diplomacy, can be reached between America, Russia and China. In any such agreement, the counters in play will be those of power and self-interest — self-interest, perhaps, in peace.

Such counsel may seem discouraging, but Christian practitioners of statecraft at the highest levels are themselves the most insistent on the extrusion of moralistic reasoning from their concerns. 'The substance of moral discussion', says Mr. Dean Acheson, 'which concerns the conduct of individuals within a society toward one another is more likely than not to be misleading if applied to the relations of one society to another.' Mr. Kennan makes another relevant point: 'It is very difficult for us to know which of the specific undertakings of government in foreign affairs might have Christian significance and which might not. If there is any one thing that is plain about international statesmanship, it is the extreme difficulty of establishing in advance the relationship between cause and effect — of gauging the likely results of one's own acts.' The precise role of the amateur in foreign affairs faces not only Christianity but democracy with a difficult question. The many intertwining issues are not susceptible to that separation into single causes which the plain man insists upon making if he is to understand them at all. In these matters, the Press itself, even the best of it, is no certain guide, for commonly the facts on which policy should be formed are hidden. An essential fact for public opinion in Britain in judging, on one vital count, the wisdom of the Munich agreement at the time it was made, was the precise state of the country's defences in September 1938. Such facts are always secret from a people, as the other vital fact, the strength of the enemy, is obscure to the government itself.

'Questions of method in foreign policy', wrote Mr. Kennan in the article already quoted, 'seem to me to be generally a much more fitting subject for Christian concern than questions of purpose.' Lord Salisbury, who set his face against all bullying and arrogance, would probably have agreed with him. 'A government', Kennan continues, 'can pursue its purpose in a patient and conciliatory and understanding way, respecting the interests of others and infusing its behaviour with a high standard of decency and honesty and humanity, or it can show itself petty, exacting, devious, and self-righteous.' Those Christians whose hobby is rebuilding the world may feel the improvement of diplomatic manners to be a poor and unexciting substitute, but for a nation to reach and maintain the standards Kennan sets out would be quite remarkable. He proposes a high standard. Honesty, for example, however necessary to the keeping of engagements, will ordinarily be less evident in the negotiations leading to their making — in the sense that no diplomat is going to put more cards on the table than he has to. The removal of self-righteousness from political utterance is something that Christians are well fitted to bring about, seeing that since Gladstone's day it has been included partly for their edification. It is best to take the sphere of foreign relations for what it is — an ever-growing body of nations struggling for their individual wants. To bring these conflicting wants into some sort of harmony is the task of cool reason and the rush of excitement which moral emotion introduces obstructs a labour already difficult. The international scene is always in movement and no settled system can contain it. Neither Communism nor what we call Western democracy is content with the place it at present occupies in the world. Both seek to extend their influence, to win new clients, to add fresh nations to their following. On each side the urge towards the expansion of power is based not merely on materialistic considerations of trading advantages and the like but on deep-rooted beliefs about the proper ordering of men and their societies. The leaders and the peoples on the two sides both assume their beliefs to be right. In the flow of history these beliefs will change, they may even merge — but to suppose at this moment that their differences do not exist, that the reality is only a conflict of power, is a facile cynicism denied by the facts. The dynamic of history is supplied by these profound clashes of opinion and will. Yet it is good for the professional handlers of the relationships of states to detach at least themselves, as far as they can, from the polemics at their back, and to deal with the plain counters of current self-interest. They cannot see clearly, any more than the leaders and peoples behind them, where the effects of their bargaining will lead. Czechoslovakia, and many other states, were the results of such bargaining at Versailles, which had an enduring settlement as its general aim, yet the upshot was totally unexpected by the bargainers. Men are driven to attempt to control the future course of history and if in planning for an ordered century they create the basis for a quiet decade their labour has been justified. The Christians, however, must believe that in the affairs of nations and the movement of history the all-powerful hands of God are at work. The Christian acceptance of belief in God's providence as well as in man's free will raises philosophical problems which are not easy to resolve. Nevertheless from Augustine downwards the idea of God's shaping history to his will, leading it to a destination of his own choosing, using for his own purposes the imperfect initiatives of men, and even their worst crimes, has been an enduring support to the minds of Christian statesmen. We have seen how Gladstone and Lord Salisbury constantly felt sustained by it. Bismarck remarked: 'The statesman cannot create the stream of time, he can only navigate upon it.' Historians come to the same conclusions as statesmen, for they see even more clearly how few major events offer any signs of having been rationally planned. The Industrial Revolution, the French Revolution, the victory of Communism in Russia rather than in the more industrialized nations where Marx predicted it — where is the evidence that any of these happenings took place according to conscious human planning? As Professor H. Butterfield puts it: 'A very considerable part of the attention of historians is concentrated in fact upon that kind of history — making which goes on so to

M

speak over our heads, now deflecting the results of our actions, now taking our purposes out of our hands, and now turning our endeavours to ends not realized.' The sense of God's great part in history compared with man's confused weakness in ordering his affairs will not lead the Christian to avoid the issues of foreign policy. But it should restrain him from excessive conviction that the next step as he sees it is the only one that may righteously be taken. If the Christian statesman does his best to advance the interests of his nation, bearing in mind that in this interlocked world those interests lie within a developing system of general order — principles, we must note, which have nothing distinctively Christian about them — he is more likely to do good in the world than if he imagines himself to possess the secret of what God wills to happen next.

Mr. Dean Acheson also advised Christians to apply their religion more to the methods of international relations than to purposes. 'Here,' he writes, 'we can and should aim high. There should be no bullying, no advantage taken of the hardship of others to drive political bargains, no lying or boasting in our propaganda or our dealings with others, no sanctimonious lecturing of others on their faults, no consciousness of our own effortless righteousness, or the thanking of God that we are not as other men.' 'Perhaps', he concludes, 'what we do is less important than how we do it.'[1]

---

[1] 'Morality, Moralism and Diplomacy', *The Yale Review*, June 1958, p. 493.

9

Christian Political Parties on the Continent

In Britain even those most convinced that Christianity has something to say in politics have stopped short of recommending Christian political parties. 'The Church as a whole', declared Temple, 'must not be attached to any political party.' The reasons for this insular attitude have been set out earlier. As Christianity in general was never attacked politically in Britain whatever disabilities remained to the dissenters after 1688, Christians had no call to rally together in their own defence. Once this was clear and Christians could be found in all parties, then it could be maintained that for them to transfer their allegiance to one body would be a poor exchange, leaving their religious interests no stronger and attracting to religion that odium which paraded differences invariably provoke. There was too, in influential thinkers like J. H. Oldham, a distaste for identifying the name of Christ with the shifts and errors that no political party can escape. As Emil Brunner put it from his viewpoint in a nation which had some experience of Christian political parties: 'The curse of the betrayal of the Name of Christ broods over the "Christian" social organization . . . we cannot tack this Name on to any of our little political banners.'

As far as Christians in western Europe go, however, the British in holding this opinion are in a minority. In France, Germany, Italy, Austria, Switzerland, Belgium and Holland, there are large Christian Democratic Parties. In Western Germany the Christian Democrats have been in power uninterruptedly since the war. In Italy they are the largest single party. In Holland the Catholic-Protestant parties, when they act together, command a majority. Clearly the policy and practice of these parties require some attention, if only to clarify the contrast in the British attitude. Fortunately there exists a useful guide in Professor Michael

Fogarty's *Christian Democracy in Western Europe 1820-1953* and
the debt of this chapter to this book is great.

The Christian parties sprang up in Europe mainly in answer to
attitudes adopted towards the Church by liberal and nationalist
movements in the aftermath of the French Revolution and
Napoleon's defeat. To begin with, politically minded Christians
were hopeful of co-operation with liberals and put away the
fears which democracy aroused. But they found slowly that
though there was much in common, there were great differences.
The strong vein of anti-clericalism in continental liberalism proved
too much for its principle of tolerance and in the course of the
century the churches' rights to manage their own internal affairs,
to maintain their own organizations, and to possess their own
schools, were all attacked. The so-called Kulturkampf launched by
Bismarck in 1873-4 after Germany had been united was animated
by the principle that in all matters the Church was subservient to
the State. Its main rigour was reserved for the Roman Catholics.
Diplomatic relations with the Vatican were broken off, a censor-
ship was imposed on pronouncements from the pulpit, lay supervision of the church schools was stiffened, the Jesuits were expelled
from Germany, and many of the bishops and priests who resisted
these measures were imprisoned. In consequence, Catholics
organized themselves politically and the Centre Party, almost
wholly composed of them, was formed in 1874. Before many
years were past, Bismarck found himself needing the help of this
party and reconciliation followed. The genesis of all the Christian
Democratic Parties was much the same, if the lay attack on religion
was less violent than in Germany. Christians organized themselves
politically the better to resist attack on their churches and schools.
They were supported by Christian workers' movements and trade
unions and drew from them much of their democratic and social
character. At the start the workers' movement was organized by
middle-class leaders, but it soon produced its own. Whether
Protestant or Catholic, the political or trade union leaders re-
joiced in standing out distinctively under their religious colours.
As a Dutch Protestant, A. Borst, put it after the last war, Christian
principles could not be given their full impact unless they were

lived out in a visible community of Christians. Not much good, he said, came from 'the little grains of salt' who had tried to add savour to neutral organizations. It was necessary for Christians to band themselves together, and for this they needed distinctive political and social doctrines. A typical statement to this effect was made in 1953 by Senator Houben of the Belgian Christian Social Party:

If politics are important and it is right for Christians to play their part in them, their action, to be effective, needs to be guided by a political doctrine. As soon, in fact, as one has in mind political action spread over a period, and proposes to attain aims defined in advance, a political doctrine is necessary to guarantee continuity and co-ordination, seeing the number of people who must act simultaneously or in succession in the different sectors and positions of political life. This is certainly true in our countries on the Continent of Europe and in our age; for we are faced with grave problems and a rapid evolution, and are at one and the same time deeply logical (to the point of regarding a precedent as an argument) and very little bound by tradition. A doctrine is indispensable, notably, to Christians, who intend to base their policy on the common good, and have in their ranks people of all environments and classes.

For the Christian, the liberal was too humanist and individualistic (and often too right-wing for a movement with strong working-class backing), while Marxist collectivism went too far to the other extreme, sacrificing freedom to a too powerful State. It was a Protestant who declared: 'The Church must condemn publicly any State which claims to be the sole warrant for its own actions.' Most of the Christian parties have sought a middle way and found themselves parties of the centre.

In their principles there are strong similarities between Protestant and Catholic parties, and we are constantly struck by echoes of views held by Gore and Temple in England. As Fogarty puts it, a Christian democrat would claim that his standpoint is ' "personalist" in the sense of bringing into account all the dimensions of personality; social as well as individual, supernatural (and therefore Church) as well as purely human'. The Conservative People's Party in Switzerland has for its basis 'the Christian conception of human personality and society'. It declares that 'respect for human dignity demands that work be valued as a personal and social achievement and as the basis of the physical and spiritual development of the individual and the family'. The Popular Republican Movement in France (M.R.P.) aims at a political, economic and social democracy that will 'guarantee respect for personal rights and civic freedoms, and ensure the primacy of labour over capital and of merit over birth or wealth'. The family is given special importance. In 1945 the Confédération Française des Travailleurs Chrétiens stated that it 'feels itself specially responsible for defending the Family. Under this it includes, along with all those material questions which affect the standard of living in a home, also moral questions concerned with restoring the stability of family life and protecting it against direct and indirect attacks'.

Regular emphasis is set on maintaining the autonomy of institutions and associations beneath the State, in line with Pius XI's encyclical *Quadragesimo Anno* of 1931: 'It is an injustice, a grave evil, and a disturbance of right order for a larger and higher organization to arrogate to itself functions which can be performed efficiently by smaller and lower bodies.' The reigning Christian Democratic Union party in Germany translates this principle thus: 'The Union is opposed to a constitution which would place at the head of the State an excessive concentration of power, which could be misused for new experiments in dictatorship. It is for that reason against the unified State, whose over-concentration of power and tendency to standardize leads to the suppression of the special ways of life of regions. . . .' This decentralization of power to the regions in Germany is paralleled throughout the Christian movement in Europe by a zeal for the rights and powers of lesser associations and for the encouragement of personal activity within them. This is particularly noteworthy in industry where great efforts are made to break down the conflict between owners and management on one side and employees on the other. Many ways have been sought to join together all working in an industrial enterprise in a common sense of sharing in responsibility and control. As a working party of Catholic industrialists, distributors and trade unionists phrased it at Bochum in 1949:

> Man stands at the centre of every economic and management problem. We recognize the right of all who work in a business to share in control over its decisions in social, personal, and economic matters. The right to joint control belongs to the natural law, under the order willed by God. For this requires that all should share in responsibility. It is to be approved in the same way as the right to property.

This is exactly in line with Gore's thinking on industrial organization.

It is perhaps this Christian stress on a weak State which has caused many Christian parties to take the lead in movements for closer international unity. The greater the respect paid to the State, the greater the jealousy for its sovereignty, which stands in the way of schemes of international co-operation. In France and Belgium (as in Portugal, where the State is Christian though not democratic), Christians have supported the association of colonies with the mother country in a wider community — though actual experience with the Congo and Algeria has not been encouraging. The European Movement in its many forms was in part initiated by the Christian parties and it has always had a strong attraction for their members for whom Europe is still the homeland of Christendom. The M.R.P. in France, for example, often supplied the Minister of Foreign Affairs during its heyday, and from this advantageous position forwarded the European idea. The European Coal-Steel community was largely Robert Schuman's creation, and the Common Market itself must be regarded as very much the outcome of Christian Democratic interest in the unification of Europe.

There is a characteristic Christian Democratic viewpoint on the world and society which is shared by all the parties, and, very largely, by politically minded Christians in England who stop short of separate political organization. Is there evidence that through the political power and influence of the Christian parties this general view is worked out and applied in legislation? In the social sphere, much evidence certainly exists. The family movement in France, for example, largely a Christian affair, led to the generous provision of family allowances. But material support for the family was not enough. It was here that the doctrines of personalism came into play. Human beings have a dignity and responsibility which they should exercise and the institutions of the State ought to encourage them to rise to their full stature. The family might be judged 'the corner-stone of the structure of society', but it was not enough to endow, still less to pamper, this fundamental human grouping. The independence and freedom of its members must be brought out, and the conviction of the importance of this was written into the administration of social security. In general, social security was created under Christian Democratic leadership as a system for increasing family incomes rather than as a supplier of services to the family. In contrast to the British Welfare State, the emphasis has been on presenting possibilities to the family through increasing its income, rather than on offering free certain specified benefits which those at the top of society judge necessary. It is a gesture of faith in human nature and in the importance of leaving to the person the right to choose well or ill on behalf of those dependent on him. This extends to the way in which social security benefits are administered. No doubt a unified system of social insurance, such as we have in Britain, is the most economical and efficient. But much is missed by administering essentially human needs through a host of anonymous clerks behind counters. In Belgium the task is done partly through friendly societies, because, it was held, the Christian friendly societies are truly human associations. The societies' officials are in touch with their members on a multitude of matters quite unconnected with social security benefits. The societies themselves are schools of Christian leadership and Christian living. Social security has been knit into the natural exchanges of society; it has been made a bond as well as a benefit. As a Belgian leader put it in 1949: 'Man is not a hermit . . . it is through full and entire involvement in the structure of society, through participation in social life in a variety of environments, that he achieves the perfection of his nature. It is for that reason essential that the environments in which he is called upon to live should be healthy and educative. . . .' In much the same way, in Germany particularly, attention has been paid to the organization of industry. The talk about the need on Christian grounds to associate the worker in the ownership and control of his place of work has not been without practical effect. The presence of a trade unionist on the supreme boards directing private industrial enterprises is witness to the strength of a vein in Christian social thought. It was shared by Gore and Temple, but had little lay backing in Britain.

Certain other characteristics of these parties may be noted. They have found it necessary to establish a formal independence of churches. If clergy join, they do so as ordinary citizens. The policies the parties seek to advance are inspired by Christian teaching delivered under the Church's authority. But inside politics, the clergy may not speak as representatives of that authority, and the political interpretation of Christianity must be left to the Christian politicians whose proper business it is. Since the War the trend, except in Holland, has been for the Christian parties to become inter-denominational. Instead of the old Catholic Centre in Germany, Catholics and Protestants work together in the C.D.U. Much the same is true in France and Belgium. All these parties offer a welcome, not unnaturally, to the non-Christian 'men of good will', but without perhaps a great deal of success.

They are broadly representative of all classes, their left wing being supplied by the Christian trade unions. Tensions inevitably result from clashes of class interest within the parties, for those who band together under the Christian title can have extremely mixed views when it comes to political action. Recruitment from right and left, coupled with the emphasis in industry on harmonizing relationships between managers and men, and possibly the instinct towards reconciliation which we have pointed to as a mark of Christianity in action, have led to the Christian parties being usually found in the centre of party alignments. To their right stand usually Conservative and Liberal groups, to their left Socialists and Communists. In Continental countries without two-party tradition, this has often given them strategical advantages out of proportion to their size, as with the M.R.P. in France, but such a position, which encourages political machination, is not an unmixed blessing.

One must now look at the comparatively short history of the Christian parties and concentrate on the blacker side of the record. Before a judgment can be made on whether the formation of specifically Christian political parties is good or bad, some attention must be paid to unworthier moments which were necessarily covered by the Christian claim. In their beginnings several of these Christian groups — none of them the parties that we have today — were tinged with anti-Semitism, not of the radical racial type but springing from a dislike of Jewish influence in society. Towards the close of the last century in Germany Adolf Stöcker, leading a Protestant social movement with strong Nationalist leanings, propagated such ideas. In the 1890s, they were taken up by a Catholic version of Stöcker's party in Austria, while at the same time in France, then immersed in the Dreyfus case, small groups of Catholic right-wing politicians were markedly anti-Semitic. None of these small bodies, all confined to the early days of the Christian political movement, could properly be styled Christian Democratic, and in none was anti-Semitism a chief plank in their platform. They were without successors. It may be held malignant to recall them. But in so important a matter as trying to establish whether politicians are wise to attach to themselves the Christian title, it is necessary to remind ourselves of instances when its use discredited religion. It is difficult, in the general weakness of the German democratic parties in face of the National Socialists, to pin any particular guilt on the Centre Party. All that can be said is that a Christian party which lived up to its name might have reacted differently. At the purely political level, in the mechanics of party combinations, the Centre abandoned after 1929 its long alliance with the Social Democrats and by this reduced the cohesion of the democratic forces. Hitler always regarded the Centre Party with enmity, which is to its credit, and, after its suppression, was vigilant against any chance of its revival. But it remains a fact that in March 1933 the leader of the Centre Party, along with the other parties, voted for the suspension of parliamentary government. In Germany Christian resistance to Nazism was conducted better by the churches than by their parties. The Italian Popular Party made quite as unimpressive a stand against the rise of Fascism, though Papal policy played here its own unfortunate part. In 1924 there was the chance of an understanding between the Popular Party and the Socialists. It is not to be said that if one had been reached Mussolini would have failed to seize power — against his revolutionary dynamic the democratic parties had no defence — but it was the obviously right move in the circumstances. Nevertheless, Pope Pius XI, who desired chiefly a concordat with the Italian State and was obsessed with the danger of Communism, exerted his influence against the Christian Popular Party's allying itself with other democratic groups. In neither Germany nor Italy did the Christian parties offer effective opposition to the political evils of the 1930s.

Another difficulty, already mentioned, rose directly from the assumption of the Christian title. Parties form most naturally on a basis of interest; they represent groups of voters each of whom look to the party for the protection or advancement of their own chief concerns. No party can afford to be backed by a single interest-group and a successful party will be looked to by many. Yet the interests behind a party should have something in common, if running the party is to be easy, and too wide a difference between them can immobilize it. If it is often possible to satisfy middle-class and lower-class members in one party, it is less easy to combine the interests of the very rich and the very poor. This is what the Christian parties have constantly sought to do and in many countries it has reduced their stability. As we have seen, the Christian political movement on the Continent originated under secularist attack on vital Church concerns like schooling and freedom of ecclesiastical appointment. These were threats to the very maintenance of their religion which all thinking Christians, both rich and poor, could readily appreciate. As long as this danger was there, it held Christians of very different class interests together. Where it grew less, a tug-of-war between richer and poorer, employers and employed, sometimes developed to the Christian party's hurt. Quite early in this century, for example, the Protestant parties in Holland suffered from dissensions because their trade union supporters were demanding shorter hours of work and a few days of paid holiday a year which employer members felt called upon to oppose. Leaders who took up the workers' demands were accused of trying to compete with the socialists. Before de Gaulle returned to power, early in the 1950s, the M.R.P. in France was continually being hamstrung by difficulties of this sort. It tried to be a genuinely bridging party, offering to those eager for far-reaching social reform an alternative to the feebleness of socialism and the dangerous strength of communism. The upper- and middle-class support which it attracted on religious grounds hampered this aim. Never holding in the peculiar conditions of French politics a majority of its own, the M.R.P. was always driven to make alliances. Those to the right were more than ever likely to cripple the party's social policies, while, although these might have been forwarded by a Communist linking, that would have been a sure way of alienating its own Christian followers. There were too the embarrassments which could be caused to a left-wing Christian party, seeking to collaborate with liberals and socialists, whenever matters of peculiarly Christian concern, like religious schooling in France, were brought into the arena. When in 1951 the French Right raised the issue of grants to church schools, and the Communists rallied to the secularist cause, the M.R.P. position was gravely shaken. Professedly a grouping where clerical and anti-clerical could meet and work together, it would not have chosen to raise the schools issue itself. Once it had been raised, the party's religious connexion made the upholding of the clerical case essential, and this in turn seriously disturbed the party's carefully fostered ties with the socialists and liberals. Thus the Christian party has not only to face the internal difficulties of finding a policy that will satisfy at one time Christian trade unionists and Christian stockbrokers, but it has an external difficulty, unsettling to any political combination it may have entered, whenever a directly religious issue appears on the stage.

Although these parties are formally independent of the Church, they cannot wholly escape its influence, particularly when fundamental religious interests seem threatened. Harassment of this sort is much suffered by the Democrazia Cristiana party in

Italy, where both the Church and Communism are strong. The aim of Christian Democrat political leaders like Sturzo and de Gasperi since the war has been to distinguish the party from its socialist-communist opponents on social and political rather than religious lines. This strategy, the same as that pursued by the M.R.P. in France, is the only one open to a party which seeks to unite all men of goodwill, liberals and democratic socialists who may be non-Christians, under one banner. But the influence of the Roman Church in Italy has worked against this harmonizing policy, because it has ecclesiastical interests of its own to defend. If the Communists gained power in Italy, it is at least possible, perhaps, as some see it, probable, that they would close Catholic schools and universities, and suppress the religious press and youth organizations. The ecclesiastical agencies, therefore, have felt obliged to buttress their interest by direct intervention in politics — a right which can be denied them in no democratic country but whose zealous exercise stultifies the non-clerical pretensions of the Christian Democratic Party. At election time in Italy the whole weight of Church organization, its parishes and its societies, is thrown into the business of getting every potential Christian Democratic voter to the polls. As Fogarty notes: 'In an Italian town at election time, pick the building with the greatest number of Democrazia Cristiana posters; it is probably the convent.' To the non-Christian, however tolerant, this must seem an introduction of sectional self-interest into the general affairs of a nation. It may well provoke hatred for the Church among those people who do not belong to it.

It is worth noting that, faced with their experience up to date, some elements in the Christian Democratic parties, though by no means a majority in any, are reconsidering the purpose and value of their Christian label. They see, first, that by the nature of the support it attracts it makes positive social policies hard to promote and, second, that it restricts the potential size of their constituency — by driving off those who are indeed not Christians but, except for the label, would vote for their policies. As we saw in our discussion of the English scene, socialism appeals to many Christians on their own grounds. What 'socialism' in this sense means, of course, it is not exactly easy to say. For the Christian it is usually, though not always, distinguished from doctrinaire Marxism. It is strongly affected by ideas of equality, by the notion of establishing a general level of good and decent living in which all may participate; 'fair shares' is a slogan that expresses it well. Christians of these views wish to identify themselves with the needs and aspirations of the broad masses of the population; their sympathies are with them and less with the professional and upper classes. Naturally such people will grow dissatisfied with a party which may receive the backing of Christian trade unionists but is restrained in its social policies by dependence on a large number of voters attracted to it by little more than religious sentiment. They see instead the large areas of common life in which men of goodwill may labour together. These people are especially struck by the example of the British Labour Party in which Christians and non-Christians pursue agreed social ends side by side, constricted neither by Marxist formalism nor by the doctrines and outlook of any church. In France, Holland, Belgium and Germany the possibilities of new political alignments, untrammelled by religion, have been discussed. In Holland a small Labour Party has actually been formed.

The chances opened by taking this new course are underlined when Christian Democrats examine the present basis of their support. They already receive as many of the votes of practising Christians as it is reasonable to expect. In Holland it is estimated that 90 per cent. of Catholics performing their religious duties vote for the Catholic Party. The percentage in Germany is lower; practising Catholics voting C.D.U. come to about two-thirds, church-going Protestants rally to the party to the extent of about 40 per cent. of their numbers. But in all the western European countries it is apparent that the Christian parties have come near the edge of their Christian constituency. Every party with a policy wishes to expand its support the better to forward it, and there is no doubt that the Christian title, in a world where Christian practice is no longer general, puts off many potential voters. Even those parties which have been at most pains to divest themselves of any denominational or even specifically Christian character have had little success in recruiting non-Christian or inactive Christian members. There are then those who would like to leave the experiment of Christian parties behind and take their chance in the open world. They are still a minority. An established Christian party or trade union is a solid core of power and influence which those who direct its fortunes are loath to throw away. Further, many sincerely convinced Christians are not happy at the picture of their co-religionists leavening the lump of religiously neutral trade unions or parties. Their point of view was well put in an address by a German to the Catholic Workers' International in 1955 — after Christian workmen in Germany had had some years' experience of a unified trade union movement:

> The situation in neutral workers' organisations is still more pernicious, that is in the so-called unified trade unions. Here too as well as in neutral political parties or employers' organisations we find people of different religious and political views. Here too the statutes guarantee religious tolerance and political neutrality. In these neutral unions the greater part of the members adhere to the socialist ideology. They are interested only in profiting from their numerical superiority and trying to introduce their ideas, that is their socialist ideals and aims, as the common basis for action. This is noticeable in the allocation of executive positions, in the appointment of officials, and in the delegation of representatives to works councils, firms' Boards, and key posts in the economy. One sees it too in their educational work, the contents of their press, and their efforts to win influence and acquire expert status in every area of life. They take no account of the views of Christian colleagues in the same union, and, in spite of the religious tolerance and political neutrality which is supposed to be guaranteed, try by means of both persuasion and compulsion — whichever happens to serve — to win over the Christians to their socialist views. Drops of water can wear away a stone, and this propaganda, working on Christian workers' minds from dawn to dusk, filters into them more and more of socialist doctrine, and gradually effaces the Christian view of life.

The notion that Christians should join together and stand together in all their activities is very strong on the Continent.

Some observers would say that the discussion so far has not touched on the main criticism which may be directed against these parties — that beside other parties their claim to be Christian is not justified in their performance. Certainly to act in politics at all is to lay oneself open to mistakes which some will describe as crimes. The Christian parties in Holland, Belgium and France may all be described as 'colonialist' by their enemies. Holland surrendered the larger part of her East Indian possessions after the war only with the greatest reluctance — and chiefly because her western allies refused to help her recover what she had lost while under German occupation in their cause. The M.R.P. stood for a French Algeria at least as far as wishing to see it federate with France, as well as supporting the long and luckless war in Indo-China. The Belgian Christian Social Party must carry large responsibility for policy in the Congo up to the ill-timed grant of independence. One of its leaders expressed the common view when he asked his compatriots: 'What would happen to our country, a high-cost producer, if we lost our outlets in the overseas territories, which in one way or another represent 70 per cent. of our foreign trade? What bankruptcies, what misery, what unemployment! Anyone with a sense of national responsibility must seek to solve the colonial problem in some other way.' As it was argued in the chapter on foreign affairs, the claim that only anti-colonialist policies are Christian has little to recommend it. But, taking into account the great division of opinion in the world on this question, there is much to be said for parties which must concern them-selves with it not sailing openly under the Christian colours. When Britain launched the Suez expedition in 1956, some Christians were in favour of it and some against, and they were distributed through all the parties, which from the point of view of their religion at the time was a happier arrangement than if they had all been enrolled within the Conservative Party.

High principles and aims are often brought low in the rough business of governing a country. None was higher than those up-held by the M.R.P. after the war and yet circumstances con-demned the party to take part in the endless and lamentable series of coalitions typical of French politics until de Gaulle revised the constitution. Its own doctrines — there is a tendency among Christian parties, seeking to work from principle, to be doctrinaire — were calculated, some English onlookers would say, to make the confusion worse. Its personalist policy led it to maintain that every citizen should feel he had a share in power and that devices for its constant exercise were desirable. The M.R.P. were zealous for proportional representation and the expression of popular will through the referendum. Unexceptional though such objectives were, they were hardly the remedies most needed by the French body politic, and though an eloquent logic could anchor each in Christian principle, the connexion to the plain man would seem tenuous and unconvincing.

What shall the judgment be between Christians in Britain who have so far rejected separate parties of their own and Christians on the Continent who have established them? Nothing in the history of the Christian parties in Western Europe suggests that they have been a disaster. But it would be difficult to maintain that their success has been impressive enough to justify the sceptical Englishman in abandoning his prejudices and following the example they have set. To say that things would have been much the same if Christian parties had not existed would be untrue. The character of the social services in Western Europe is coloured by Christian views. Yet they are not the only Christian views that might have been applied. It is not, for instance, immediately clear that the continental emphasis on increasing family income rather than on supplying free services to the family is an ideally Christian solution. The argument that a parent should be free in the exercise of his responsibility is compelling, but so is the objection that a father ought not to be allowed, when it is possible to prevent it, to use his freedom to his children's hurt. Nevertheless, if the special merit of the principles behind Christian Democratic schemes of social security is granted, it has still to be asked whether the gain is important enough to justify the apparatus of Christian parties. Western Germany, Holland, and Belgium have been ruled since the war by Christian Democratic governments or by governments in which Christian parties have been strongly represented. They are countries which can hold their heads high in the world and no sensible British citizen would wish to assert a general superiority over them. We take them as European

N

countries of worth, as we take our own to be. But if it were to be suggested that in them we might find among the mass of people, in their cultural life, in their politics and administration, a deeper moral sense and a higher moral practice than our own, we should demand strong evidence and examine it carefully. No one who knows these three countries would imagine such evidence was there to produce. Yet it should surely exist, in a convincing degree, if the application of Christian principles to politics, in which their governments believe, had been successfully made. In England, men like Sir Stafford Cripps, Canon Collins, and Sir Richard Acland have argued powerfully about what could be accomplished if Christianity were made the mainspring of political action. We see before our eyes in Europe cases where this has been attempted by good men, where Christian governments have been long in power, with at their back a wealth of carefully meditated Christian theory and a large body of Christian social organizations, from trade unions to family, youth and professional associations of all kinds. The spectacle is not in the least deplorable; it is no more than disappointing. We see governments which act in ways not greatly unlike our own and peoples in whom, for all the differences, we see the likeness of ourselves. This after all is the test. To risk the Christian name in the hazards of politics is justified only if the good results are large and obvious.

Great and undoubted gains must be required, because the dangers are great also. The organization of politics on religious lines can on occasion be a divisive force in the nation and no service to Christianity. It emphasizes the distinction between believer and unbeliever. Fortunately no severe traces of this potential evil have shown themselves in Western Europe since the war, though it is perhaps in Italy, where Church influence over the Christian party has been most apparent, that the danger is nearest. The record of history suggests that the frontier between religion and anti-religion, when accentuated, can become a centre of passionate conflict. France gave modern proof of this during the nineteenth century and at the beginning of the twentieth. Trouble can start even between two religious allegiances, and if, for instance, a union of Eire and Ulster were ever to come about, its difficulties would be the greater, one must feel, if the population were split up in Catholic and Protestant parties.

A plausible Christian reply to this would be to say that the nation as such is not of foremost concern and that whatever may happen in the country as a whole, Christianity itself may be strengthened by its followers forming political organizations of their own. In a world where so many have fallen away, in a society purely humanist in character, Christians tend to lose their sense of community together. As the Christian life depends on this sense of belonging, it is vital to put Christians into touch so that they may be sustained by each other. This is less a political than an evangelistic argument; it is to maintain that Christians are stronger in faith when they band together to perform the various tasks of life. The few isolated Christians in neutral political parties, trade unions, professional and social organizations, have small chance of exerting any effective influence — so the argument would go — and, worse than that, the strongly secularist environment inclines them themselves to laxity and discouragement. Just as the faith of a Christian is warmed when he stands in a packed congregation in a great cathedral, seeing himself surrounded for once by people who share his belief, so, it is argued, that same faith of his will be best supported, if he is a doctor, say, by his joining a professional organization of other Christian doctors, and, if he wishes to be active in politics, by entering a party made up of fellow Christians. As a strategy for the Christian mission in the world, this course of separation is not to be despised. There was originally a sense in Christians of being 'over against' the world which they condemned. A policy of banding together on every possible score not only strengthens the individual Christian, but it may attract the non-Christian, moved by this display of solidarity, and so act as a converting force. Necessarily, the upholders of these views would say, the separate organization of Christians tends to increase the distance between them and the rest, but emphasizing our distinctiveness increases the efficiency of our mission. 'He that is not with me is against me; and he that gathereth not with me scattereth.'

Different traditions, different circumstances, justify different courses of action. When religion is under attack, it may well be advisable for Christians to use the democratic conventions and form parties in their own defence. Yet it is possible to sacrifice spiritual life to worldly strength. Politics is to the Christian a secondary business. He has first, as St. Ignatius put it, to consider whether what he does ministers to the greater glory of God and the salvation of his own soul. Certainly the duty of Christians is to show forth to the world as much as they can of the love of God, in their relations together and to everyone, so that Christ may be lifted up and draw all men to Him. In the worship of the Church, in the life of religious communities, in works of charity and in Christian social organizations, a strong attractive power may lie, speaking to the outside world. But political parties and associations cannot speak with the same pure voice. At their highest they represent the interests, the secular needs, of the Churches. Where it is a question of survival, they may have reason behind them, but it is less in ordinary times. An organized religious interest, struggling for its own ends on the hustings and in parliaments, is no more attractive to the outsider than any other sectional selfishness. It is not wrong for a class, or an industry, to use politics for its own protection; in democratic politics it is an understood thing. But somehow, it is an English feeling, religion should fight its battle by other means.

Further, in a political party or association, a trade union, for example, we necessarily see men pursuing aims and policies which have no religious bearing whatsoever. If men are organized politically, they will spend the greater part of their time, rightly, pursuing what is to be pursued in politics. A great part of a Christian trade union's concern, as it is of any union, is simply to improve the wages and working conditions of its members, and this must sometimes be done in competition with other claimants. When a coalition is formed from parties of which one is Christian, the leaders of this Christian party, being politicians, are properly eager to secure as many ministerial posts for themselves as they can. It is the nature of a politician to desire power; if he did not desire it he would not be a good politician. But these aims and ambitions, legitimate enough when forwarded in the ordinary

way of the world, seem less in place under the sign of the Cross.
'A little leaven leaveneth the whole lump.' The banding together of Christians in their own parties may give them a sense of
warmth and security, but it cuts them off to some extent from their
fellow citizens. They are not totally cut off, of course. In the street,
in following the arts and sport, men and women mix freely whatever their ultimate beliefs, but the withdrawal of politics from
ground religiously neutral reduces the number of meeting points.
It is true that the secularist environment of the modern world is
insidious and that it is easy for Christians to fall into a weak conformity with it, but a Christian strategy cannot be based on the
assumption of Christian weakness. 'Vos estis lux mundi!' That is
what Christians are meant to be. It may seem foolish to apply
this divine encomium to the broken-backed Christians of modern
times, but however dim the light may have become, the command
is to show it. Christians must mingle with the crowd and be seen;
it is their evangelistic task, and it cannot be so well advanced if
Christians, instead of joining with other men in common tasks,
organize themselves in separate groupings.

No rule is to be made of this. To condemn what Christians have
done on the Continent would be presumptuous and unjustified.
If what they have done in their parties is compared with what
British Christians have done inside neutral bodies, the balance of
good or ill achieved will not be found greatly different. All that
may possibly be said is that Continental experience offers no
cogent reason for the British to change their own tradition. It
does at least preserve Christianity from the taunts which its
followers draw on to their faith when they behave as other men
do, as inevitably they must in politics. The harsher decisions of
war and peace are better taken by men, acting according to the
inspiration of their consciences one trusts, but making no open
profession of accepting a higher guidance than that of human
reason. This would seem to be a humble approach to matters
sometimes intensely difficult, whose settlement will often stop far
short this side of perfection.

10

Instruments of God

IN these days, when our increasing mastery of nature and power to plan our own environment seem securely established, there are temptations to drag in Christianity where it is hardly at home. We change things with an accomplished rapidity never seen before, and the feeling of many is that the changes should be in a Christian direction. But we have tried to indicate that this is not as possible as it may seem. The concerns of politics are different from those of religion and when attempts have been made to unite them, as in the Middle Ages, the results have been discouraging — at this distance, for example, the Crusades appear to have little in them of the Gospel light.

The Christian can never escape the tension caused by his dual allegiance. He is a citizen of this world which, though fallen and sinful, was created by God and is yet used by God for the realization of His purposes. But the Christian is called to citizenship of another world — and as a Church member already belongs to it, the Kingdom whose rule is love. He is led to attempt to apply the rule of the Kingdom to the affairs of this fallen world, his other home, and it will not fit. He may start off with great hopes, but in the end, it is always the same, the application fails. It should not surprise us. Does anything in human experience suggest that love may be institutionalized or legislated for?

Sometimes people speak as though the spirit which animated the Good Samaritan has been expressed by the establishment of the Welfare State. If a man is found half-dead by the side of an English road, the agencies of the State will perform for him each one of the Samaritan's acts; they will bind up his wounds, attend to his recovery, supply him with money if he needs it. But there is in reality no significant link between the Good Samaritan and the Welfare State. The Samaritan in his day acted over and above what nature and reason required, out of love. The Welfare State in our day is a rationally chosen means of distributing resources so as to meet human needs. It is organized self-interest issuing in self-help; it is a refined modern extension of the defensive mounds which surrounded a primitive settlement.

The organized satisfaction of human wants belongs to the natural order. Christians do not despise this order, for it is God's creation. He has placed them in it; from it only may they find Him. It is their road, their throughway, and for the natural order they have as much responsibility as other men. The exercise of this responsibility in company with other men calls for no form of Christian inspiration. If such were needed, the Creator would have set men impossible tasks in the series of States that existed before the Christian revelation.

Christianity, one believes, is less about this world than about the Kingdom to come, and the ethics of that Kingdom, the ethics of the Gospel, cannot be applied in this sin-corrupted world — except, and then only in moments of grace, in personal relationships with God and man. What is often miscalled Christian morality is usually no more than natural morality. The Christian supports natural morality because it too springs from God, but the Crucifixion did not take place in order to call attention even to the Ten Commandments, let alone a largely rational system of ethics. Christ came to earth to preach the Kingdom and the outgoing love which characterizes it, which we are called upon to show for God and for each other. This is Christianity, a supernatural religion, and it is this which leaves it so largely irrelevant to politics, set in the natural order.

It is surely this distinction between the natural and the supernatural order which our Lord makes in the celebrated saying, 'Render unto Caesar the things that are Caesar's and unto God the things that are God's.' We may see the matter more clearly by contrasting the Greek view of the State with the Christian. For Aristotle, the State was the means by which the Good Life was realized. He envisaged no conflict between a man's religion and his duty to the State, because for him, broadly speaking, God and Caesar were one. But when Christians gained power in the world and so had to consider the question of the State, they drew a clear distinction which the ancients did not make. Church and State are ranged against each other; there are two swords, not one; the Middle Ages saw an unending dispute over the delimitation of the two spheres of authority. God and Caesar, Church and State, *Civitas Dei* and *Civitas terrena* — one sees in practical arrangement and intellectual concept alike a characteristically Christian division. The distinction may throw light on the findings of our inquiry. It is revealing that those who believe most strongly that Christianity may be related to politics, like Cripps, tend to hold a Greek view of the State. They feel there should be one city only, not two; this leads them to dream of raising the Kingdom of God on earth. They part company with traditional Christian attitudes and in our view they are mistaken.

But if politics can never be made Christian, in any way that satisfies such a definition, this does not mean that Christians are not called to take part. They are particularly called to take part by the side of other men. The natural order in which all men live was created by God and it must be sustained by men. Such work for a Christian is a work of love. God loves his children and loving Him means to love them, and the arena of love is the world; its sinfulness is no reason for turning our backs on it. Serving God's purpose in this way is to show love, but love is not to be caught in a principle or a law. No principle of love can be appealed to which even gives us clear guidance in our dealings with our neighbour. As Emil Brunner says: 'We never know what is right for us, nor what is best for the other person. We go astray when we think that we can deduce this from some principle. . . .'

The politician takes up his career as the farmer or the engineer or the craftsman takes up his. Many influences come into play— family, special opportunities, particular inclinations. No divine call is usually heard, but the young Christian, making his choice, will seek, as Shaftesbury did, to relate it to God's will. He will believe that he, like all men, is an instrument of God's purposes, and if he enters politics it is in this solemn understanding that he should begin. As Brunner writes: 'I have to accept thankfully the place, in which I am now set, from the hands of Providence, as the sphere of my life, as the place in which ... I am to meet my neighbour in love.' There is great value still in the idea of vocation, which Luther expressed in his famous reference to the dairy-maid. In her work on the farm, he said, in doing her daily duty as a dairy-maid, she could and should serve God and her neighbour and this was more important than all those other duties of hers, which might be described as specifically religious. God does not disdain to use this world, with its nations, States, and associations, and we must not. In using it we become entangled with the sin which is found in its every part, but into this predicament we have been called, ordered, by God Himself, and our share in this sin is covered, so Christians believe, by the redeeming sacrifice of His Son. The Christian is called upon to act beside other men and no assurance is given him that he will sense God's purpose better than they. He can no more aim to be a Christian statesman than a Christian engineer. Politics has at any one time its own techniques, aims and standards, vary though they may, and in the light of them as they are in his lifetime, the Christian's effort must be to make a good politician and no more. He stands here on a par with the non-Christian, just as there are no denominations in the science of physics. His religion will give him no special guidance in his public task, as it will do within his personal relationships with close neighbours; but it can, and should, endow him with a greater energy and a profounder seriousness before his task than he would have had without it — that is, if his religion means as much as Gladstone's did to him. It is as Brunner puts it:

> The Christian must take an active part in politics because there, if nowhere else, he learns that we are poor sinful human beings, who with the best will in the world cannot do the real Good. He must also take an active part as a citizen of the State, because there he must show whether he really cares about the weal or woe of his brethren, whether he really is in earnest about active love. Only when we know how a man acts in the sphere of the State have we to some extent a reliable criterion by which to judge whether faith has a real penetrating influence on his life or not.

There are temptations peculiar to a politician even in a democracy, and choices which are sometimes terrible for a man who

has in his mind the thought of the Kingdom and its commands as
well as the knowledge of his duty to serve in this world. But the
call to Christians to enter politics is still uttered, we must believe,
in countries which are not democratic. Each choice must to some
extent be governed by circumstances — for our whole argument
has been that there are no general rules. But if one accepts the view
that Christians are called upon by God to play their part in the
politics of this sinful world, then those Christians who live in
countries with Fascist or Communist régimes may feel bound to
enrol in Fascist or Communist politics, though keeping their
minds clear of the paganism of the one and the atheism of the
other. From our democratic vantage-point, we assume rather
easily that the duty of Christians under such régimes is to oppose
them. We may sympathize with the Christian who lies low
out of fear, but one of goodness and courage would, we suppose,
feel bound to resist. As has been said, all turns upon circumstances.
No régime is sacrosanct and an attempt at change which would be
foolish when the Government is strong becomes feasible when the
Government is weak. But where a Communist régime, for
example, is strongly entrenched, as in Russia, it may well seem to
an Eastern Orthodox Christian that in the special circumstances
of his country, if he is to heed the call to play a part in politics at
all, he should do so in co-operation with the prevailing Communist forces. In spite of its errors and cruelties, the Communist
Party in Russia is sustaining, developing and using its part of the
world created by God.

The truth is we do not know what politics may demand. We
are commanded to enter but in a sense we do so blindfold. At one
moment, all is stable and quiet; the choices are respectable and
need give a Christian little anxiety. At the next, some convulsion
or political catastrophe overtakes the country or the world, and
the evils between which choices have to be made grow gigantic
and whatever a Christian decides to do, he may feel, will be a
denial of his religion. That is not so; he must show courage and
act according to his own best lights and those of the men at his
side. He has accepted the call to politics; he must follow it to the
end. However dark the choice, moreover, however horrifying

the future it may open, God is still there, as concerned as ever for the world He has made. A non-Christian may scorn this picture of God 'as concerned as ever for the world' when His creatures may at some future date be found attempting to destroy themselves in nuclear warfare. But for the Christian it is the true picture. God never turns away in horror from the world; His eyes are never averted; for as long as His purposes require, He is using it, and He stands at the side of the politician when he determines the issue of life or death for his fellow men.

Politics necessarily involves judging before the time. Men are condemned or defended by their contemporaries long before all the evidence has become available, and we must remember that much of the evidence, how the issue actually appeared to the man in his own mind, how he grappled with it, what early influences of his upbringing affected him, can never be known at all to any except God. Yet snap judgments will always be made, most of all of politicians. The world judges by results; we must suppose that God will judge more by motives. It is at least possible, as things stand today, that the hand which formally and technically releases large-scale nuclear war on the world will be Christian. Such a war, we must hope, will never be waged, but if such a calamity came about, as the forces are now arranged, and with the views held on both sides, everyone must admit the possibility of a Christian's holding major responsibility. Many would say that such a man had betrayed his religion, rejecting in one moment the Gospel message of love and the reasoned counsels of the Natural Law to preserve the created world. Nevertheless it is not open to the Christian to say now of this man, any more than he may say it of any other man, that he will be condemned by God.

So much emotion covers the issue of nuclear warfare, that we shall not choose it as our main example of those more fearful political choices which Christians, with so little definite guidance, are called upon to make. Instead, we shall consider briefly the subject of political assassination, because in this discussion the feelings of fewer readers will be hotly engaged. Murder as a political weapon is generally rejected; few, if any, of the opponents of South Africa's racial policies approved of the attempt made in 1960 upon the life of Dr. Verwoerd, the Prime Minister. Yet political murder is still a fairly frequent occurrence, and in 1961, for example, the dictator of Dominica, Trujillo, met his end in this way. Much was written by Christians in earlier years on this matter, as they considered the means of redress open to peoples labouring under foreign oppression or a ruler who outraged their consciences. In the sixteenth century, when tyrannicide was a favourite topic, the Huguenot publication *Vindiciae contra Tyrannos* examined exhaustively the general question, 'Whether it is lawful, and if so, to whom, in what manner, and to what extent, to resist a prince who is violating the law of God?' Even in medieval times the deed was held appalling enough to be thought of only as a last resort. The tyrant was to be remonstrated with, rebuked by the national assemblies and urged to reform, before any attempt on his life could be sanctioned on Christian grounds. Aquinas stopped short; he favoured resistance to an unjust régime but in simple pragmatical arguments he rejected assassination. Bad men, he thought, more often undertook tyrannicide than good men, and, since bad men find obeying kings no easier than obeying tyrants, the recognition of the private citizen's right to kill tyrants involved more chance of losing good rulers than being relieved of bad. Much later S. T. Coleridge gave a wise opinion:

I think with Machiavel and with Spinosa, for many and weighty reasons assigned to those philosophers, that it is difficult to conceive a case, in which a good man would attempt tyrannicide, because it is difficult to conceive one, in which a wise man would recommend it. In a small State, included within the walls of a single city, and where the tyranny is maintained by foreign guards, it may be otherwise, but in a nation or empire it is perhaps inconceivable, that the circumstances which made a tyranny possible, should not likewise render the removal of the tyrant useless. The patriot's sword may cut off the Hydra's head; but he possesses no brand to stanch the active corruption of the body, which is sure to reproduce a successor.

Much Christian argument has been on the other side. The views of the Spanish Jesuit, Mariana, are not without relevance today, when we still have in mind the achievements and crimes of Hitler and Mussolini. Mariana agreed with his medieval predecessors that before recourse was had to assassination the unjust ruler should be approached through the national assemblies or parliaments. But if the assemblies were not permitted to meet or to act — or if they had become, as we may add from modern experience, the mere creatures of the dictator — then the citizen was justified in killing the tyrant at his discretion. He believed that giving respectability to the doctrine of tyrannicide would have good political effects, for by its very existence it would have a restraining effect upon rulers, reminding them that if they oppressed their subjects they might expect attempts upon their lives and that at all times the authority of their people was above their own.

It will be seen that Christians apply to the practice of assassination the plain arguments of natural reason. Is it practicable? Do the circumstances promise a good result? These are the questions they raise. Yet they are discussing the political usefulness of murder. It throws light upon the nature of the political realm into which Christians, as we have argued, are called by God to enter. They cannot escape the dread choices which the doctrine of the lesser evil from time to time inexorably presents. Generally speaking, the opinions of Coleridge are admirably to the point. Further, in any functioning democracy, even of the South African sort, it ought to be morally impossible for a voting member of the democracy (as distinct, perhaps, from the disfranchised) to contemplate the political assassination of particular elected persons, who, far from being tyrants, have been appointed to power by the freely expressed will of their peoples. However, this does not allow the Christian to put the question out of his head. It is true that the strong basic structure of the greater modern States, such as Soviet Russia, removes any political utility from the assassination of particular rulers. There are a hundred capable of filling a sudden gap. But the special circumstances of Germany under Hitler show that there are sometimes other possibilities even in modern States, and in Western discussions of the Army conspiracy of July 1944 against his life, which failed, one does not detect any criticism on ethical grounds of the attempt itself. In fact, Hitler's case exactly suited the Christian advocates in past centuries of the respectability of political assassination. He was a tyrant oppressing large sections of his nation, and he was irreplaceable, because much of his power was bound up with his own unique qualities. It was his irreplaceability which clinches the argument. There were other powerful personalities at the head of the Nazi party and it is unlikely that it would have disintegrated immediately upon Hitler's death. Yet if he had been struck down as late as 1939 the removal of his mesmeric hold would almost certainly have changed the whole balance of forces within Germany and it would have been reasonable to suppose that war might have been avoided, at least at that time. Political assassination is generally execrated by Christian and non-Christian alike, and rightly so, but we have produced an instance where its utility would in the light of later history be conceded by most good men. If they are rare, occasions can arise when the good Christian politician may have to order a killing.

It is easier to speak of a divine call to politics if it is conceived of as a beneficent activity for improving the human lot. That is one side only of the picture, and it ignores the coercive powers which belong to the State. The dispersal of riotous crowds by rifle fire, the refusal of a reprieve to a man condemned by the judiciary, the decision to resort to war, the order, in certain circumstances, that a life should be stopped — there are moments in politics when these things have to be done and they are moments which will come again. A Christian in politics may evade them no more than another kind of man. They arise out of the sin that is in the world, in the Christian as much as in all men; yet though action is mixed with sin, action must be taken. It is not for Christians to contract out of the human responsibility for running this world which, in spite of everything, is God's world.

The Christian who is an active party politician will face temptations peculiar to his calling which perhaps encourages pride, the first of the cardinal sins, more than any other way of life. To point to such temptations is not to say that all politicians succumb to them, and there is no intention here to blacken a whole profession. It is merely to draw attention to occupational hazards which can create attitudes especially injurious to the frame of mind which a

Christian should seek to possess. A politician must take the lead, if not at all levels at least in some, and his supporters expect this of him. A candidate for Parliament, called out of the anonymous obscurity of ordinary life to be his party's representative, tastes from the very beginning a new kind of existence, and this is still true though his chances of actual election are exiguous. He is raised high on platforms, he makes speeches, performs ceremonies; he is always in the public eye and his supporters, jealous for his honour which is theirs, will seek for him the highest place at banquets. It is a small world, this constituency in which he moves, but a section of it has chosen him as its leader. He stands for his followers; for their sake he must endeavour to exhibit his virtues and hide his vices. He must carefully cloak any natural concern he may have for his own interests and career, for the only purpose that he is expected to have before him is the public good. Like an actor, he plays a part, but he plays it more continuously, and the exercise is a little insidious, for he is playing the part of himself, only larger than he knows himself to be. Lord Longford, then Frank Pakenham, wrote a useful analysis of these aspects of the political life in an article called ' "Grey Eminence" and Political Morality' in the *Political Quarterly* (Oct.–Dec. 1942), which was later discussed in Dr. J. H. Oldham's *Christian News-Letter* (8 January 1947).

From the first the political candidate is confronted with a succession of pressure groups — for Sunday observance, Church schools, temperance, old-age pensioners and the like — all promising votes in exchange for his pledged support for their cause. The candidate of a strong party nationally, standing for one of its safe seats, is able to meet these approaches sympathetically but to withhold promises which he knows his party will not honour. A candidate more weakly placed, seeking all the votes he can muster, is more tempted to offer worthless pledges. (Christian citizens active in the local sphere have a duty to show some understanding of the candidate's difficulties in such matters.) The temptations of electioneering are many. The Gospel insistence on doing good in private, of taking the lower place, of avoiding a Pharisaic parade of righteousness — all of it is almost necessarily overborne. Self-advertisement is essential to a candidate; electors must be made aware and admiring of him if they are to give him their votes. He is compelled to make a public show of himself, his virtues and talents. In general terms, a Christian must regard this as part of the price that must be paid for entering, on God's call, into the politics of an imperfect world. Benedetto Croce in his *Politics and Morals* established a humanist position which Christians may also accept: 'The initial situation is given in each case; the men with whom we have to deal are always what they are; their ideas, their prejudices, their good or bad dispositions, their virtues and their defects furnish the material on which and with which we must work, and there is no way of substituting for them more pleasing material.' It is necessary to gain co-operation for political enterprises and to this end, Croce considers, it is perfectly proper to soothe men's illusions, flatter their vanity and speak to them in terms, sometimes, of their most superficial ideas. No doubt there are times when a politician may act as an educative force — indeed, all politics is a form of education — but of no man is it more demanded that he should come down to the level of his audience. He must establish a connexion with them; to disdain the contents of simple minds is almost to deny the democracy which most politicians in Britain profess. This is not to suggest of course that any politician should become the slave and mouthpiece of popular opinion. That is not required of him, and Burke said all that needs saying about the duty of a Member of Parliament to his constituents. But a politician is in these days expected to speak to the electors in their own language, to start from what is already in their heads, and if he will not show this much concern there remains little reason why they should give him their votes.

Nevertheless, it is clear that the counsel to keep oneself 'unspotted from the world' comes with a special urgency to the Christian in politics. It is, of course, impossible to fulfil. But the Christian must be aware of what his vocation requires him to do; he must keep the counsel before him as a restraint against the complete abandonment of himself to the pursuit of popularity; he has to examine in private what he has done in public; he has to guard his aspirations. Maintaining the order of God's created world requires of him acts and attitudes which are in conflict with God's other call to enter His Kingdom. The lower of the two standards, the two moralities, must not crowd out of his mind the image of the higher. So long as he preserves that image, by daily contrasting it with his practice in his vocation in this world, his falling short of it will be covered at the last by God's mercy. The tension a Christian should feel, set as he is between the natural and supernatural orders, is hard to catch and to explain. The non-Christian reading here the advice to a Christian to act in politics as other men do and recollect, rather than apply, the counsels of supernatural morality, may possibly condemn religion as totally ineffectual. He would be wrong. The habit of recollection erects in the Christian mind a disposition to resist complete surrender to the world. Surrender there must be, if the world's work is to be done, but there is, or should be, in the Christian's mind a resistance to a complete capitulation to these worldly values. This marginal resistance, though the margin only be narrow, while it upholds the Christian's links with the Kingdom, can also serve to raise temporal standards. Much of this process must lie undetected, but we cite a possible example quoted in an earlier chapter. It may be that one instance of the working of this marginal resistance is to be found in Wilberforce's condemnation of Dundas in 1805. If he took this course in answer to the promptings of a Christian conscience more exacting than the demands made by society at that time, his action served to strengthen the doctrine of ministerial responsibility, which society has found valuable.

Power corrupts, as Acton noted, but power is what the politician pursues and what to a greater or lesser extent he possesses. The least of them has a certain power in his own constituency — and the sense of power comes out in various ways. The public meeting, though a feature of all elections, is not quite what it was — the television screen has usurped part of its place — but it still retains something of what its employment by Victorian Liberalism gave it, when as Mr. Lovell Cocks notes in *The Nonconformist Conscience*:

o

The huge audiences, the hymns or songs they sang, the mounting excitement, and, above all, the oratory — all combined to proclaim to the world the numbers and influence of those who supported the cause, and to bring to those supporters a deepened conviction of the nobility of their aims and of the unspeakable wickedness of the evils they had gathered to denounce.

He went on to describe the effect of meetings on the politicians who addressed them.

The public meeting assailed the orator with strange and subtle temptations. Few of his hearers had come to listen to a reasoned exposition of the case; the minds of most of them were already made up, and they had come to rejoice in the strength of their cause and to hail the approaching day of its triumph. In this apocalyptic atmosphere even the doubters were more likely to be swayed by the emotional stress of the occasion than by arguments. And when we take into account the effect of the cheering crowd on the speaker's own sub-conscious mind, we are not surprised that the masters of assemblies have sometimes become their slaves. Not that Gladstone and Bright ever pandered to the selfish passions of their hearers; but the influence of the massed levies of puritanism they addressed is clearly traceable in their speeches. Their appeals are couched in the language of moral idealism. Every political issue becomes a sharp cleavage between right and wrong. They use the whites and blacks and avoid the half-tones.

If few politicians possess the faculty of men like Lloyd George and Aneurin Bevan for dominating huge audiences by the spell of words, most from time to time experience the afflatus which comes from having stirred a crowd. 'He played on all the strings of the human heart', wrote Thomas Jones of Lloyd George, 'and matched with each the mobile landscape of his face and bodily posture — the alluring smile, the scowling visage, the thrilling whisper, the eloquent pince-nez dangling from its black silk ribbon, the menacing finger, the arms outstretched to the utter-most.' If the grand style of oratory is now less attempted by those at the centre of things, it still has exponents on the periphery, whose emotions sometimes carry themselves and others away. The Christian with such powers has to watch himself very narrowly. Different though his methods are, the politician who can succeed on television — quietly confident, sincere, modestly displaying a heartfelt sympathy with ordinary folk — needs to examine himself as much as the old platform orator. Successful public utterance is a great stimulus of pride. It does not do for a politician in his public performances to admit doubt or ignorance. He must appear fully in command of himself and his task; he must show the confidence in himself which he expect others to have. All this can enter into the settled habit of his mind.

Lord Longford, in his *Political Quarterly* article, noted that the politician has not only to persuade vast numbers of his fellow-men of the superiority of his views and of his personality, but also 'to collaborate with vast numbers of his fellow-men to the point of ardently espousing and publicly recommending doctrines with which he is frequently in imperfect sympathy and to which on occasion he may be strongly antagonistic'. Party politics necessitates the acceptance and at times the propagation of views with which individual members may not agree. Resignation is open to any one at any time, and a fair number of politicians avail themselves of it on serious points of principle. There may be no moral element in such a course; it may mean no more than that the man has a different judgment from that of his party on the way the future will turn and he resigns so as the better to enjoy the rewards of prescience at a later date. Frequently, however, the resigner believes that a moral issue is involved and when he feels thus strongly it is for the health of politics that he should be willing to stake his career. Nevertheless, if politicians resigned every time they disagreed with their party's course of action, politics would become impossible. Party loyalty contributes to the stability of government and no one can quarrel with the moderate means generally employed for its enforcement. On occasions it has its uglier side, for groups can be crueller and less forgiving than persons. 'We'll break you for this' are words recently reported to have been shouted after a young dissentient minister as he left a meeting of his party in a House of Commons committee room. Parties can show a hard ruthlessness in preserving themselves. And a certain hardness is a quality almost necessary in politicians.

Lloyd George used to say that courage was the gift especially needed in politics, and with it often goes the will to power and leadership. 'The urge to be first' is characteristic of the born politician and a man who denies himself this particular ambition, which can exist in him obviously or hidden away, is unlikely to go far. Some men climb quietly, like Lord Attlee, some more combatively like Ernest Bevin and Aneurin Bevan, but the desire to climb must be expected. Men respect fighting quality in a man; Sir Winston Churchill's lonely struggle in the 1930s, his refusal to be discouraged by isolation, stood him in good stead when this country and its politicians faced the danger of war. Some statesmen are like those battering rams used in medieval sieges under whose cover and assault power other men pressed to the attack. Gentleness and humility are not to be found in such tigerish characters who nevertheless can always expect to win success in politics, if their pugnacity is balanced by patience and a shrewd head. How much that men prize in their politicians is summed up in the moral Sir Winston Churchill chose to prefix his *The Second World War*:

> In War: Resolution
> In Defeat: Defiance
> In Victory: Magnanimity
> In Peace: Goodwill.

They are virtues of the natural order, but virtues none the less.

The environment of the politician is rough, worldly and exacting. It imposes great physical strains. The demands of constituents, the need to master to some extent a succession of difficult matters, the constant travel, the perpetual argument, the smoking and the drinking (though there are those who abstain from both), the many calls for public appearances and writing, the unending struggle for place or for influence over those who hold place — all these make for a life which is intensely hard. It leaves little time or energy for the pursuit of religion, though for this the convinced Christian will determine to keep a place.

This vocation to which God calls some Christians, it will be seen, is unfriendly in many ways to the Christian life. When Sir Harold Nicolson suggested to Lord Curzon that Scawen Blunt seemed to him to be a highly conceited and belligerent person, he got the reply, 'But aren't we all?' Certainly the profession of politics encourages in a marked degree pride, emulation, duplicity, self-seeking and disputatiousness. A Christian cannot free himself entirely from these worldly impulses. To ask a politician to forgo pride altogether is like asking a medieval knight to abandon the concept of honour. It is a snare rising out of the natural order which if one wishes to participate in the world's affairs one cannot entirely escape. It is one of the motive forces of political life; in Gladstone it came out in that firm sense he had of righteousness. It is absurd to expect a politician not to seek his own advancement, or to avoid the dispute in which he may show his mettle or the duplicity sometimes demanded by political craftsmanship.

Some men, it will be noticed, miss or resist these temptations more than others. If Cripps was at times too egotistical to listen to what others said, in Lansbury the traces of pride are harder to find and he was not a self-seeking man — though he was factious. Some make a temperate entry into politics — only half immersing themselves as it were — and, being less committed, are less taken by its lures. Lord Halifax perhaps, a devout practising Christian, seems to have kept himself well outside the hurly-burly. But if some have greater means of resistance, they are all open to the special temptations of their trade.

The Christian politician must see all this and admit all this, as a man possessing a dual loyalty to the *Civitas Dei* and to the *Civitas terrena*. He has to find time, in his physically exhausting day, for self-examination and prayer — moments when he consciously sets against the higher call his actions in response to the lower, which is still of God. He must not be blind to what sin contributes to his life and to the essential activity in which he has found his vocation. He has to recollect how much in the public world, which God has bidden him to enter, is a hurt and an affront to God. On his ears should fall always certain of the Reproaches, those one could say were aimed at the politician, sung movingly on Good Friday in the ancient churches of western Christendom:

Ego dedi tibi sceptrum regale; et tu dedisti capiti meo spineam coronam.

Ego te exaltavi magna virtute: et tu me suspendisti in patibulo crucis.

Popule meus, quid feci tibi? aut in quo contristavi te? responde mihi.[1]

It will be an aid to the Christian politician, more necessary to him than to others, to keep before him the thought of death and judgment. As Jeremy Taylor said, 'He that will die well and happily must dress his soul by a diligent and frequent scrutiny.' But above all as a Christian living his life in the world of politics he must look to the personal relationships that it brings. He will be a good politician, loyal as it lies within his power and conscience to his party, contributing to its policies, sharing in the dire decisions to which they sometimes lead. In all this, he will be as other men. But it is important that in the rough and tumble of politics, in ways that are appropriate to him and appear quite natural to others, in the corridors, committee rooms and eating places, he should set an example of love. It calls for no excess, no stupidity; but he should be accessible, open, warm, and no confidence of the heart given him should be betrayed. Other men should see something about him — not that he is ascetic, or pious, or a crank — but that there is in him a friendliness, a willingness to help, an outgoingness. For all around him, in the courts of power, are his neighbours, and to them he gives what Christianity has made of him. It is not so much in policy or statecraft that his religion is to be found, though both may be touched by it, as in his relations with his fellow men.

After taking many decisions on which his religion gave him little guidance, after living among temptations subtler than most men endure, and more damaging to the soul, the Christian politician comes one day before the judgment of God. He is indeed acting under it all the time. How may he be fairly judged by rules never entirely clear to him? In private life the sense of guilt

---

[1] I gave thee a royal sceptre: and thou hast given me a crown of thorns.

I have exalted thee with great strength: and thou hast hanged me on the cross.

O my people, what have I done to thee? or in what way have I afflicted thee? answer me.

is keener; the wrongs one has done stand clear. In politics the rights and wrongs of action are obscure. Mistakes — every politician knows he makes them; when does a mistake become a sin?

But it is not only on his private life of human relationships that a politician will be judged; his motives and attitudes in public life will be called to account. If the rules in this sphere are vaguer, they exist. There is the good disclosed by natural reason which it is for every man to follow and there is the higher call of God's Kingdom which every Christian hears. A politician may often be perplexed and torn between the two moralities, but we may believe that when he acts below the mean of them, he is not unaware of failure. He has no cause to fear the judgment of his opponents or public opinion. Certainly a politician who falls from place after being condemned by public opinion merits his failure; it is part of his trade to keep public opinion behind him. But to the issue of his final judgment, the outcry of Press and people, invariably ignorant of all that was in train in the situation and in his mind, is irrelevant and hardly worth attention. In May 1940, the House of Commons debated the conduct of the War and the failure of our attempt to counter the German invasion of Norway. Chamberlain was still Prime Minister; he had striven hard for peace and afterwards was required to lead his country in war, a task to which he was unfitted. In the debate our weakness and lack of preparation became increasingly obvious and exasperation mounted. There came a point when a speaker turned passionately upon Chamberlain and cried, 'In the name of God, go.' Chamberlain did resign and Winston Churchill took his place. But when we try now to judge Chamberlain — and how unfitted we are to judge in any final sense, either as ordinary men or as historians — we do not hold against him as a man his failure to inspire as a war leader. It was an office thrust upon him for a short time, and he failed in it, not morally, but technically.

It is no easier for us to pronounce on those politicians who succeed. What may we make of Bismarck, a deeply religious man? He believed intensely in the nationhood of Germany, and nationalism in his day did not receive the disrespect which is its lot in ours. To create modern Germany, he went to war with Austria, with Denmark and with France, and in this course he believed profoundly that in the eye of God he was securing the destiny of his country. If the strengthening of the German State and the expansion of its territories by force were crimes, most of the other statesmen of Bismarck's day were criminals. We recall Gladstone's attack on Egypt and Salisbury's patient ambition to raise Britain's power.

Brunner makes a good distinction here.

It is not the Christian politicians (*Realpolitiker*) of the *Bismarck* type who are the danger, but the theorists who hang on their coat-tails and begin to justify what those men did, with a sense of deep responsibility in the sight of God as right at that moment, in a general theoretical way; theorists who derive the right of an amoral type of politics from that which these politicians, as a rule, did as a necessity of State, but which weighed heavily upon their souls.

Machiavelli is the most famous of such theorists. His indifference to political morality, even of the natural order, springs from his basic assumption that the world and men are evil through and through. He says:

Whoever organizes a state and arranges laws for the government of it must presuppose that all men are wicked and that they will not fail to show their natural depravity whenever they have a clear opportunity, though possibly it may lie concealed for a while.

This is a simplification which Christians, with others, are sometimes tempted to accept. But the depravity is not total; the goodness of men is as obvious as their badness. It is this double quality of every man and every situation which creates the difficulty of the Christian politician. Policies which ask too much from men are impractical; policies which ask too little, acts implying a contempt for men or the value of their lives, are repugnant. 'Cesare Borgia was accounted cruel; but it was to that cruelty that he was indebted for the advantage of uniting Romagna to his other dominions' — Machiavelli's tripping maxims are far removed in spirit from Bismarck's earnest building of a greater Germany, which was for him a moral cause. Caught as they are in the stream of events and opinion, less free than they seem to act as they will, statesmen must often feel that the judgment seat of God will be more understanding of their political strivings than the parliaments of their fellow men. Any man, looking back over his life, will recall many deliberate actions which, as it were, can be settled only between himself and God. He will discover things done by him, possibly at the end of a chain of sins and errors leaving him no good choices, which he knows cannot be defended, even before men. His only hope is in that understanding which is called mercy. This is even truer of the politician.

At the climax of our Lord's life on earth, He was confronted with the politician, the procurator of Judaea, the agent of the Emperor. Pilate was in Jerusalem to maintain order and authority, and Rome like all successful ruling powers was severe with her administrators who failed in this elementary task. The Jews were well known as restless subjects, prone to riot and rebellion. Pilate had already dealt savagely with some of them; in fact his handling of a later outbreak cost him his post. When Jesus was taken before him, the leading Jews demanding His execution with an excited crowd at their back, Pilate was concerned with two principles by which his country set store — order and justice. As often in political decisions, these two goods appeared in conflict; it was not possible to pursue them both. To do justice to the man before him would provoke a tumult and the breakdown of order. Pilate hesitated before his dilemma; he attempted to shift his responsibility on to the Jews who were demanding a life. But, in fact, he had taken his decision, which was sensible, and in natural-law terms moral. He chose to preserve order, which was a good choice, because when order breaks down innocent lives are lost. Other Romans, including Julius Caesar, had tried to show an understanding of the peculiar religious susceptibilities of the Jews. Here, on the count of a religion which he did not understand, Pilate knowingly denied justice to one man for the sake of saving the lives of others — and his own career. Our Lord, as we know, did not judge this politician harshly: 'Thou wouldest have no power against me, except it were given thee from above: therefore he that delivered me unto thee hath greater sin.' Pilate is not sinless. But in this saying our Lord shows His understanding and acceptance

of the political profession. The power of politicians comes from
above — not only from their Government (Pilate was the servant
of a Government, to which he was responsible), but from God
Himself, the fount of worldly order. Politicians, vice-regents of
God, necessary to his purposes, may expect from Him a judgment
different from that made of them by their fellow men. But God's
judgment they must face, and at the last like all men they must
cry:

> Recordare, Jesu pie,
> Quod sum causa tuae viae
> Ne me perdas illa die.[1]

The Christian politician must aim to act so that at the end he
may utter this appeal in hope and without fear.

[1] Remember, Jesus, that it was for me you lived your life; save me at the last.

Further Reading

(Dates, except when specified, refer to English publication.)

Cullman, O., *The State in the New Testament*. 1957.

Gierke, Otto, *Natural Law and the Theory of Society*. Introduction by Ernest Barker. 1950.

Gore, Charles, *Christ and Society*. 1928.

Wood, H. G. and others, *The Kingdom of God and History*. 1938.

Troeltsch, Ernst, *The Social Teaching of the Christian Churches*. 1931.

Cambridge Medieval History.

Carlyle, R. W. and A. J., *A History of Medieval Political Theory in the West*. 1950.

D'Entrèves, A. P., *The Medieval Contribution to Political Thought*. 1939.

— —, *Aquinas: Selected Political Writings* (ed.). 1948.

Powicke, F. M., *The Christian Life in the Middle Ages*. 1935.

Rivière, Jean, *Le Problème de l'Église et de l'État au temps de Philippe le Bel*. Louvain, 1926.

Tawney, R. H., *Religion and the Rise of Capitalism*. 1926.

Weber, M., *The Protestant Ethic and the Spirit of Capitalism*. 1930.

Bennett, J. C., *Christians and the State*. 1958.

Berdyaev, Nicolas, *Slavery and Freedom*. 1943.

Brunner, Emil, *The Divine Imperative: a Study in Christian Ethics*. 1937.

Butterfield, H., *Christianity and History*. 1950.

Cecil, Lord Hugh, *Conservatism*. 1912.

Collins, Diana, *Christian Action*. 1949.

COPEC, *Reports* (12) presented to the Conference on Christian Politics, Economics and Citizenship at Birmingham (1924). 1925.

Cripps, Sir Stafford, *Towards Christian Democracy*. 1945.

Croce, Benedetto, *Politics and Morals*. 1946.

D'Arcy, M. C., *The Sense of History*. 1959.

Dawson, Christopher, *Beyond Politics*. 1939.

Ehler, S. A. and Morrall, J. B., *Church and State through the Centuries*. 1954.

Eliot, T. S., *The Idea of a Christian Society*. 1939.

Fogarty, Michael, *Christian Democracy in Western Europe 1820–1953.* 1957.

Greenslade, S. L., *The Church and the Social Order.* 1948.

Iremonger, F. A., *William Temple.* 1948.

Jenkins, Daniel, *Equality and Excellence.* 1961.

Lindsay, A. D., *The Two Moralities: Our Duty to God and to Society.* 1940.

Macmurray, John, *The Clue to History.* 1938.

Maritain, Jacques, *Freedom in the Modern World.* 1935.

— —, *True Humanism.* 1938.

Mauriac, François (and others), *Le Communisme et les Chrétiens.* Paris, 1937.

Mayer, J. P., *Political Thought: the European Tradition.* 1939.

Micklem, N., *The Theology of Politics.* 1941.

Oldham, J. H., *The Churches Survey their Task* (Report of the Oxford conference). 1937.

Pike, James A., *Doing the Truth.* 1956.

Prestige, G. L., *The Life of Charles Gore.* 1935.

Niebuhr, H. Richard, *Christ and Culture.* New York, 1951.

Niebuhr, Reinhold, *Moral Man and Immoral Society.* 1936.

— —, *The Nature and Destiny of Man.* 2 vols., 1941, 1943.

Raven, C. E., *Christian Socialism 1848–1854.* 1920.

Reckitt, Maurice B., *Maurice to Temple.* 1947.

Sturzo, L., *Church and State.* 1939.

Talmon, J. L., *The Origins of Totalitarian Democracy.* 1952.

Temple, William, *Christianity and Social Order.* 1942.

Thompson, Kenneth W., *Christian Ethics and the Dilemmas of Foreign Policy.* Duke University Press. 1959.

Vidler, Alec R., *The Orb and the Cross.* 1945.

Zimmern, Sir Alfred, *Spiritual Values and World Affairs.* 1939.

Index

24848

PRINTED IN GREAT BRITAIN
BY ROBERT MACLEHOSE AND CO. LTD
THE UNIVERSITY PRESS, GLASGOW